OECD

MONETARY STUDIES SERIES

MONETARY POLICY
IN THE
UNITED STATES

1974

The Organisation for Economic Co-operation and Development (OECD) was set up under a Convention signed in Paris on 14th December, 1960, which provides that the OECD shall promote policies designed :

— to achieve the highest sustainable economic growth and employment and a rising standard of living in Member countries, while maintaining financial stability, and thus to contribute to the development of the world economy;
— to contribute to sound economic expansion in Member as well as non-member countries in the process of economic development;
— to contribute to the expansion of world trade on a multilateral, non-discriminatory basis in accordance with international obligations.

The Members of OECD are Australia, Austria, Belgium, Canada, Denmark, Finland, France, the Federal Republic of Germany, Greece, Iceland, Ireland, Italy, Japan, Luxembourg, the Netherlands, New Zealand, Norway, Portugal, Spain, Sweden, Switzerland, Turkey, the United Kingdom and the United States.

**

CONTENTS

3

Appendices

٭٭٭

LIST OF TABLES AND CHARTS

TABLES

CHARTS

4

FOREWORD

This report forms part of a series of special studies on monetary policy undertaken by the Secretariat of the OECD at the request of the Economic Policy Committee. Each country has increasingly to formulate its own monetary policy within an international context. The purpose of these studies is to provide a better framework for the analysis of national monetary policies, and for international consultation regarding the use of monetary policy in Member countries for domestic demand management and balance of payments adjustment.

The need for detailed analysis on the working of monetary policy in different countries had been felt for various reasons:

i) In the recent period increased use has been made of monetary policy, and in more countries than previously, as a means of controlling demand, and as a consequence more evidence is becoming available as to the nature of its impact. It is useful to examine this evidence on an international basis and to compare the effects on demand of monetary policy in different countries.

ii) The volatility of international capital movements has increased. Though the scale of the effects to be attributed to monetary policy is difficult to quantify, the question is clearly of considerable importance for monetary authorities. Since the effects depend on the relative posture of monetary policies in different countries, they can clearly best be evaluated in the context of studies which examine the joint effects of different national monetary policies in at least the major financial countries.

The internal effects of monetary policy depend greatly on the economic and financial structure of the economy including the size of the public debt, the role of banks as financial intermediaries in the saving/investment process, the way in which housing is financed, and the scale and nature of consumer credit. These factors differ much from country to country. The external effects of monetary policy also depend to some extent on general institutional factors peculiar to different countries, and, in some cases, on the use made of policy instruments particularly designed to have external effects.

A series of country studies has, therefore, been envisaged which assembles the evidence about the working of monetary policy, taking into account differences in the economic and financial structure and the ways in which they have affected the choice of monetary instruments and the transmission process through which monetary policy has affected the financial and real sectors of the economy.

It has been decided to confine these studies, at least initially, to five or six countries whose monetary policies have been most important in influencing international capital movements. This report on the United States follows the studies on monetary policy in Japan, Italy and Germany, which have been already published. The next report will be concerned with monetary policy in France. It is also planned to publish a general report synthesizing the separate studies on these countries and also covering the experience of the United Kingdom in the use of monetary policy.

The present study was prepared by the Monetary Division of the Department of Economics and Statistics, with valuable assistance from other members of the Department. It was discussed at meetings of official experts from the Member countries to be covered by the studies. The view and analysis presented in this series of monetary studies are, however, not necessarily those of monetary authorities concerned, and the reports are published on my sole responsibility.

Emile van LENNEP
Secretary-General

March 1974.

INTRODUCTION

The purpose of the present study is to describe monetary policy in the United States since 1960. The policy instruments available and· the effects of changes in these instruments on financial markets and on the real economy are analysed. Monetary policy is throughout defined as synonymous with the actions of the US central bank, the Federal Reserve System. The survey ends at the end of 1971, but some references to subsequent changes in policy have been included.[1]

The task of describing monetary policy in the United States is easier and more difficult than for other countries. It is easier because US monetary experience is generally much better documented than that for other countries, and because the availability of data relating both to financial markets and to disaggregated components of demand makes detailed analysis possible. It is more difficult because the richness of the statistical material has not led to unanimous findings in empirical work on the effects of monetary policy. Although the most heated debates on the conduct of monetary policy seem to be over, considerable disagreement remains with respect to the details in handling particular policy phases and to the methodology for assessing empirical evidence. The methodological issues are highly technical; the reader is referred to a special background study prepared for the OECD [32]*. The availability of this study makes it unnecessary for the present study to go into the detailed econometric arguments concerning the relative merits of different methods. However, it has been necessary to be highly selective in presenting the evidence; and therefore a caveat against any excessively firm interpretation of the conclusions reached is appropriate at the outset.

Part I describes a background to the use of monetary policy, in the form of the main cyclical experiences of the US economy, the changing use of fiscal policy and the main characteristics of financial markets and the financing by sectors. *Part II* describes the individual policy instruments used by the Federal Reserve System. It also reviews combinations of these instruments, and the overall constraints which political or other factors have imposed on their use. *Part III* assesses the transmission mechanism by which changes in the monetary instruments have affected financial markets and through them the major components of demand, prices, employment and the current balance of payments; it includes a discussion of the impact of changes in US monetary policy on capital flows and the Euro-dollar market. The survey of the transmission mechanism draws heavily on a large-scale econometric model developed jointly by

---

1. Several other descriptions of US monetary policy are available. For a thorough review of policy instruments and their use, see in particular [27] and [101].

* The numbers in brackets refer to the bibliography at the end of this study.

economists in the Federal Reserve System and in two universities: the so-called FMP model.[2] Evidence from econometric research primarily relates to average responses over the period included in the sample. *Part IV* supplements this evidence with a brief review of how policy was actually used in four phases during which the authorities attempted to influence, in a major way, the course of the economy. These periods are two phases of expansion, namely 1960-62 and 1970-71, and two periods of restraint, 1966 and 1969. The review ends with an illustration, by means of simulations with the FMP model, of the order of magnitude of the impact from monetary restraint on aggregate demand. *Part V* offers some concluding observations. There are four appendices: a chronology of monetary measures taken; a description in more detail of open market operations, which have been the main policy instrument; a review of residential investment and the housing market; and an account of the scope for changing the structure of interest rates through debt management and open market operations and the implications of this analysis for capital flows in and out of the United States.

---

2. Federal Reserve Bank—Massachusetts Institute of Technology—University of Pennsylvania; preliminary versions of the model have been published in various articles, notably [18], [19] and [86], but no comprehensive survey has as yet been made available. The model is occasionally referred to as the MPS model.

I

THE ECONOMIC AND FINANCIAL BACKGROUND
FOR MONETARY POLICY

a) MAIN CYCLICAL EXPERIENCES: MAJOR COMPONENTS OF DEMAND, EMPLOY-
MENT, PRICES AND THE BALANCE OF PAYMENTS

During the 1960s, there were two relatively brief periods in 1960 and
in 1969 when total real demand declined in the United States. A more
precise dating of the business cycle phases is considerably facilitated by
the work of the National Bureau of Economic Research (NBER). According to the indicators developed by the NBER, the period since the beginning
of 1960 may be divided as follows:

up to 1960 QII: final stage of 1958-60 upswing;
1960 QII to 1961 QI: downswing;
1961 QI to 1969 QIV: upswing;
1969 QIV to 1970 QIV: downswing;
1970 QIV onwards: upswing.

A broadly similar picture is found from the two main indicators of capacity
and actual output (Chart 1). The 9-year upswing which started in 1961
was the longest in the history of the United States; it reflected initially a
sustained effort by the authorities to restore a high degree of employment.

From the middle of 1965 through the end of 1969, the economy was
operating at, or even above, the level defined by high employment output;
as a corollary, unemployment was typically somewhat below 4 per cent.
During this period of delicate demand/supply balance, a so-called "mini-
recession" (or "growth recession") took place. The precise dating of this
mini-recession is not free from controversy; the rate of growth of GNP
in current dollars declined from the beginning of 1966 until the end of
the year, but there was no absolute decline in real GNP as was the case
in the two standard recessions. Real GNP decelerated more sharply
during 1966 and its growth rate became marginally negative in 1967.I. The
rate of growth of the index of industrial production behaved almost iden-
tically. Based on these series, the growth recession coincided virtually
with the calendar year 1966 and thus divided the long upswing into three
sub-periods, with the latter two periods corresponding closely to the phase
when the authorities were seeking to manage an economy operating close
to capacity.

1961.I-1966.I: upswing;
1966.I-1967.I: mini-recession;
1967.I-1969.IV: upswing.

11

Chart 1. SOME MAIN INDICATORS OF THE DEMAND/SUPPLY BALANCE

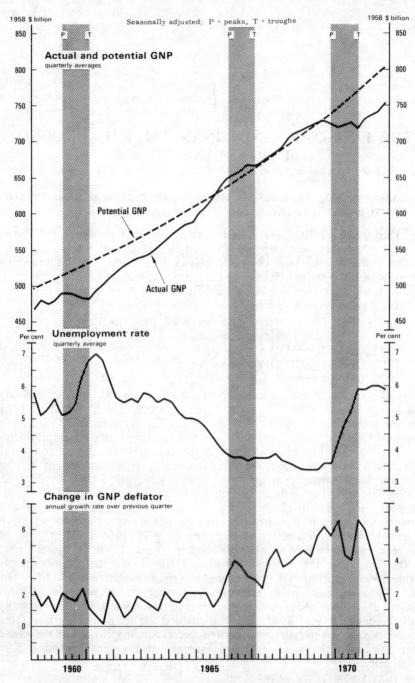

NOTE. Shaded areas represent periods of economic slowdown or recession.
Sources: Business Conditions Digest and National Income Accounts.

It is useful at this point to compare and contrast the behaviour of the composition of real demand in the three recessions, the two real recessions and the mini-recession of 1966 (Table 1). For this purpose it is helpful to define two sub-aggregates of total demand: *(i)* gross private capital expenditure, defined as gross private investment plus expenditure on consumer durables; and *(ii)* gross private capital expenditure *excluding* investment in inventories. The first concept corresponds to private expenditures typically undertaken to a significant extent with borrowed funds, while the second excludes the most volatile element of investment, inventory accumulation. The second concept isolates a demand component the sensitivity of which to financial changes is particularly well established by econometric studies.[1]

Using these concepts, it is clear that both of the standard recessions were dominated by the behaviour of gross private capital expenditures, which fell by about $15 billion (1958 prices) in each case. The percentage decline, however, was smaller in the second period, primarily because inventory accumulation fell less sharply and because residential construction, which had fallen in the first recession, merely levelled off in the second. On the other hand, the percentage declines in gross private capital expenditure excluding inventories were very similar at around 6.5 per cent in each of the two periods. The two recessions, during which the percentage falls in real GNP were nearly identical, thus had strong similarities. Both were dominated by declines in gross private capital expenditure and exhibited closely similar behaviour in terms of fixed investment. The growth recession of 1966 showed different characteristics; gross private capital expenditures (excluding inventory investment) declined about 3 per cent, but the weakening of demand was dominated by expenditures on consumer durables, which declined by 2.5 per cent, and in particular by residential construction which declined by more than 25 per cent. The tentative conclusion that emerges from this inspection of the three recessions is that private-sector capital expenditures played an important role in all three.

It is not possible to make a similar comparison between the long upswing of 1961 to 1966 and the recent upswing starting in the fourth quarter of 1970, because the latter is still under way (as of late 1973). It seems, however, that the recovery from the 1969-70 recession was rather slower than the corresponding recovery from 1960-61, and that an unusually large part was played by residential construction and expenditures on consumer durables. Another factor which may significantly have delayed the upswing in the recent phase is the decline in net exports from the United States; there was no significant contribution to changes in GNP from this component during the 1960s. A further difference is that Federal government expenditures played a much more active role in 1961 to 1966, when they were rising very sharply, than in the recent phase.

Special interest attaches to cyclical movements in residential construction: *(i)* it has been argued that the housing cycle has tended to become more pro-cyclical than was the case in the 1940s and 1950s; and *(ii)* cycles in residential construction are thought to have been sharply affected by

---

1. One other component of demand, consumer non-durable expenditure, though it is less sensitive to financial changes than private fixed investment, may weigh more heavily in estimates of the total impact of monetary policy because of its large share in GNP (see page 80).

13

TABLE 1. MAIN EXPENDITU
SEASONALLY ADJUSTED ANN

	1960 II - 1961 I			1961 I - 1966 I		
	1	2	3	1	2	3
1. Consumer Non-durables	2.5	0.9	−35.2	68.6	25.0	42
2. Consumer Durables	−3.9	−8.6	54.9	31.3	75.0	1
3. Gross Private Investment	−11.1	−15.1	156.3	41.6	66.7	25
4. Producers' Plant and Equipment	−2.7	−5.7	38.0	26.9	59.9	16
5. Inventory Change	−7.2	..	101.4	12.9	..	7
6. Residential Structures	−1.1	−5.0	15.5	1.9	9.1	1
7. Federal Government Expenditure	1.2	2.4	−16.9	9.0	17.2	5
8. State and Local Government Expenditure	1.7	3.9	−23.9	13.3	29.3	8
9. Net Exports	2.5	..	−35.2	−1.0	..	−0
10. GNP	−7.1	−1.4	100.0	162.8	33.7	100
11. Gross Private Capital Expenditure (2 + 3)	−15.0	−12.6	211.3	72.9	70.0	44
12. Gross Private Capital Expenditure less Inventory Change	−7.8	−6.8	109.9	60.0	55.8	36

1. Change ($ billion).
2. Percentage change.
3. Change as percentage of GNP change.
Source: Survey of Current Business.

monetary policy. As regards the first point, it is obvious that the housing cycle has not in the past typically coincided with the general cycle (Chart 2), but that investment in housing on several occasions has tended to move counter-cyclically. In the early post-war cycles, housing investment did not turn down sharply in recessions, and the rise during the upswings tended to peak well ahead of overall economic activity. In recent recessions, however, and particularly in 1966, the decline in housing has been substantial, and the subsequent upswings both in 1967-68 and following the end of 1970 have been unusually strong. This increasingly clear tendency for housing construction to fluctuate cyclically has been a source of concern to policy makers both for social and political reasons and because it has tended to weaken one of the stabilising mechanisms that appeared to operate in earlier business cycles. The role of monetary policy in influencing cyclical movements in residential construction will be reviewed in Parts III and IV and in Appendix III.

Neither the background to monetary policy decisions nor the assessment of policy effects can be adequately analysed without looking at the cyclical movements in the two domestic objectives which have dominated the formulation of economic policy since 1960: the unemployment rate and the movement of prices. The percentage of unemployed in the total civilian labour force did not decline much during the 1958-60 upswing, and it rose during and even beyond the subsequent recession (Chart 1) from 4.7 to 7.2 per cent; the end of 1961 saw a sharp fall to approximately

	1966 I - 1966 IV		1966 IV - 1969 IV			1969 IV - 1970 IV			1970 IV - 1971 IV		
	2	3	1	2	3	1	2	3	1	2	3
.2	1.8	39.5	38.9	11.1	60.7	9.4	2.4	−101.1	8.3	2.1	23.4
.9	−2.6	−12.1	13.3	18.7	20.7	−7.8	−9.2	83.9	16.4	21.4	46.3
.4	4.2	28.0	−0.2	−0.2	−0.3	−7.0	−6.5	75.3	11.7	11.6	33.0
.4	3.3	15.3	7.5	10.1	11.7	−6.2	−7.6	66.7	6.0	6.6	16.9
.7	..	49.0	−12.3	..	−19.2	−1.8	..	19.4	−0.7	..	−2.0
.8	−25.4	−36.9	4.6	27.1	7.2	1.0	0.5	−10.7	6.4	28.3	18.1
.6	10.8	42.0	3.8	5.6	5.9	−8.4	−11.7	90.3	0.8	1.3	2.2
.6	4.4	16.6	10.9	17.8	17.0	3.0	4.2	−32.2	3.4	4.5	9.6
.2	..	−14.0	−2.6	..	−4.1	1.5	..	−16.1	−5.1	..	−14.4
.7	2.4	100.0	64.1	9.7	100.0	−9.3	−1.3	100.0	35.4	4.9	100.0
.5	1.4	15.9	13.1	7.3	20.4	−14.8	−7.7	59.1	28.1	15.8	79.4
.2	−3.1	−33.1	25.4	15.6	39.6	−13.0	−6.9	139.8	28.8	16.5	81.4

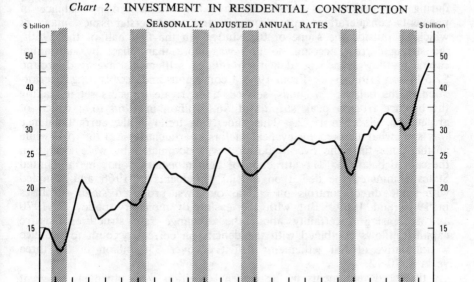

Chart 2. INVESTMENT IN RESIDENTIAL CONSTRUCTION

SEASONALLY ADJUSTED ANNUAL RATES

NOTE. Shaded areas represent periods of economic slowdown or recession.
Source: Business Conditions Digest.

15

5.5 per cent. This was followed by a rather steady decline until the onset of the mini-recession, but from the third quarter of 1967 the level began to edge down further, reaching 3.4 per cent towards the end of 1969, well below the target figure for unemployment formulated at the beginning of the 1960s. During the 1969 recession, unemployment rose sharply to about 6 per cent (a change which in relative terms was considerably greater than that of the 1960-61 recession); it remained around this level through 1971 and then gradually declined to around 5.5 per cent in mid-1972 and close to 5 per cent towards the end of that year.

It is not easy to discover a cyclical pattern in the behaviour of prices. From 1960 through 1965 the United States enjoyed a high degree of price stability with the GNP price deflator rising by less than 2 per cent a year. Subsequently, over a period coinciding with the intensification of the Vietnam conflict and the appearance of levels of real GNP close to or even in excess of potential, the rate of price increase began to accelerate, rising to 5.6 per cent in 1970. In the second half of 1971, the rate of increase fell sharply following the imposition of the price and wage freeze (Phase I) in August; it picked up moderately in 1972 to 3.0 per cent. Thus, in common with a number of other countries, the United States has experienced a long-run tendency for the rate of price changes to accelerate since the early 1960s, with a rather slow response to the easing in demand pressures at the end of the period. It was this unusually slow response which persuaded the authorities to supplement traditional demand management instruments by direct control over wages and prices. Apart from the initial effect of the Phase I freeze, it is not yet clear whether the new policies have significantly reduced the sensitivity of the rate of change of prices to variations in demand pressure.

The question of how much the conduct of US monetary policy during this period was or should have been influenced by balance of payments considerations raises complex and controversial issues, many of which lie outside the scope of this study. In the first half of the 1960s, the strong current account position was more than offset by substantial capital outflows, and the deficit on official settlements averaged around $2.5 billion (1960-64). From 1965 a continuous and accelerating deterioration in the balance on goods, services and private transfers set in, taking the balance from a peak surplus of $6.5 billion in 1964 to a deficit of around $6 billion in 1972. This underlying trend in the current balance was somewhat masked by cyclical factors (particularly in 1969-70), while at the same time the overall position was dominated by wide swings in the capital balance. The attraction of tight monetary policy in the United States eliminated the deficit on official settlements in 1966 and, coupled with some direct controls on capital outflows, produced small surpluses in 1968 and 1969. But with the easing of monetary policy in 1970 and increasing uncertainty about the exchange rate structure, massive capital outflows combined with the deficits on current account to produce a cumulative official settlements deficit of over $50 billion in the three years 1970-72.

These developments in the external position were obviously of great concern to the monetary authorities. But it would nevertheless seem that they had only a relatively marginal influence on the general thrust of monetary policy. There was clearly no conflict between internal and external considerations during the tight money phases of 1966 and 1968-69. Throughout the rest of the period, there was generally a conflict between the policies required to achieve the main domestic objective of a high and stable level of employment and those designed to bring the balance of payments closer to equilibrium. Four reasons can be put forward as to why the internal considerations prevailed:

    i)   the small size of the foreign sector; exports constituted only 4 to 5 per cent of total demand and the net current deficit, even in 1972, amounted to less than one half per cent of GNP;

   ii)   a growing conviction that the external disequilibrium was due to a divergence in the competitive positions of the United States and its main trading partners, and hence not of a kind which it would be appropriate to try to remedy through demand management policy;

  iii) a widely-held view that because of the international role of the dollar it was not possible for the United States to change its exchange rate at its own initiative; and

  iv) the role of the dollar as a reserve currency; as a result of that role, the large deficits had little direct impact on domestic monetary conditions.

The near-isolation from any monetary consequences of external imbalances is a feature that has distinguished the United States from other economies and has attracted the attention of foreign observers.[2] External surpluses and deficits, measured on an official settlements basis, affect domestic reserve money when, as is normally the case in other countries, the imbalance is settled by a transfer of external reserve assets. Thus, under the simple pattern of the gold standard, reserve money was reduced by an external deficit settled in gold and increased by a surplus. The money supply was accordingly forced to vary by a multiple amount depending on institutional arrangements governing the relationship between assets and liabilities of the central bank and commercial banks, as well as on the distribution of reserve money between the banking and non-banking private sectors. The United States itself, in an earlier period, provided an illustration of this mechanism. The growth of the US gold stock was by far the most important single source of reserve money prior to 1914 and remained significant in the interwar period. Subsequently, the role of variations in the gold stock and other non-dollar international reserve assets has been relatively much less important, as an increased share of external disequilibria—since 1958 mainly deficits—has been settled by an accumulation of claims on the United States by foreign official holders. Unlike settlements in reserve assets, such liability financing usually leaves reserve money unaffected, since it merely represents a change in ownership—from domestic and foreign private units to foreign

---

2. In comparing the United States with other countries, it must be recalled that the monetary authorities in all countries attempt to sterilise any unwanted external impact on domestic monetary conditions. However, the instruments for doing so may not always be available, and dwindling external reserves may limit the options available to the authorities. The position of the dollar as a reserve currency during the period under study significantly diminished the scale of sterilisation operations which would otherwise have been required, and it reduced the constraining effect of external reserves.

official institutions or vice versa—of domestic securities and bank liabilities.[3] Table 2 illustrates the extent to which liability financing has come to dominate in the settlement of US payments imbalances. For the period 1960-71 as a whole, only 24 per cent of the gross imbalance of over $62 billion on official settlements was financed through a change in reserve assets.[4] The proportion of reserve financing reached a minimum (10 per cent) in 1971, the year of maximum deficit; nonetheless, this year saw the largest decline in reserve assets recorded: a reduction of $3 billion. Over the twelve-year period, the average annual change in reserve assets was $1.3 billion, a relatively modest but not insignificant amount compared to the size of open market operations and other domestic sources of reserve money.

A preliminary conclusion is therefore that the use of the dollar as an international reserve asset reduced the need for open market operations to offset the impact of the widening external deficit on US domestic monetary conditions. The accumulation by foreign central banks of claims on the United States—mainly in the form of Treasury bills and certificates (including special issues to official institutions of non-marketable certificates of indebtedness, essentially the so-called Roosa bonds) and to a minor extent in the form of bank deposits—implied that the downward pressure on domestic reserve money was reduced to proportions which were modest compared to the huge financial market in the United States. The extent to which the preliminary conclusion must be modified because of secondary effects in US financial markets will be reviewed below (pages 61-65).

External considerations did, however, have some influence on the techniques used to implement monetary policy, and on the search for other measures to stem the capital outflow. This can be seen, for example, in the attempt to "twist" short-term interest rates up relative to long-term rates in the expansionary phase in the early 1960s, the introduction of the Interest Equalisation Tax in July 1963 and in the various programmes to restrain both bank and non-bank foreign investment introduced during the second half of the decade. The efficiency of these measures will be commented upon below (Parts III and IV and Appendix IV).

b) THE MEASUREMENT AND IMPACT OF FISCAL POLICY

Fiscal policy, the other main instrument of demand management apart from monetary policy, has been used actively in the United States on several occasions during the period under review. Though some of the changes made have not been motivated primarily by considerations of short-run demand management—examples are tax reforms for greater equity and the growth of expenditures for military purposes—the timing

---

3. If, however, liability financing results in a shift of foreign official funds from the private banking system to a Federal Reserve bank or vice versa, the impact on reserve money is similar to that from a change in the stock of gold or any other international reserve asset. In practice, such transfers played a negligible role during the period under discussion.

4. Netting out deficits against surpluses, the net imbalance was a deficit of $54 billion, 20 per cent of which was financed through a decrease in reserve assets, mainly gold. The reserve-financing proportion for the years of deficit (1960-67 and 1970-71) was much lower (23 per cent) than for the two surplus years 1968-69 (48 per cent).

TABLE 2. THE BALANCE ON OFFICIAL SETTLEMENTS AND ITS FINANCING[1]

$ million

	1960	1961	1962	1963	1964	1965	1966	1967	1968	1969	1970	1971
Balance on Official Settlements (OECD definition)	-3,458	-2,042	-3,333	-2,262	-1,518	-851	-109	-2,972	1,505	2,789	-10,948	-30,709
Financed by:												
Non-Reserve Financing (+ = increase)	1,012 (29.3)	1,437 (70.3)	1,797 (54.0)	1,883 (83.3)	1,348 (88.8)	-404 (-47.5)	-636 (-583.5)	2,897 (97.5)	-626 (41.5)	-1,591 (57.0)	8,059 (73.6)	27,665 (90.1)
Changes in Liabilities (incl. BIS)	958 (27.7)	742 (36.3)	1,117 (33.6)	1,557 (68.9)	1,363 (89.8)	33 (3.9)	-964 (-884.4)	3,344 (112.5)	-758 (50.2)	-1,504 (53.9)	7,815 (71.4)	27,439 (89.4)
Special Transactions	54 (1.6)	695 (34.0)	680 (20.4)	326 (14.4)	-15 (-1.0)	-437 (-51.4)	328 (300.9)	-447 (-15.0)	132 (-8.3)	-87 (3.1)	244 (2.2)	226 (0.7)
Reserve Financing (+ = decrease)	2,445 (70.7)	606 (29.6)	1,533 (46.0)	377 (16.7)	171 (11.2)	1,256 (147.5)	745 (683.5)	74 (2.5)	-883 (58.5)	-1,198 (43.0)	2,891 (26.4)	3,043 (9.9)
Change in Gold (incl. IMF)	2,003 (57.9)	857 (42.0)	890 (26.7)	461 (20.4)	125 (8.2)	1,699 (199.5)	748 (686.2)	1,192 (40.1)	1,170 (-77.5)	-978 (35.1)	334 (3.1)	844 (2.8)
Currency Assets	—	-116 (-5.7)	17 (0.5)	-113 (5.0)	-220 (-14.5)	-349 (-41.0)	-540 (-499.4)	-1,024 (-34.4)	-1,183 (78.4)	814 (-29.2)	2,152 (19.8)	381 (1.2)
Reserve Position in IMF	442 (12.8)	-135 (-6.6)	626 (18.8)	29 (1.3)	266 (17.5)	-94 (-11.0)	537 (492.7)	-94 (-3.2)	-870 (57.6)	-1,034 (37.1)	389 (3.5)	1,350 (4.4)
SDRs (excl. allocations)	—	—	—	—	—	—	—	—	—	—	16 (0.1)	468 (1.5)

Figures in brackets represent percentage of balance on official settlements.

1. The OECD " balance on official settlements " (excluding the allocation of SDRs) is conceptually slightly different from the US " balance on official reserve transactions " (excluding the allocation of SDRs), the main difference being the inclusion, as a financing item, below the balance on official settlements line, of " special transactions ", in the recent period representing essentially non-scheduled repayments of US government assets which are treated as a long-term capital flow in the US balance on official reserve transactions. In Table 11 special transactions have been assimilated with liabilities towards foreign official institutions. A more refined analysis would have disaggregated special transactions and treated each type of them according to their primary monetary effect. Also, as a rule, only changes in reserves and liabilities to officials resulting from actual balance-on-official-settlements financing were retained. Thus, changes in the gold stock due to IMF gold deposits and investment or changes in SDR holdings due to allocations were omitted.

Source: Survey of Current Business.

of fiscal policy must be reviewed in relation to the cycles observed in the real economy. In the review of four particular phases of monetary policy in Part IV, more detailed comments will be made on the conduct of fiscal policy in these periods. The present preliminary review attempts only to give an overall assessment of the contribution of fiscal policy.

The use of monetary and fiscal policy, in the United States as elsewhere, is not determined jointly by a single authority. Indeed, to judge by the frequency with which Federal Reserve publications have urged more active use of fiscal policy, one may conclude that the stance of fiscal policy, or expectations as to the scope for its change, have had to be accepted by the monetary authorities as a datum—and at times a constraint—in the formulation of its own policy. Thus in certain situations which, from a cyclical point of view, called for restraint, the Federal Reserve was compelled to provide all of the restraint while fiscal policy remained expansionary (see page 22 and Part IV).

The means of measuring the impact of the Federal government budget on the economy has progressively become more refined in recent years. In 1960 the impact was measured primarily with reference to the surplus or deficit, on a national accounts basis, of the Federal government budget, but there were several competing measures. The Economic Report of the President [21] began in 1962 to use the concept of the "full employment budget" as an indicator of the thrust of fiscal policy. Though somewhat refined during subsequent years, and often labelled "high employment" instead of "full employment" budget to avoid the arbitrary definition of full employment, this concept has been retained as the main measure of the fiscal impact. In the review of individual policy phases below, the present study will make use of this concept for the purpose of assessing the macroeconomic thrust of policy. But it will be necessary, in addition, to look at the actual surplus on deficit of the Federal budget on a cash basis, since this concept is relevant from a liquidity viewpoint.

Though convenient, the full or high employment budget has several weaknesses as an indicator of the thrust of fiscal policy in the short run. Its estimation involves difficult problems of judgement, and is at times quantitatively ambiguous; see Lotz [67].[5] Despite these weaknesses, use will

---

5. High employment expenditures are measured as actual expenditures adjusted for the difference between unemployment benefits at high and actual employment. High employment receipts are obtained by applying to a national high employment real GNP, revalued at current prices, the taxation function imposed by the fiscal authorities. Hence calculated changes in high employment receipts contain two elements: (i) changes in high employment GNP multiplied by the initial tax function, and (ii) the change, if any, in the tax function, i.e. the element of discretionary fiscal policy, multiplied by the initial level of high employment GNP. It follows that if expenditures at high employment are constant and the tax function is unchanged—a situation which could be classified as unchanged fiscal policy—the high employment surplus will rise because high employment GNP is rising along a trend growth curve. Thus an unchanged fiscal policy is more restrictive than inspection of the surplus or deficit would suggest. The conceptual problem is compounded by using simply the full employment surplus as an indicator, a procedure which implies that a unit increase in expenditures has the same impact regardless of its origin and is equivalent to a unit decrease in revenues. A third criticism of the change in the high employment surplus as a fiscal indicator is that a change in fiscal policy at the actual level of income implying a higher deficit may, translated into its high employment equivalent, imply a higher surplus or a smaller deficit because the slope of the tax function has changed; this would occur if steeper progression in income taxes had been introduced.

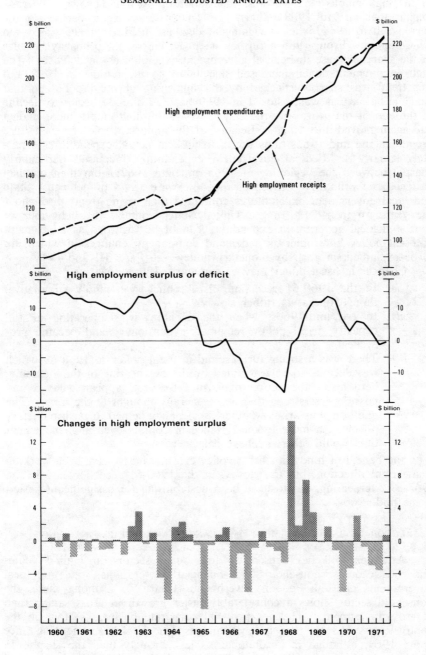

Chart 3. THE IMPACT OF FISCAL POLICY:
THE HIGH EMPLOYMENT SURPLUS

SEASONALLY ADJUSTED ANNUAL RATES

High employment expenditures

High employment receipts

High employment surplus or deficit

Changes in high employment surplus

NOTE. The high employment budget is defined on National Income Accounts basis.

Source: Federal Reserve Bank of St. Louis.

21

be made of the measure in Part IV with rough allowance for the bias towards restriction outlined in the footnote. As measured by the changes in the high employment surplus, the stance of fiscal policy was generally expansionary up to 1968 (Chart 3). There was a slight decline in the surplus up to 1964, when a significant decrease in direct taxes was voted by Congress. From 1965 a further steep decline set in, primarily because of the sharp increase in Federal government expenditures on defence. The high employment deficit increased sharply up to the middle of 1968, but this trend was sharply checked by the tightening of fiscal policy in that year. The surplus was restored in 1969 but had already begun to decline at the end of the year. By the end of 1971, the high employment budget had again moved into deficit. Because of the important role of expenditure growth in the mid-1960s, it is useful to look at actual expenditures separately (Chart 4). Federal government expenditures increased particularly sharply between the beginning of 1965 and late 1967; from then on they flattened out primarily because of the downward trend of defence. State and local government expenditures continued their rising trend throughout the years up to 1971. In the United States context, the behaviour of state and local government expenditure cannot be regarded as an element of fiscal policy but rather as a demand component, changes in which are to be explained, in part, by monetary policy (see Parts III and IV).

Changes in fiscal policy may be summarised as follows[6]:

i)   In the 1960-61 recession, fiscal policy was mildly stimulative, though operating rather slowly.

ii) In the mid-1960s, when the economy was operating at full capacity, fiscal policy remained expansionary and became pro-cyclical.

iii) There was a strong turn-around in fiscal policy in 1968-69 which was deemed to be warranted by the overheating of the economy; here again the action may, in retrospect, appear delayed and possibly less strong than was generally thought at the time. The question thus arises whether fiscal policy helped to push monetary policy to a more extreme stance in counter-cyclical management than would otherwise have been necessary.

With the benefit of hindsight, fiscal policy can be said to have been working in the right direction, but too slowly, in the 1960-61 recession and in the 1968-69 overheating, but to have been destabilising for a significant period in the mid-1960s.

c) SECTOR SAVING/INVESTMENT IMBALANCES AND THEIR FINANCING

Attention will be focused on four main sectors in United States financial accounts: households, non-financial corporations, state and local governments and the Federal government (Chart 5). Among these, the household sector shows a considerably faster growth in gross saving than in gross investment. The non-financial corporate business sector, on the contrary, invests more than it saves, and its deficit has been widening since about 1964, although in absolute terms less strongly than the surplus in the household sector. State and local governments have been in small

---

6. For a more thorough discussion, see e.g. Okun [80].

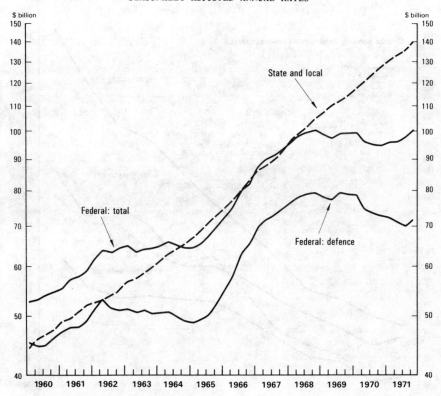

Chart 4. GOVERNMENT EXPENDITURES
SEASONALLY ADJUSTED ANNUAL RATES

Source: Business Conditions Digest.

and rather stable deficit throughout the period. The Federal government, as is to be expected, shows larger fluctuations than the other sectors; its deficits were very sizeable in 1967 and from 1970 onwards, while there was a large surplus in 1969.

Looking in more detail at individual sectors, the net saving of *households* relative to personal disposable income has moved up sharply over the 1960s. The share of total savings accumulated in the form of financial assets has increased, while there has been a corresponding decline in capital expenditures relative to gross funds available (Table 3). It is a striking feature of the US economy that households are very active in financial markets both as borrowers and lenders. The share of borrowing in gross funds available has remained approximately constant at just less than 20 per cent. Though the annual data do not reveal cyclical movements clearly, it can be seen that the form in which households have accumulated financial assets has varied considerably and that this variation has been correlated with the cycle. For example, in 1966, a year of monetary restraint, household purchases of credit-market instruments were

23

Chart 5. THE SAVING/INVESTMENT BALANCE OF MAIN SECTORS

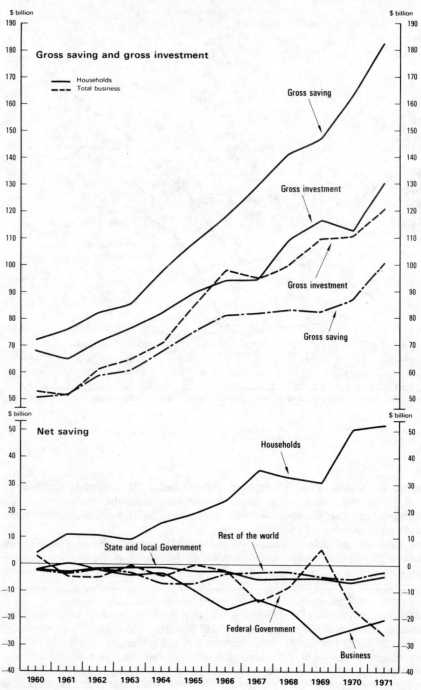

Source: Federal Reserve Bulletin.

around one-fourth of their net acquisition of financial assets, while in the following year the share fell to just over 6 per cent. This readiness to substitute various financial assets is discussed further in Part I *(d)*.

In the *non-financial corporate business sector,* the flow of internal funds has not kept up with the growth of total gross investment (Table 4). As a result, the share of external funds in total financing has gone up from little more than one-fourth to close to one-half at the end of the period under study, although again there has been considerable cyclical variability. Borrowing has been mainly in the form of long-term issues of securities; in comparison with most other countries, corporate business in the United States relies relatively little on bank loans, which have constituted on average less than 20 per cent of total external funds. However, late in economic upswings short-term financing has been almost as important as long-term borrowing. These movements have been reversed in recessions and periods of restraint. In 1960-61, for example, the decline in the rate of short-term borrowing accounted for two thirds of the decline in external finance, and in 1969-70, short-term borrowing (mainly bank loans) fell by nearly 50 per cent more than the total use of external funds, though that decline was largely offset by increased long-term borrowing. In both 1966-67 and 1969-70, declines in the rate of expansion of trade credit were very important (Part IV); in the 1969-70 phase, non-financial corporations were particularly strained in their dependence on short-term finance. A general conclusion is that the last two slowdowns found the business sector uncomfortably illiquid at the peak of the boom and that during both periods it was necessary to adjust the composition of marginal liabilities quite sharply. At the same time, the accumulation of financial assets was markedly reduced. This double adjustment put heavy strain on particular financial markets, e.g. the commercial paper market in mid-1970, and made corporations financially vulnerable at and shortly after cyclical peaks. In consequence, however, the non-financial corporate sector has shown considerable and apparently increasing flexibility in its financial arrangements.

For the reasons outlined earlier, the arrangements for the finance of *housing* are of particular interest from the viewpoint of monetary policy. Residential construction expenditures have moved over the 1960s parallel to mortgage borrowing (Chart 6); to what extent this relationship may be interpreted as a causal link from financing to real activity will be discussed further in Part III. Here it will suffice to note that the main lenders in the mortgage market are, in order of importance, savings and loan associations, mutual savings banks, commercial banks and life insurance offices. A more detailed account of housing finance and the housing cycle is given in Appendix III.

It has been a major problem in the conduct of monetary policy that, as the economy has approached a situation of overall excess demand, as was the case in the years 1965 through 1968, other sectors, notably the corporate business sector, have been able to bid financial and hence real resources away from the housing sector through the operation of the interest rate mechanism. Interest rates offered by the institutions primarily engaged in the housing market have exhibited considerable stickiness, primarily because their earning assets have been dominated by loans contracted in periods of much lower interest rates than those prevailing in the 1960s. Accordingly, when interest rates have risen in other financial

Table 3. FLOW OF FUNDS: HOUSEHOLD SECTOR

	1960	1961	1962	1963	1964	1965	1966	1967	1968	1969	1970	1971
Percentage ratio of:												
Personal Saving to Personal Disposable Income	4.9	5.8	5.6	4.9	6.0	6.0	6.4	7.4	6.7	6.0	7.9	8.2
Net Acquisition of Financial Assets to Gross Funds Available	27.5	34.0	35.5	37.6	37.4	39.1	39.5	39.7	38.8	32.3	43.2	39.8
Capital Expenditure to Gross Funds Available	75.4	69.8	69.3	67.8	65.2	64.5	66.3	61.6	62.0	65.4	61.0	57.4
Borrowing to Gross Funds Available	19.8	18.2	20.3	24.1	22.3	21.7	16.6	15.4	19.7	17.4	11.6	19.6
Net Financial Investment to Gross Investment	9.2	18.3	18.0	16.6	18.8	21.2	25.6	28.3	23.6	18.6	34.2	26.0

Source: Federal Reserve Bulletin.

Table 4. FLOW OF FUNDS: NON-FINANCIAL CORPORATE SECTOR

	1960	1961	1962	1963	1964	1965	1966	1967	1968	1969	1970	1971
Percentage ratio of:												
Saving to Total Gross Investment	78.7	68.2	69.7	69.4	77.8	68.2	68.2	69.2	62.0	56.6	64.7	65.8
Saving to Gross Investment in Real Assets	88.2	97.0	95.0	96.3	96.9	90.1	79.4	85.4	81.0	70.7	73.1	82.2
Short-term Borrowing to External Funds	26.4	6.3	13.0	16.8	22.1	29.9	24.5	22.0	26.8	33.6	17.3	7.5
Long-term Borrowing to External Funds	54.3	52.9	42.0	36.6	42.2	24.6	39.9	57.6	37.2	37.2	74.6	73.8
Liquid Assets to Total Gross Investment	-8.0	7.3	5.8	7.4	1.8	3.1	-4.1	5.4	5.3	-0.5	-1.1	9.7
External Funds to Total Funds	28.9	36.9	35.6	34.6	29.7	40.0	39.0	37.8	43.8	48.9	41.4	45.4

Source: Federal Reserve Bulletin.

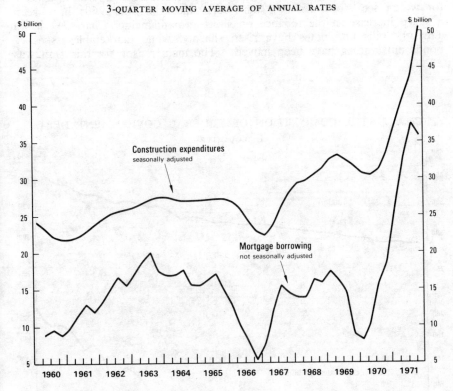

Chart 6. RESIDENTIAL CONSTRUCTION:
INVESTMENT EXPENDITURES AND BORROWING

3-QUARTER MOVING AVERAGE OF ANNUAL RATES

Sources: Business Conditions Digest and Federal Reserve Bulletin.

markets, funds have been attracted away from the mortgage lending institutions, cutting off a substantial part of traditional flows. The government,
recognising that this process went too far in 1966, intervened more
actively in 1969 to protect the mortgage market from some of the effects
of monetary restraint.

The deficit of the *public sector* has been financed through the issuance
of securities. Very large issues have been made by both the Federal
government and its agencies and by state and local governments; total
public issues typically have been somewhat larger than corporate issues of
bonds and stocks combined. The size and composition of the Federal
government debt is of particular interest to the monetary authorities
because of the necessity of co-ordinating debt management with the use
of monetary policy instruments in general and open market operations in
particular. Some comments on the short-run problems created in periods
of heavy Treasury financial operations—so-called even-keel periods—will
be made in Part II; here the main concern is with longer-run trends in
the methods of financing Federal government deficits. While the pattern

27

of new Federal issues of debt instruments did not change much during
the first half of the 1960s (not even during the period of "Operation Twist",
for which see Appendix IV), the years since the mid-1960s have seen
a sharp increase in the reliance on short-term financing (Chart 7). Both
Treasury bills and notes have risen sharply, while marketable issues of
bonds outstanding have been halved. The main reason for this shift was

Chart 7. THE COMPOSITION OF FEDERAL GOVERNMENT DEBT
END-QUARTER

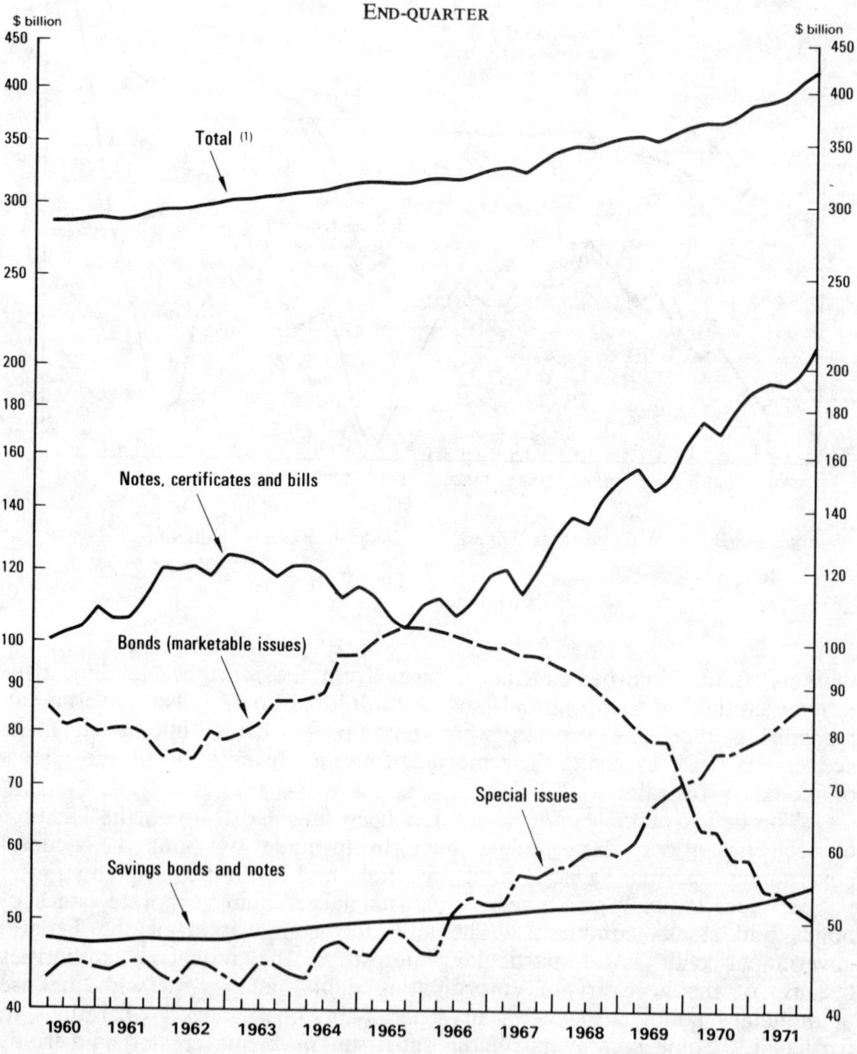

1. Total includes (not shown separately) convertible bonds, non-interest-bearing
debt and non-marketable debt other than savings bonds and notes.
Source: Federal Reserve Bulletin.

28

a statutory interest rate ceiling on Treasury bond issues (see also page 36). Issues of non-marketable savings bonds and notes were negligible during this period.

While the securities issued by the Federal government and its agencies generally yield competitive rates, the securities of state and local governments enjoy a particular advantage in that the interest income has been exempt from Federal income tax, an exemption which has enabled the state and local governments to attract funds at a lower cost than would otherwise have been possible. The yield on such instruments (state and local government Aaa bonds) has generally been one half to one percentage point lower than on comparable Federal issues.

d) COMMERCIAL BANKS AND NON-BANK FINANCIAL INSTITUTIONS

The distinguishing feature of the US financial system is the very large number of individual banks. At the end of 1971, there were about 13,700 commercial banks. This diffusion reflects, *inter alia,* the legal restrictions on branch banking, which is entirely prohibited in some states, permitted to a limited extent in others, and fully allowed in some. Rather less than half of the total number of banks are members of the Federal Reserve System and thus are directly subject to the discretionary actions of the monetary authorities, but these banks account for over 80 per cent of deposits (Table 5). Member banks of the Federal Reserve incur obligations and receive privileges. The most important obligation is the requirement to maintain minimum reserves against defined classes of liabilities. The main privileges are the right to use the facilities of the Federal Reserve to clear cheques, transfer funds and obtain currency; and the ability to borrow from the Federal Reserve subject to certain criteria as described in Part II. Most published statistics until recently classified member banks into reserve city banks and country banks[7] and sub-classified them by size of deposits, revealing the enormous variety of the banking business. However, since November 1972 banks are classified only according to size for the purposes of reserve requirement ratios (see page 56).

The assets which Federal Reserve member banks are required to hold as reserves—currency and deposit balances at Federal Reserve banks— are non-interest-bearing, and banks are not legally required to join the System.[8] In deciding to join or leave the system, an individual commercial bank is likely to make a careful assessment of the costs and benefits of membership. This balance is not invariant for individual banks over time; accordingly banks both leave and enter the system. During the first

---

7. This distinction was not solely one of location. Some banks which were located in reserve cities (i.e. those where Federal Reserve offices are placed) were classified as country banks because of the nature of their business activities.

8. Banks in the United States may obtain charters either from the Federal government or from the government of the state in which they are located. Only the former are required to become members of the Federal Reserve System. Non-member banks as well as members are eligible for coverage under the government insurance programme, the Federal Deposit Insurance Corporation (FDIC). Since the 1930s, the FDIC has insured depositors against loss of their deposits up to specified maximum amounts. This measure has, in the opinion of most observers, contributed more than any other to the stability of American financial institutions compared with that observed prior to the depression of the 1930s.

29

TABLE 5. BANKS' ASSETS AND LIABILITIES
END-YEAR, $ BILLION

	TOTAL BANKS			Member Banks			Reserve City Banks			Country Banks			Non-member Banks		
	1960	1965	1970	1960	1965	1970	1960	1965	1970	1960	1965	1970	1960	1965	1970
ASSETS															
Loans	217.5 (45.9)	371.5 (53.8)	567.4 (54.5)	99.9 (46.1)	169.8 (54.2)	253.9 (54.5)	62.9 (47.5)	106.5 (56.0)	154.5 (55.0)	37.0 (44.0)	63.3 (51.4)	99.4 (53.8)	17.7 (43.2)	31.9 (49.9)	59.6 (53.8)
Securities	144.6 (30.5)	186.2 (27.0)	259.9 (24.9)	65.7 (30.3)	81.8 (26.1)	112.0 (24.1)	31.8 (24.0)	41.8 (22.0)	57.3 (20.4)	30.9 (36.7)	40.0 (32.5)	54.7 (29.6)	16.2 (39.5)	22.6 (35.4)	35.9 (32.4)
Cash Assets	98.0 (20.7)	113.7 (16.5)	175.1 (16.8)	45.8 (21.1)	52.8 (16.8)	81.5 (17.5)	31.0 (23.4)	35.4 (18.6)	56.1 (20.0)	14.8 (17.6)	17.4 (14.1)	25.4 (13.8)	6.4 (15.6)	8.1 (12.7)	12.1 (10.9)
Other	14.1 (3.0)	19.3 (2.8)	39.6 (3.8)	5.2 (2.4)	9.0 (2.9)	18.2 (3.9)	6.8 (5.1)	6.5 (3.4)	13.1 (4.7)	1.4 (1.7)	2.5 (2.0)	5.1 (2.8)	0.7 (1.7)	1.3 (2.0)	3.2 (2.9)
TOTAL ASSETS OR LIABILITIES (as percentage of total banks)	474.2 (100.0)	690.7 (100.0)	1042.0 (100.0)	216.6 (45.7)	313.4 (45.4)	465.6 (44.7)	132.5 (27.9)	190.2 (27.5)	281.0 (27.0)	84.1 (17.8)	123.2 (17.8)	184.6 (17.7)	49.0 (8.6)	63.9 (9.3)	110.8 (10.6)
LIABILITIES															
Total Deposits	422.8 (89.2)	607.9 (88.0)	865.7 (83.1)	193.0 (89.1)	275.5 (87.9)	384.6 (82.6)	117.0 (88.3)	164.8 (86.6)	222.7 (79.3)	76.0 (90.4)	110.7 (89.9)	161.8 (87.6)	36.8 (89.8)	56.9 (89.0)	96.6 (87.2)
Demand Deposits	290.6 (61.3)	339.3 (49.1)	451.4 (43.3)	134.1 (61.9)	154.5 (49.3)	203.6 (43.7)	87.2 (65.8)	95.5 (50.2)	127.8 (45.5)	47.0 (55.9)	59.0 (47.9)	75.8 (41.1)	22.3 (54.4)	30.3 (47.4)	44.2 (39.9)
Time Deposits	132.2 (27.9)	268.7 (38.9)	414.3 (39.8)	58.9 (27.2)	121.0 (38.6)	181.0 (38.9)	29.8 (22.5)	69.3 (36.4)	94.9 (33.8)	29.0 (34.5)	51.7 (42.0)	86.1 (46.6)	14.5 (35.4)	26.7 (41.8)	52.3 (47.2)
Borrowing	0.2 (0.0)	8.6 (1.2)	38.0 (3.6)	0.1 (0.0)	4.2 (1.3)	18.6 (4.0)	0.1 (0.1)	3.9 (2.1)	16.8 (6.0)	0.0 (0.0)	0.3 (0.2)	1.8 (1.0)	0.0 (0.0)	0.2 (0.3)	0.8 (0.7)
Capital Account and Other	51.2 (10.8)	74.2 (10.7)	138.3 (13.3)	23.5 (10.8)	33.7 (10.8)	62.4 (13.4)	15.4 (11.6)	21.5 (11.3)	41.5 (14.8)	8.1 (9.6)	12.2 (9.9)	21.0 (11.4)	4.2 (10.2)	6.8 (10.6)	13.4 (12.1)

Figures in brackets represent percentage of total.

Source: Annual Report of the Board of Governors of the Federal Reserve System.

half of the 1960s, there was a slight increase in the number of member banks; but since the mid-1960s the membership of the Federal Reserve System has dwindled at a somewhat faster pace than it increased in the first half of the decade. Concern over the decline in the number of member banks of the Federal Reserve System has to some extent motivated the form in which changes in policy instruments have been made in recent years (see Part II). It also has led the Board of Governors to request on several occasions—most recently in January 1974—that the Congress pass legislation requiring most non-member banks to meet the System's reserve requirements.

The environment for banking is highly competitive. In attracting deposits, banks compete not only with each other but, in the case of longer-term deposits, also with other financial intermediaries (notably savings and loan associations and the mutual savings banks) and with open market assets such as Treasury bills and commercial paper. Competition depends upon transaction costs, the characteristics of the assets involved and the extent to which portfolio owners are aware of and are prepared to act upon opportunities for substitution. On their side, banks have shown a considerable capacity to innovate: the 1960s saw the growth of markets for negotiable time deposits (known as certificates of deposit, or CDs), commercial paper (issued by bank affiliates) and Euro-dollars. In part, these innovations were prompted by the restrictions pertaining to the payment of interest on deposits. No interest may be paid on demand deposits, and the so-called regulation Q imposes a ceiling on the interest rates that may be offered on time and savings deposits.[9]

As already noted, US portfolio owners have demonstrated high sensitivity to variations in interest rate differentials between financial assets over major cyclical phases (Chart 8); substantial shifts among deposits of various kinds—bank and non-bank and by maturity—as well as between longer-term deposits and financial market instruments, seem to have taken place during the phases of restrictive monetary policy in 1966 and 1969. The main econometric studies on asset choices are, however, not unanimous in their findings.[10] Much of the disagreement may be due to differences in methods used; cross-section studies generally find a lower degree of substitutability than do time-series studies. The conclusions of the latter are subject to the reservations that interest rates on competing assets tend to move parallel to one another, and that the non-price characteristics of assets are not invariant even over so short a time as a decade; illustrations of financial innovations during the 1960s have already been offered. The empirical studies do broadly agree that the degree of substitution is highest between deposits of comparable maturity in banks and non-banks, notably savings deposits in commercial banks and in savings and loan associations or mutual savings banks; it is less high, but still very significant, between longer-term deposits and financial market instruments such as Treasury bills or commercial paper; it is lower between deposits of different maturity, e.g. between commercial bank demand deposits on the one hand and time and savings deposits in banks or non-banks on the other.

---

9. Two different types of banks (member banks of the Federal Reserve System and non-member banks insured by the FDIC) are subject to this control (see pages 52-53).

10. Important contributions have been made by Feige [29 and 30], Hamburger [41], Lee [66] and Edwards [22].

SEASONALLY ADJUSTED ANNUAL RATES

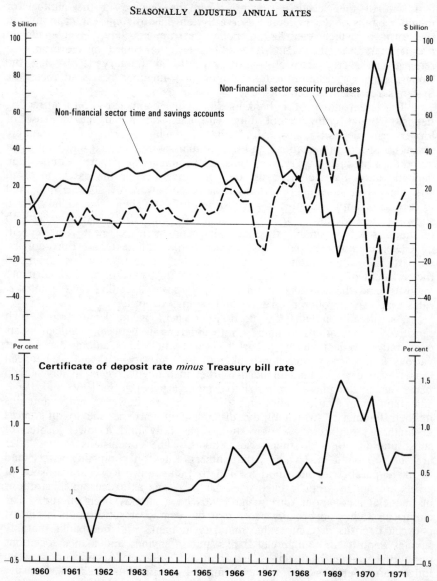

1. Data for the Certificate of Deposit Rate are available only from 1961.
Source: Federal Reserve Bulletin.

The degree of substitutability between demand and other deposits has important implications for the definition of the monetary aggregates; the findings suggest that a narrow definition of the money stock—currency

32

TABLE 6. THE STRUCTURE OF COMMERCIAL BANK LENDING

	$ billion			Percentage of total		
	1960	1965	1970	1960	1965	1970
Commercial and Industrial including Open Market Paper	43.1	70.9	112.5	35.9	35.1	35.8
Agricultural	5.7	8.2	11.2	4.8	4.1	3.6
Loans for Purchasing or Carrying Securities	5.1	8.3	9.9	4.3	4.1	3.1
Loans to Financial Institutions	8.1	15.2	34.8	6.8	7.5	11.1
Real Estate Loans	28.7	49.0	72.5	23.9	24.2	23.1
Other Loans to Individuals	26.4	45.3	65.8	22.0	22.4	20.9
Other Loans	2.9	5.2	7.6	2.4	2.6	2.4
Total	120.0	202.1	314.3	100	100	100

Source : Federal Reserve Bulletin.

plus demand deposits with commercial banks (M_1)—may be a more meaningful behavioural concept than a more broadly defined aggregate.[11] The ownership of demand deposits has been surveyed regularly in recent years;[12] just less than one third of the deposits are held by households in their capacity as consumers, slightly more than half by non-financial business and the rest mainly by other financial institutions. The observed variations in M_1 therefore reflect the behaviour of rather heterogeneous economic agents.

Bankers also operate in a competitive environment as lenders. Their main customers are industrial and commercial corporations. The maturity of loans is typically short by international comparison, and it is customary to require large borrowers to keep a compensating balance in a demand deposit account with the bank; this requirement may effectively increase the interest cost to the borrower by 20 to 30 per cent. However, competition puts tight limits to the extent to which commercial banks can increase the costs of borrowing. In particular, in their lending activity, the banks have to compete closely with funds raised through the issue of open market paper. Overall, the rationing effects of reduced availability of bank loans to the private sector seem to be less severe than in most other countries.

The structure of commercial bank lending displays considerable longer-run stability, despite some cyclical variations (Table 6). During the 1960s, total lending increased about 2½ times, but the share of commercial and industrial loans remained roughly unchanged at little more than

11. Partly for this reason the policy simulations in Part IV report on policy effects in terms of M_1. However, the FMP model, on which these simulations are based, incorporates significant elements of substitution between demand deposits and other financial assets. The degree of substitutability also may be expected to increase in the future as greater use is made of Negotiable Orders of Withdrawal (NOW) accounts and similar devices which essentially enable time deposits to be used for transactions purposes. See [31].
12. For a detailed description, see [26], June 1971, p. 466.

one-third. This category of loans is of special interest since it reflects movements in gross capital expenditure as defined above; therefore, the monetary authorities have to a significant extent, particularly in the phases of restraint in 1966 and 1969, judged the effects of their policies by their impact on the availability and cost of industrial and commercial loans. Particularly significant in most periods as an indicator of cost is the prime rate, normally a minimum interest rate charged to particularly credit-worthy customers. There has generally been some tendency for the share of commercial and industrial loans (and often of loans given at prime rate) to rise in phases of restraint, while other forms of lending are being held back.[13]

Though commercial banks are prohibited from investing in (as well as underwriting) corporate stocks and customarily acquire few corporate bonds, they are by far the most important private buyers of most categories of government bonds. They are traditionally most interested in securities with under one year's maturity issued by the Federal or state and local governments. The banks generally regard these highly liquid securities as secondary reserve assets; such assets constitute the most important source of short-term finance for the banking system. Discounting at the Federal Reserve banks is a marginal source of short-term finance (since it is considered as a privilege and not a right, so that the banks are generally reluctant to rely on it continuously); and though the Federal funds market (see pages 39-40) is an important source of short-term finance for individual banks it usually is not for the banking system as a whole.[14]

Among the *non-bank financial intermediaries,* two types are particularly important, namely savings and loan associations and mutual savings banks. Savings and loan associations number almost 6,000 and their assets are about one-third of those of commercial banks at the present time (see also Table 7). Regulations of their activity vary according to states, but their lending powers are generally restricted to real estate and share account loans. At the end of 1970, real estate loans accounted for more than 85 per cent of their total assets. The main source of their finance is a special type of savings deposits. The mutual savings banks are much less numerous. Their total assets are half as large as those of the savings and loan associations. They are also heavily specialised in lending for housing; at the end of 1970, real estate loans comprised more than 70 per cent of their total assets. But in contrast to the savings and loan associations, they can also hold corporate debt instruments and some equity issues. In several states, they may also make consumer loans. They rely largely on savings deposits for the source of loanable funds, although some states permit them to accept demand deposits.

These two types of thrift institutions compete with commercial banks for collecting savings deposits. Although the regulation on maximum interest rates payable on savings accounts, such as passbook accounts, has

---

13. This effect is in accordance with the conclusions of the theory of credit rationing. During phases of restraint, banks may be expected to try to increase the share of low-risk loans, i.e. loans to large corporate customers in their total portfolio; see in particular Jaffee [54], Chapter 3, which uses various measures of this share as an index of the tightness of credit rationing in the bank loan market.
14. This statement does not apply in periods in which the authorities are aiming to stabilise the Federal funds rate, as will be discussed further in Part II and Appendix II.

TABLE 7. RELATIVE IMPORTANCE OF PRIVATE FINANCIAL INTERMEDIARIES

$ BILLION

	1960	1961	1962	1963	1964	1965	1966	1967	1968	1969	1970
TOTAL ASSETS											
Commercial Banks	256.3 (48.7)	277.4 (48.4)	296.0 (47.9)	311.8 (46.9)	345.1 (47.3)	375.4 (47.4)	402.9 (47.8)	405.7 (48.7)	500.2 (49.5)	530.7 (49.6)	572.7 (49.9)
Savings and Loan Associations	71.5 (13.6)	82.1 (14.3)	93.6 (15.1)	107.6 (16.2)	119.4 (16.4)	129.6 (16.4)	133.9 (15.9)	143.5 (15.5)	152.9 (15.1)	162.3 (15.2)	176.6 (15.4)
Mutual Savings Banks	40.6 (7.7)	42.8 (7.5)	46.1 (7.5)	49.7 (7.5)	54.2 (7.4)	58.2 (7.4)	60.9 (7.2)	66.4 (7.2)	71.2 (7.0)	74.1 (6.9)	79.0 (6.9)
Others	158.4 (30.1)	170.7 (29.8)	182.4 (29.5)	195.8 (29.4)	211.3 (28.9)	228.6 (28.9)	244.8 (29.1)	264.9 (28.6)	285.9 (28.3)	303.7 (28.4)	320.0 (27.9)
Total	526.8 (100.0)	573.0 (100.0)	618.1 (100.0)	664.9 (100.0)	730.0 (100.0)	791.8 (100.0)	842.5 (100.0)	925.5 (100.0)	1,010.2 (100.0)	1,070.8 (100.0)	1,148.3 (100.0)
MORTGAGE LOANS											
Commercial Banks	28.7 (24.8)	30.3 (23.7)	34.3 (23.6)	39.1 (23.6)	43.7 (23.6)	49.4 (24.2)	54.1 (25.1)	58.7 (25.4)	65.3 (26.2)	70.3 (26.4)	72.3 (25.8)
Savings and Loan Associations	60.1 (52.0)	68.8 (53.8)	78.8 (54.3)	90.9 (54.8)	101.3 (54.7)	110.3 (54.0)	114.4 (53.0)	121.8 (52.8)	130.8 (52.4)	140.3 (52.6)	150.6 (53.7)
Mutual Savings Banks	26.7 (23.1)	28.9 (22.6)	32.1 (22.1)	36.0 (21.7)	40.3 (21.7)	44.4 (21.8)	47.2 (21.9)	50.3 (21.8)	53.3 (21.4)	55.9 (21.0)	57.8 (20.6)
Total	115.5 (100.0)	128.0 (100.0)	145.2 (100.0)	166.0 (100.0)	185.3 (100.0)	204.1 (100.0)	215.7 (100.0)	230.8 (100.0)	249.4 (100.0)	266.5 (100.0)	280.7 (100.0)

Figures in brackets represent percentage of total.

Source: The Report of the President's Commission on Financial Structure and Regulation, December 1971.

35

enabled these institutions to maintain higher deposit rates over commercial banks, the interest differential between the thrift institutions and commercial banks in recent years has tended to narrow.

Finally, there is a large group of other intermediaries which are highly active in long-term financial markets. The most important of these are life insurance offices and pension funds, the main recipients of contractual savings. These intermediaries invest most of their loanable funds in bonds and shares. Life insurance companies are also important lenders in the mortgage market. Their real estate credit is more than half as large as that of savings and loan associations.

e) SHORT-TERM AND LONG-TERM FINANCIAL MARKETS

In the United States, the *bond market* is generally taken to encompass three broad classes of securities: government (and Federal agency including central government enterprises) obligations, state and local government securities, and debt security issues of private (financial and non-financial) corporations. Foreign issues are a relatively minor element in the US capital market; they are under-written and marketed much like corporate issues. Generally the total of outstanding *public (Federal government and agency)* security issues[15] has increased steadily since the war. While the net security issue has displayed rather wide year-by-year fluctuations in volume, there has been a pronounced shortening of the terms of new issues, with the very long-maturity bonds (over 20 years) losing ground to the medium-term notes (1-5 years) and rather long bonds (5-20 years). Treasury bills as a proportion of the total marketable issue have shown a similarly strong upward trend (Chart 7). The issuance of long-term bonds was hindered until 1971 because of a statutory interest ceiling (4½ per cent) on Treasury bond offerings combined with Congressional prejudice against new issues at a discount below par. On the demand side, all bond markets in the United States enjoy a large element of private support: in November 1972, private investors held almost 60 per cent of public debt. If the comparison is confined to marketable government securities, the proportion increases to about 70 per cent. Within the private sector, purchases by the commercial banks, the households (mainly savings bonds), and the foreign and international buyers recently have been of roughly equal importance and together account for about 75 per cent of private investors' holdings of public debt. While the proportion of this debt held by the first two categories has remained more or less constant during the period under observation, the increase in the foreign holdings has risen sharply since late 1971—a development largely reflecting the large deficits in the United States balance of payments (see pages 17 and 62-64).

State and local governments, together with such specialised municipal bodies as school districts and transportation authorities, rely heavily on capital market funds for their substantial financial requirements. Their debt instruments, the *state and local government securities* (commonly called municipal securities), are typically of the long-term variety and are exempt from Federal income tax. The issues are of two broad types: "general obligations" and "revenue" (or "enterprise") bonds; the latter type is secured only by the revenues from the activities financed by the issues, i.e.

---

15. All Federal government and agency issues are fully taxable.

TABLE 8. BOND AND SHARE MARKETS
END-YEAR, $ MILLION

Holders:	Total[1]		Bonds[2] Federal Government and Agencies		State and Local Government		Corporate and Foreign		Shares	
	1964	1970	1964	1970	1964	1970	1964	1970	1964	1970
Monetary Institutions	120,325 (11.7)	171,804 (12.3)	85,891 (54.1)	99,987 (52.3)	33,535 (36.1)	69,296 (48.3)	899 (0.8)	2,521 (1.2)	—	—
Federal Reserve Banks	30,462 (3.0)	36,177 (2.6)	30,462 (19.2)	36,177 (18.9)	—	—	—	—	—	—
Commercial Banks	89,863 (8.8)	135,627 (9.7)	55,429 (34.9)	63,810 (33.4)	33,535 (36.1)	69,296 (48.3)	899 (0.8)	2,521 (1.2)	—	—
Insurance Companies and Pension Funds	191,661 (18.7)	284,276 (20.2)	20,467 (12.9)	15,235 (8.0)	17,655 (19.0)	22,684 (15.8)	96,067 (82.4)	142,635 (69.2)	57,472 (8.7)	103,722 (12.0)
Other Financial Institutions	44,715 (4.4)	73,508 (5.2)	12,496 (7.9)	16,053 (8.4)	1,145 (1.2)	1,332 (0.9)	5,668 (4.9)	13,333 (6.5)	25,406 (3.9)	42,790 (5.0)
Federal Government	11 (0.0)	4	11 (0.0)	4	—	—	—	—	—	—
State and Local Government	15,213 (1.5)	22,780 (1.6)	9,161 (5.8)	13,379 (7.0)	2,223 (2.4)	2,751 (1.9)	3,829 (3.3)	6,650 (3.2)	—	—
Non-financial Enterprises	12,313 (1.2)	16,665 (1.2)	9,783 (6.2)	7,518 (3.9)	2,530 (2.7)	9,147 (6.4)	—	—	—	—
Households	621,660 (60.6)	815,407 (58.0)	16,266 (10.3)	38,139 (19.9)	35,915 (38.6)	38,182 (26.6)	9,251 (7.9)	39,698 (19.3)	560,228 (85.3)	699,388 (81.0)
Rest of the World	19,343 (1.9)	20,249 (1.5)	4,586 (2.9)	1,008 (0.5)	—	—	922 (0.8)	1,141 (0.6)	13,835 (2.1)	18,100 (2.1)
Total	1,025,241 (100.0)	1,404,693 (100.0)	158,661 (100.0)	191,323 (100.0)	93,003 (100.0)	143,392 (100.0)	116,636 (100.0)	205,978 (100.0)	656,941 (100.0)	864,000 (100.0)
Relative Importance (in % of total)	100.0	100.0	15.5	13.6	9.1	10.2	11.4	14.7	64.1	61.5

1. Figures in brackets represent percentage of total.
2. Includes only marketable issues with original maturities of more than one year.

Source: OECD Financial Statistics.

by the success of a state or local governmental service. The two types together account for nearly all of the total issue, the general liability obligation being roughly twice the size of the revenue issue. The markets for state and local government securities tend to be less stable than the corporate and government bond markets; acquisitions by the individual purchaser groups, and not least by the banks, have varied a great deal in the short run in accordance with changing monetary conditions. At present the commercial banks are by far the most important single group of holders, their share of the assets amounting to nearly half the total issue (Table 8). By contrast, households, which up to 1965 accounted for a larger share of the issue than the banks, now hold little more than a quarter. The third major purchaser-group, the insurance companies, have increased their holdings more or less in step with the overall trend. Due to fragmentation, these securities do not command a ready secondary market.

Finally, the *corporate debt security issue* (including foreign bonds floated in the US markets) has expanded very considerably, more than doubling during the last decade and a half. It overwhelmingly takes the form of business liabilities. They are usually single-dated long-term issues, though in a few cases serial maturities are offered, and like the Federal government and agency securities they are fully taxable.[16] Corporate debt securities are placed almost exclusively with long-term institutional investors: life insurance companies, corporate non-insured pension funds and state retirement funds, all of which have an expanding contractual inflow of savings. Within this group, the life insurance companies are marginally more important than the private and state and local government pension and retirement funds. The household sector accounts for a much smaller proportion of the issues but has expanded its holdings at a very fast rate (Table 8).

New *corporate issues of stock* are a relatively minor source of funds, in the aggregate, despite the systematic easing of investment regulations in recent years in favour of shares. The reluctance of corporations to issue new shares is largely a consequence of stockholder resistance, which in turn results from the expense and uncertainty involved in the issuance of new stock. There are basically two types of (domestic or foreign) *shares:* corporate (common and preferred) stock and open-end investment company (mutual fund) shares. While the outstanding volume of the latter has increased at a faster rate than that of the former, corporate stock still accounts for the lion's share of the total (just under 95 per cent in 1968). While additions to the supply of stocks have been small, the demand for shares on the part of institutional investors has intensified considerably in recent years with the result of a decline in holdings by individuals. This shift from individual to institutional ownership is continuing in step with the general shift towards institutional savings.

The United States *money market,* which deals with a wide range of assets with maturities of less than one year, embraces some 15 per cent

16. As indicated above, foreign security offerings are underwritten and marketed much like corporate issues, and the two forms will be dealt with together in the following. However, it is worth noting that underwriting commissions for foreign securities are relatively large. This fact, together with the Interest Equalisation Tax and the voluntary foreign credit restraint programme for financial institutions (see page 87), has substantially limited the market, particularly for certains types of foreign securities to which these programmes applied when they were in force.

TABLE 9. MAJOR MONEY MARKET CLAIMS
END-YEAR, $ BILLION

Type of claim	1968	1969	1970	1971
Short-term securities[1]:	*147.0*	*162.3*	*173.3*	*174.8*
US Treasury bills	74.0	79.8	87.2	97.5
Other Treasury issues	45.5	48.6	46.6	32.9
Federal agency securities	19.4	23.2	24.9	25.2
State and local government securities	8.1	10.7	14.6	19.2
Other short-term claims[2]:	*67.6*	*76.2*	*92.6*	*100.2*
Negotiable certificates of deposit	23.5	10.9	26.1	34.0
Commercial paper	20.5	31.7	31.8	30.8
Federal funds (inter-bank loans)	5.6	8.6	13.5	17.4
Bank call loans to brokers and dealers	7.7	6.7	8.6	9.3
Bankers' acceptances	4.4	5.5	7.1	7.9
Euro-dollar borrowings	6.0	12.8	5.7	0.9
Gross total, major instruments[3]	214.6	238.5	265.9	275.0

1. Includes only issues maturing in one year or less, except for " other Treasury issues " which includes some debt maturing in up to two years. Federal agency issues include some loan participation certificates. State and local securities totals have been interpreted from fiscal-year data.
2. Negotiable CDs are issued in amounts of $ 100,000 or more, as reported by weekly reporting banks. Federal funds data are as given in call reports for all commercial banks.
3. The figures are gross because some claims may finance others included in the table; for example, negotiable CDs may supply funds to banks making call loans. Some interbank Federal funds borrowings are re-lent to other banks and thus are counted twice.

Source: Treasury Bulletin, US Bureau of the Census, *Governmental Finances*, Federal Reserve System.

of the entire credit market. Like the rest of the credit market, the money market is based in New York City, though market participants typically have direct links to financial markets elsewhere in the country. The money market is also in continuous and close communication with foreign markets. Domestically, the major participants are the large financial and non-financial corporations and the commercial banks (Table 9). The former group placed a large amount (as much as two-thirds in 1970) of their liquid funds in money market claims. In order to meet short-run changes in deposits, the commercial banks also keep a part of their earning assets in money market paper which is shiftable to other bank and non-bank holders. The Federal government is the major borrower from the money market; it directly accounts for 60 per cent (or, together with government agencies, 70 per cent) of the market's generally available claims. Most of these short-term claims are 3-12 months' bills—an issue on which, as indicated on page 36, the Treasury has come to rely more heavily in recent years for government financing.

An important sub-market, the so-called Federal funds market, is essentially an inter-bank market where banks with reserve balances in excess of requirements offer to lend them on a day-to-day basis to banks deficient in reserves. Thus commercial banks may adjust their reserve positions by borrowing from other banks, in addition to borrowing at Federal Reserve banks or selling securities in the market. Since the mid-1960s there has been a tendency for many large banks to be almost continuous borrowers in the Federal funds market.[17] The Federal funds

17. For a more thorough discussion, see Boughton [7].

rate is a highly sensitive indicator of shifting pressures in this very short end of the market. The banks are very active in all other sub-markets as well, though non-financial corporations play important roles in the markets for Treasury bills, certificates of deposit (CDs) and commercial paper. The bill market is the most important of these, and the three-month bill rate is another important indicator of shifting money market pressures. The existence of active secondary trading facilities and the wide participation by banks and non-banks have made the bill market a most efficient, broad, and active market; through it, the Federal Reserve System conducts the great bulk of its open market transactions.

II

THE INSTRUMENTS AND THE DESIGN
OF MONETARY POLICY

a) THE STRUCTURE OF THE FEDERAL RESERVE SYSTEM AND THE SCOPE
FOR POLICY INSTRUMENTS

Monetary policy in the United States is conducted by the Federal Reserve System, which is not a single central bank, but rather twelve Federal Reserve banks forming part of a single central banking organisation. The responsibility for control of the many instruments of monetary policy available to the Federal Reserve System is complex. The following chart reproduced from the IMF study by Ralph Young shows the relationship between the Board of Governors, the Federal Open Market Committee and the principal instruments through which monetary policy has been conducted (Chart 9). The Federal Open Market Committee, which meets approximately every four weeks, has developed into the main policy-making body; its members are the seven members of the Board of Governors, the President of the Federal Reserve Bank of New York, and four of the remaining eleven Federal Reserve bank presidents serving in rotation.

The principal instruments used in conducting domestic monetary policy during the period 1960-71 have been:[1]

1. Open market operations;
2. Variations in the Federal Reserve discount rate;
3. Variations within defined limits of the reserve requirement ratios of member banks against defined classes of liabilities;
4. Variations in the maximum rates of interest payable by banks on defined classes of time and savings deposits (Regulation Q).

---

1. Other actions by the monetary authorities may supplement the impact of changes in the principal instruments. In particular, the Federal Reserve has powers accorded by a long series of regulations to regulate various financial transactions, notably those relating to the stock exchange. It is a common characteristic of these powers that they have not been designed as instruments of counter-cyclical monetary policy. The most important of them are those pertaining to margin requirements —i.e. the percentage of the market value of a security which the purchaser has to provide out of unborrowed funds—for the purchase, with borrowed funds, of defined classes of marketable claims. Originally the requirement covered equities only, reflecting its origin in the determination to avoid a repetition of the speculative excesses in the stock market of 1928 and 1929. The margin requirement has now been extended to cover convertible bonds, stocks issued by mutual funds and a limited group of securities traded over the counter. Administratively the margin requirements are implemented by four separate regulations: G, T, U and X. Changes in margin requirements take place when the Federal Reserve finds that there is excess or deficient liquidity in the stock market.

Chart 9. STRUCTURE OF FEDERAL RESERVE AUTHORITY FOR CREDIT AND MONETARY REGULATION

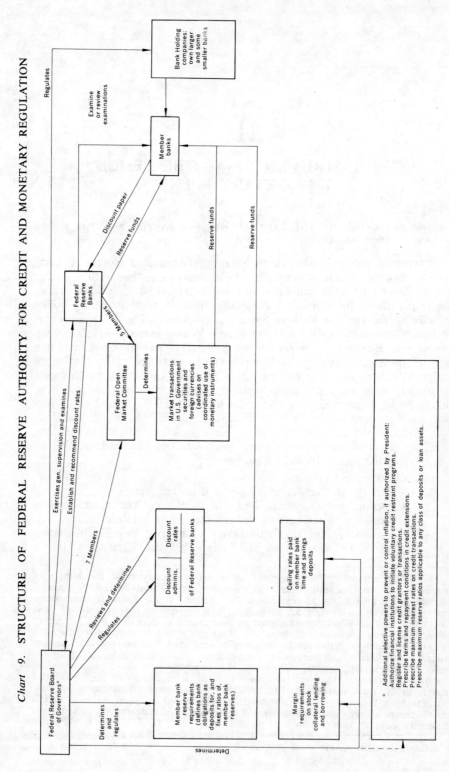

Source: "Monetary Policy and its Instruments in the United States", Ralph A. Young, IMF.

It may be noted that since 1952 the Federal Reserve System has had no power to vary the terms of consumer credit. The Federal Reserve does possess a variety of means of influencing public opinion and the political process through its many publications, speeches by Board members and the virtually continuous commentaries provided throughout the country by the Presidents and senior officers of the Federal Reserve banks to local financial and business communities.

"Moral suasion", defined as informal central banking advice or requests to commercial banks, backed by implicit threats of loss of central banking goodwill in the event of a failure of any bank to respond, appears to have had relatively little place in the conduct of US monetary policy. There are exceptions to this, however; in both 1966 and 1969, moral suasion was employed during the two periods of monetary restraint. Thus in September 1966, a letter was sent out by the Board of Governors to member banks instructing them not to continue selling municipal securities at the rate observed during the summer months. Banks complying with this request would be granted special facilities at the discount window. But, in general, the Federal Reserve traditionally has relied upon the response of individual banks to the influence it can have on money market conditions through the instruments under its control. In brief, the method of conducting monetary policy is a market system, as opposed to an administrative system in which the central bank can maintain direct contact with each of a relatively small number of commercial banks.

b) OPEN MARKET OPERATIONS

Open market operations have become the Federal Reserve System's primary control instrument over member-bank reserves and short-term interest rates such as the Federal funds rate and the three-month Treasury bill rate. Operations are conducted for the System by the Federal Reserve Bank of New York through a group of about 20 security dealers. These dealers are required to satisfy the System regarding their conduct of business. The actual operations of the manager of the Federal Open Market account ("the Desk" for short) consist of three types of transactions:

1. Outright purchases or sales;
2. Purchases of securities under agreement to resell at an agreed price within 15 days (repurchase agreements);
3. Sales of securities under agreement to repurchase at a known price, usually within 3 days (sale-repurchase agreements).

The securities used in these transactions are predominantly direct or fully guaranteed US government securities, since the government securities market is the broadest and most active. They also include US government agency securities, the market for which has developed substantially in the past few years. The Desk also purchases a small amount of prime bankers' acceptances with less than 6 months maturity, mainly to help promote a more effective secondary market in such issues. Transactions effected under repurchase agreements often constitute the major portion of total operations (Table 10). The outright transactions as well as others are predominantly in Treasury bills rather than long-term securities. No net sales were made of securities with a remaining life of over one year during the period under study. Even the purchase of these securities,

43

TABLE 10. OPEN MARKET OPERATIONS, 1971

TABLE 10. OPEN MARKET OPERATIONS, 1971

$ MILLION

	Outright Transactions in US Govt. Securities by Maturity				Repurchase Agreements (US Govt. Securities)		Pur-chases of other Secu-rities net	Net Change[1]
	Treasury Bills			Other				
	Gross Pur-chases	Gross Sales	Re-demp-tions	Net Pur-chases	Gross Pur-chases	Gross Sales		
January	1,515	1,547	327	—	2,298	2,298	2	–357
February	5,347	5,153	—	484	4,183	4,183	–5	673
March	2,600	2,523	240	542	6,561	5,242	271	1,968
April	2,033	1,298	50	197	5,085	6,404	–268	–707
May	1,163	248	—	128	4,076	4,076	56	1,099
June	1,893	1,165	37	63	1,165	1,165	–49	705
July	2,067	1,617	127	—	3,044	3,044	–7	316
August	1,709	1,024	—	108	2,184	1,951	121	1,148
September	1,818	1,088	83	283	3,697	3,930	–64	634
October	772	1,133	—	—	2,616	2,616	36	–326
November	1,129	1,070	200	755	5,003	5,003	250	862
December	3,055	1,981	—	105	4,830	3,607	449	2,850
Total	25,101	19,847	1,064	2,665	44,741	43,519	789	8,866

1. Net change in US government securities, Federal agency obligations and bankers' acceptances. Sales, redemptions and negative figures reduce System holdings; all other figures increase such holdings.

Source: Annual Report of the Board of Governors of the Federal Reserve System, 1971.

however, marks a change of Federal Reserve policy relative to the 1950s. During that period, the Federal Reserve confined its actions to the short end of the market in the belief that the outstanding volume of long-term securities was too modest to withstand substantial dealings by the System. The abandonment of this so-called "bills only" (or "bills preferably")[2] policy in 1961 was considered a significant change by outside observers. The Federal Reserve also conducts open market operations in foreign currencies; but these operations are of no major significance for domestic monetary policy.[3]

The impact of open market operations on member-bank reserves is illustrated in Chart 10, where the elements influencing reserves are classified into their major components. The main policy component is the change in the System's holdings of US government securities, which is virtually equivalent to the net volume of open market operations.[4] Most

2. For an authoritative interpretation of this policy, see notably R. Young and C. Yager [102].

3. For a description see R. Young [101], Appendix to Chapter III.

4. The term "Federal Reserve credit" is often used to denote the policy instrument; see e.g. the review of simulations in Part III. This concept includes, in addition to open market operations, also various relatively minor sources of reserve money, of which the most important is float: credit extended to member banks through the System's function as a clearing agency. For practical purposes, Federal Reserve credit and open market operations may be regarded as synonymous terms.

Chart 10. SOURCES AND USES OF RESERVE MONEY
ANNUAL CHANGES

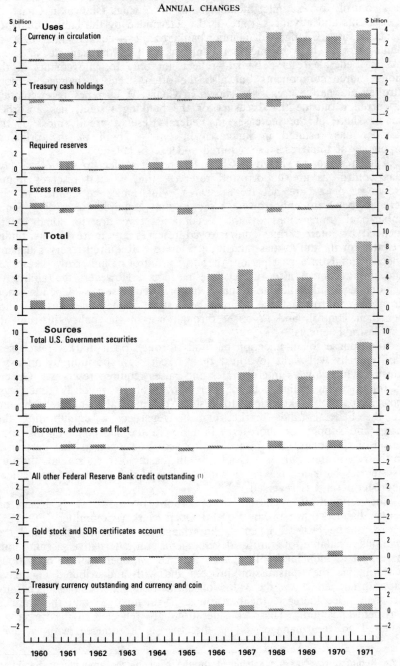

1. Minus other Federal Reserve accounts and Federal Reserve liabilities and capital.

Source: Annual Report of the Board of Governors of the Federal Reserve System.

of the other sources and uses of reserves are not subject to complete policy control; for example, member-bank borrowings (shown in Chart 10 as "discounts and advances") are partly determined by the banks' demands for such loans. Changes in member-bank reserves—defined since 1960 to include currency held by member banks as well as the deposits of those banks at Federal Reserve banks—reflect not only the movements in the various source components but also the often sizeable changes in non-controlled alternative uses. As shown in Chart 10, currency in circulation (i.e. currency outside the Treasury or the banking system) has absorbed a major share of the increases in Federal Reserve credit; most of the remainder has resulted in increases in one or both of the principal components of total reserves: required and excess balances.[5]

Total reserves as shown in Chart 10 are not subject to so close a day-to-day control as are unborrowed reserves, that is total reserves minus borrowings; or as are net free reserves, which may be defined as the difference between unborrowed reserves and required reserves. Since member-bank borrowings at the Federal Reserve are to some extent influenced by interest rates, unborrowed reserves are more closely under the control of the authorities than total reserves. Required reserves depend on deposit totals in a past period; therefore, control of unborrowed reserves would imply control also of net free reserves. However, the ability of the monetary authorities to control unborrowed reserves depends upon their ability to forecast the sources of reserve money in Chart 10 not under their control, and to offset through use of the policy instruments any undesirable effects.

In response to an injection of funds through open market purchases, banks typically will want to adjust their free reserve position by an asset expansion which lowers interest rates and raises required reserves. Generally, this banking adjustment of portfolio positions involves time lags. Deposit expansion takes time to restore commercial bank equilibrium; since the Federal funds market can be regarded as equilibrating the demand and supply for short-term liquidity in the short run during such a period of adjustment, the immediate impact of net open market purchases is on the rate in this market. Gradually, the easing of rates spreads through the system as bank asset expansion proceeds and the downward movement in short-term rates is reversed.

The conduct of open market operations by the Desk is based on directives handed down by the Federal Open Market Committee (FOMC).[6] The aim of the FOMC, given its knowledge of the recent past and the predictions available of future developments on alternative assumptions with respect to monetary policy, is to arrange for open market operations which will, via the transmission process and with a distributed lag, have an appropriate effect on the value of ultimate target variables: generally the rate of price increase, the percentage of unemployed and the balance of payments position. These considerations are reflected in the directives formulated to the manager. The directive is introduced with a one-

---

5. Required reserves are calculated on the basis of the amounts of liabilities, mainly deposits, held by each bank in the second week prior to the computation. See page 56.

6. A more complete account of FOMC procedures and strategy may be found in Appendix II.

paragraph review of recent policy trends and of the objectives pursued by the authorities; a second paragraph contains the instructions which are to guide the Desk over the period to the next meeting of the Committee. The directive is made public three months after the date of the FOMC meeting and subsequently is published in the *Federal Reserve Bulletin* [26] and in the *Annual Reports* [25] with an indication of the votes cast in its adoption. The directive itself is preceded by a short review of recent economic trends and by indications in qualitative terms of expectations for the next quarter or so. The forecasts of the real economy on which the decisions of the Federal Open Market Committee are based are not, however, made public.

There have been important changes since 1960 in the formulation of the open market directive.[7] During the years up to 1969, there was heavy emphasis on *money market conditions*. Generally money market conditions are thought to be definable in terms of at least three variables:

1. the Federal funds rate,
2. the net free reserves of member banks, and
3. the three-month Treasury bill rate (Chart 11).

In view of the nature of the money market (pages 37-40), these three variables summarise the main features of changes in the market. The manager is typically given a range to which these variables should conform within the period up to the next FOMC meeting. Conflicts obviously may arise among the instructions given with respect to the variables. In an exact world, the quantity variable—net free reserves—would be related by stable asset demand functions to the two interest rates, and the three target variables would merge into one. The Desk, with only one instrument, Federal Reserve purchases of securities, could operate on one target only; in principle, it could achieve the chosen target exactly. But stable, i.e. fully predictable, asset demand functions do not exist; in practice, a given range of net free reserves may, at different times, co-exist with very different Federal funds rates. In general, the definition of policy in terms of money market conditions does not leave the Desk with any simple mechanical rule of action; an interpretation of the directive will usually be required.

From 1966 through early 1970, the directive contained a so-called *proviso clause*. Following the instructions relating to changes in the money market conditions, there was added a clause in the form, "provided bank credit... remains on a projected course." As a practical approximation, bank credit typically has been measured through the liability side of balance sheets of the commercial banks, including at first only deposits, but subsequently also non-deposit funds, the expanded concept being known as the "adjusted bank credit proxy". In general, given the prevailing definition, the *proviso clause* was symmetrical in the sense that the Desk was expected to make money market conditions easier than otherwise stated if the rate of growth of the proxy fell significantly short of its projected growth, or conversely to tighten conditions if it significantly exceeded the range of rates projected. The origin and time horizons of projected rates of growth cannot be inferred from the directive, but according to Axilrod [4], p. 17, the projection was usually for one month

---

7. The evolution of the directive through the 1960s is explained in Axilrod [4].

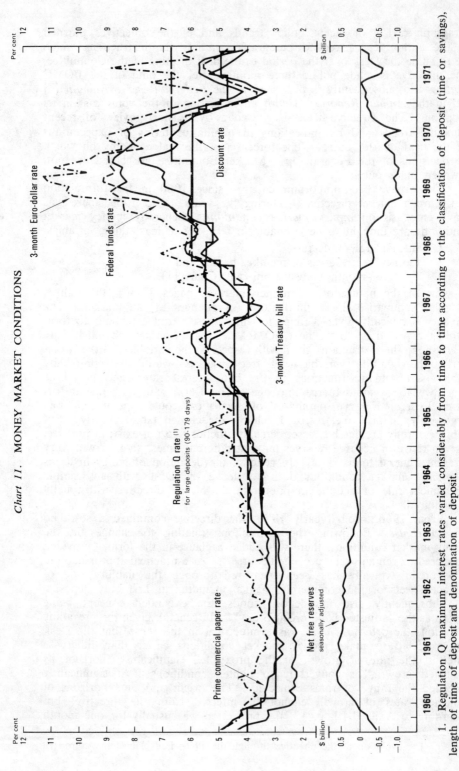

Chart 11. MONEY MARKET CONDITIONS

3-month Euro-dollar rate

Federal funds rate

Discount rate

3-month Treasury bill rate

Regulation Q rate [1]
for large deposits (90-179 days)

Prime commercial paper rate

Net free reserves
seasonally adjusted

1. Regulation Q maximum interest rates varied considerably from time to time according to the classification of deposit (time or savings), length of time of deposit and denomination of deposit.

The highest ceiling was set on 21st January, 1970 on single maturity time deposits of 1 year or more for deposits of $100,000 and over.

Source: Federal Reserve Bulletin, Business Conditions Digest, World Financial Markets.

and was based on a quantitative interpretation of money market conditions as defined above. The directive contained no information regarding the permissible size of the deviation, or on whether the Desk should revise money market conditions if significant errors appeared after the first, second or third week of the policy periods. Since the Desk's control over even unborrowed reserves is not perfect, it is plausible to suggest that control over the bank credit proxy could not be firm in the short run, even if the change in the proxy were a stable function of current and past changes in unborrowed reserves; therefore, large percentage errors in the bank credit proxy may have to be accepted. Moreover, though the Desk's control over bank credit depends upon the method by which this concept is calculated, the estimates available to the manager will in any case contain some error; if so, there may be—in addition to uncertainty regarding the response of the proxy to open market operations—uncertainty about what is actually happening to bank credit. For these reasons one may infer that at least in the short run a major function of the *proviso clause* relating to the bank credit proxy or some other monetary aggregate was to check whether the real economy was on the course projected and considered acceptable by the monetary authorities; see Appendix II.

Since early 1970, *monetary aggregates* have been given greater prominence. Initially the order of importance between the monetary aggregates referred to in the *proviso clause* and the money market conditions was reversed. Thus, the directive was amended to instruct the manager to achieve certain growth rates in the monetary aggregates provided that money market conditions were consistent therewith. The Federal Open Market Committee remained eclectic in its formulation of these additional targets: both the narrow money supply (M_1), the broad money supply, i.e. including longer-term deposits at commercial banks (M_2), and the bank credit proxy were used in the directive. As analysed in further detail in Appendix II, the introduction of this modification of the directive led to considerable difficulties, partly because the demand for money appeared to become less stable during the years 1970 and 1971. The reasoning behind this introduction of monetary aggregates as an important target for the Federal Reserve System has been given by Brimmer [10].[8]

Since the end of the period here under study, the directive has undergone further modifications. The definition of money market conditions has been given more precision by modifying and putting relatively more emphasis on bank reserves. The preferred definition of bank reserves is now that of "reserves to support private member bank deposits" (RPD) which excludes reserves held against inter-bank deposits or government deposits. This measure is considered preferable to total reserves because short-run fluctuations in government and net inter-bank deposits tend to be large and unpredictable and are usually not of major significance for policy. It is as yet too early to evaluate the effects of changing to this new formulation of the directive.[9]

---

8. Occasionally the terminology that the monetary aggregates are an "intermediate" target has been used to distinguish them from the "operating", i.e. very short-run targets. Since the distinction between the two types of targets cannot be made precise, depending as it does on the proximity of the variable to the instruments of policy, this terminology is not used in the present study. But the substantive issues involved in controllability of various targets are reviewed in Appendix II.

9. For a preliminary explanation of the new policy see *inter alia* Ruebling [89]; for a review of 1972 experiences see *Federal Reserve Bulletin* for June 1973 [26].

The several modifications of operating procedures introduced in recent years suggest that the Federal Reserve has not yet adopted a firm view as to what it can or should aim to control through manipulation of its major policy instrument. Indeed operating procedures have been under constant review over the last few years, partly as a result of criticism by academic economists, partly in response to the continuing attempts of the FOMC to devise more efficient short-term procedures. The preliminary conclusion is that no single procedure can be said to be optimal for all time periods. In operating on either an interest rate or a quantity variable reflecting money market conditions, the Desk has the major advantage of having a high degree of control; it has the means to bring about in the short run any desired change in the Treasury bill rate[10] or the Federal funds rate. Similarly, but with less than full precision and with some time lag, the Desk could achieve a target level of free reserves, though with no greater accuracy than that with which the non-controlled sources of reserve money (and the currency drain) can be predicted. But the usefulness, from the viewpoint of controlling the monetary aggregates, of adopting one of these procedures depends on the relative stability of the links from either of them to the monetary aggregates. The issue in the formulation (or emphasis) of instructions regarding money market conditions is, as Pierce and Thomson [83] have shown, whether the relationship between reserves and the money stock is more predictable than that between the selected short-term rate and the money stock. The relative predictability hinges in turn on the stability of the money demand and supply functions, as described in more detail in Appendix II; if the money supply is the more stable, the pursuance of a reserve target will give better control of the monetary aggregates. The 1972 shift in operating procedures towards more emphasis on a reserve target reflects an acceptance by the FOMC of the hypothesis that operating on reserves should tend, on average, to make the monetary aggregates more predictable. This recognition is not surprising following the apparent instability of the demand for money experienced in 1970-71; but it is not one that is necessarily valid for all time.

The aim of monetary policy is, however, wider than control of the money stock. It is to influence aggregate demand in such a way that the ultimate policy objectives are more closely approximated. The issue is therefore whether changes in the aggregates exert an important influence on income, so that by controlling the monetary aggregates the authorities may also be confident that they are exercising the desired impact on aggregate demand. If not, interest rates—in this case the longer-term rates relevant as expressions of the cost of capital to spenders—may provide a superior policy target. This is an issue which, in a way analogous to the discussion of money market conditions, hinges on the relative stability of two sets of relationships; on the one hand the demand function for money and on the other hand the investment and saving functions.[11] It

---

10. The short-run controllability of the Treasury bill rate provides a justification for analysing policy changes as originating from an exogenous (policy) change in the bill rate. See the discussion of policy simulations on pages 71-72.

11. Technically speaking, the issue is whether the LM or the IS curve is the more predictable in the simplified presentation of general equilibrium introduced by Hicks; see in particular Poole [85].

would make little sense to aim to control the monetary aggregates—even assuming that the technical problems of such control, referred to in page 50, have been resolved through experimentation with "appropriate" operating targets such as RPD—if these aggregates turned out to be poor predictors of movements in income, employment and prices. The increasing emphasis on monetary aggregates since the mid-1960s reflects that the Federal Reserve System has come to place greater reliance on the informative content in the money stock and other aggregates. This development does not imply that the Federal Reserve has become "monetarist"; as noted above, the choice of an operating target depends on the relative predictability of the demand for money functions and the investment and savings functions, rather than the relative degree of interest elasticity of these two functions; see e.g. Mayer [73]. The view reflected in several policy actions in recent years and even more clearly in the econometric research done by or in co-operation with the staff of the Board of Governors is indeed the eclectic one that *(i)* the effects of monetary policy are largely transmitted through interest rates; but *(ii)* the monetary aggregates often convey more information about the current thrust of monetary policy. These issues can be discussed only in connection with the review of the transmission mechanism undertaken in Part III (see also Part IV*(a)* and Appendix II). But it must be underlined that the choice of policy targets is not an either-or; there may be grounds for expecting that in some periods the investment-saving functions are sufficiently stable for long-term interest rates to constitute a policy target superior to the monetary aggregates. In practice, it is therefore likely that the authorities will wish to keep an eye on both types of financial variables.

c) DISCOUNT RATE CHANGES

Member banks may, for approved purposes, borrow from the Federal Reserve bank of their region by discounting. In practice the method of borrowing is for the member bank to offer its own promissory note secured by government securities. The rediscounting of eligible paper is now very rare. Neglecting emergency situations, the terms of access to the discount window are governed by Regulation A. Discounting is regarded as a privilege, not a right, and is normally expected to be a temporary measure taken to offset unexpected losses in reserves. Persistent borrowing to take advantage of interest rate differentials would not be permitted. Any renewal of discounts beyond the original maximum period of 15 days brings into operation an increasingly strict surveillance procedure. There are no general rules as to the ceilings on borrowings of individual banks. The Federal Reserve does not systematically vary its administration of the discount facilities cyclically except by changing the discount rate. The restrictions on the supply side of the market may be reinforced by reluctance of member banks to borrow.[12] In a fairly active year in the 1950s about 20 per cent of member banks borrowed at one time or another, and similar percentages have been observed in the periods of monetary restraint in 1966 and 1969. The percentage is very much higher

---

12. Historically such a reluctance is thought to have been very widespread; see e.g. Holland [48]. But borrowing has tended to become a more important feature of commercial bank activity in the post-war period.

—of the order of 70 per cent—for banks in the large financial centres alone. But even in recent periods of monetary restraint, member-bank borrowing did not amount to more than 3 to 4 per cent of required reserves and less than ½ per cent of deposits.

The discount rate is in principle fixed by the individual Federal Reserve banks, but their decisions are submitted to the Federal Reserve Board which "reviews and determines" the ultimate action. A fixing of the discount rate may therefore be regarded as a joint responsibility of the Board of Governors and the individual Federal Reserve banks. It is changed in discrete steps, generally of ¼ of ½ of a percentage point. Although the Federal Reserve's discount policy has become somewhat more flexible since 1970, the discount rate in the period under review moved at relatively infrequent intervals. Thus, the discount rate not only has remained below the rate on commercial paper, but was at times also left lower than the Federal funds rate and the Treasury bill rate. For example, in the early months of both 1970 and 1973, the discount rate was left at a level about 1.5 percentage point below the Federal funds rate. In such periods, when the discount rate did not act as a penalty rate, total borrowing at the Federal Reserve was controlled more importantly through non-price guidelines that define appropriate use of the discount window, as, indeed, the terms of Regulation A described above suggest.

The consequences of a change in the discount rate may be decomposed into two elements: the impact on interest rates and on borrowing of member banks, and the effect on expectations. A change in the discount rate, unborrowed reserves being constant, changes the cost of temporary borrowing at the Federal Reserve; thus a rise in the discount rate tends to reduce the demand for borrowed reserves, although some doubt remains as to the size of its response. A rise in the discount rate is restrictive also because it tends to increase the demand for free reserves at any given level of deposits. There is at the same time an effect on the interest rates charged by banks to their customers. The most detailed study available on the commercial loan market suggests that a one percentage point increase in the discount rate tended during the tight money periods in the late 1960s to result in an increase in the commercial loan rate of 36 basis points in the same quarter and 33 basis points in the following quarter.[13] The discount rate is also thought to affect expectations in financial markets, because changes in it are interpreted as a signal of a change in monetary policy. To the extent that the discount rate tends to follow, rather than lead, movements in market rates, changes in it may provide a confirmation that changes in observed money market conditions were in fact approved by the Federal Reserve and thus reflect policy. They also may suggest that further changes are in prospect.

d) REGULATION Q MAXIMA

Potentially Regulation Q is a powerful weapon. The power to fix ceiling rates on bank deposits may be used jointly with open market operations to bring about shifts in interest rate differentials between the Treasury

---

13. See Jaffee [53], p. 115.

bill market and deposits with a comparable maturity in the banking system. By changing such interest rate differentials, the non-bank public, and particularly the large corporations, could be made to shift funds in large quantities between the banking system and the money market. As already mentioned in Part I, the degree of substitution in corporate liquid holdings between time deposits in the form of negotiable certificates of deposits (CDs) and short-term money market instruments is very considerable. The purpose of using this instrument was to reduce the access of banks to deposit funds in periods of monetary restraint; this limitation was expected to constrain the expansion of bank loans, particularly to industrial and commercial customers. This reasoning, which may essentially be classified as an availability theory of bank credit, did not have the predicted effects when used in 1966 and 1969 (see the description of these policy phases in Part IV below); commercial banks managed to offset much of the run-off of CDs by attracting funds from abroad and through the commercial paper market, and their lending to industrial and commercial borrowers was protected further from the effect of restraint by a reduction in holdings of securities; see pages 55-56.

The fixing of maximum interest rates on bank deposits also regulates the competitive position between banks and other institutions, notably the non-bank financial intermediaries. In recent periods of rising interest rates, the savings and loan associations and mutual savings banks have found it difficult to offer competitive rates because their assets are to a large extent tied up in loans contracted at the lower interest rates prevailing prior to the mid-1960s. In the absence of any regulation of bank deposit rates, there would have been a very strong tendency for individual depositors to shift funds out of these savings and loan associations and mutual savings banks and into closely substitutable deposits with commercial banks.[14] The monetary authorities found such shifts undesirable, as they endangered the viability of an important category of financial institutions and pushed the brunt of monetary restraint too heavily onto the housing market for which these institutions are the main source of finance. From 1966 a distinction has been introduced in Regulation Q between two categories of deposits: large deposits, defined as those in excess of $100,000 and typically involving large banks, and small time and savings deposits below this amount. Following the run on non-bank financial intermediaries in 1966, a ceiling was imposed on the smaller deposits in both banks and savings institutions; subsequently this ceiling was maintained below that on large deposits. Thus, since 1966, Regulation Q has basically had a dual purpose (although in fact the regulation now distinguishes several classes of deposits; see Table 11 and page 56. The first objective has been to protect some of the more vulnerable financial institutions from growing competition with larger banks in the deposit market during

---

14. It may be noted that while empirical work tends to find that long-term deposits with banks and non-banks are close substitutes (page 31) the substitutability between deposits with non-bank institutions and money market instruments, such as Treasury bills, is more limited. While individual holders of savings deposits with savings and loan associations do respond in some measure to a change in the appropriate interest rate differential, the size of the response is limited by institutional factors, such as the minimum denomination of bills; the latter was raised in 1969-70 from $1,000 to $10,000, thus taking the purchase of Treasury bills outside the reach of most individual holders of non-bank savings deposits.

TABLE 11. REGULATION Q MAXIMA

PER CENT PER ANNUM

TYPE OF DEPOSIT	EFFECTIVE DATE[1] Jan. 1 1957	Jan. 1 1962	July 17 1963	Nov. 24 1964	Dec. 6 1965	July 20 1966	Sept. 26 1966	Apr. 19 1968	Jan. 21 1970	June 24 1970	May 16 1973	July 1 1973
Savings deposits	3	...	...	4	4	4	4	4	4½	4½	4½	5
Less than one year	...	3½	3½	...	...	...	...	...	...	...	...	...
1 year and over	...	4	4	...	...	...	...	...	...	...	...	...
Other time deposits												
Multiple maturity[2]:												
30-89 days	1	1	1	4	5½	4	4	4	4½	4½	4½	5
90 days to 6 months	2½	2½	...	...	...	...	...	...	...	...	...	...
90 days to 1 year	...	...	4	4½	5½	5	5	5	5	5	5	5½
6 months to 1 year	3	3½	...	...	...	...	...	...	...	...	...	...
1 year and over	3	4	4	4½	5½	...	...	...	...	...	...	...
1 year to 2 years	...	...	...	...	...	5	5	5	5½	5½	5½	...
1-2½ years	...	...	...	...	...	...	...	...	...	...	...	6
2 years and over	...	...	...	...	...	5	5	5	5¾	5¾	5¾	...
2½ years and over	...	...	...	...	...	...	...	...	...	...	...	6½
4 years and over[3]	...	...	...	...	...	...	...	...	...	...	...	n.c.
Single maturity:												
less than $100,000:												
30-89 days	...	...	...	...	...	5½	5	5	5	5	5	5
90 days to 1 year	...	...	...	...	...	5½	5	5	5	5	5	5½
1 year to 2 years	...	...	...	...	...	5½	5	5	5½	5½	5½	...
1 - 2½ years	...	...	...	...	...	...	...	...	...	...	...	6
2 years and over	...	...	...	...	...	5½	5	5	5¾	5¾	5¾	...
2½ years and over	...	...	...	...	...	...	...	...	...	...	...	6½
4 years and over[3]	...	...	...	...	...	...	...	...	...	...	...	n.c.
$100,00 and over:												
30-59 days	...	...	...	...	...	5½	5½	5½	6¼	n.c.	n.c.	n.c.
60-89 days	...	...	...	...	...	5½	5½	5¾	6½	n.c.	n.c.	n.c.
90-179 days	...	...	...	...	...	5½	5½	6	6¾	6¾	n.c.	n.c.
180 days to 1 year	...	...	...	...	...	5½	5½	6¼	7	7	n.c.	n.c.
1 year and over	...	...	...	...	...	5½	5½	6¼	7½	7½	n.c.	n.c.

1. n.c. = no ceiling as of the date shown.
... = category not applicable as of the date shown.

2. Multiple-maturity time deposits include deposits that are automatically renewable at maturity without action by the depositor and deposits that are payable after written notice of withdrawal. The distinction between multiple- and single-maturity deposits has been incorporated in Regulation Q since July 20, 1966. This table includes all "other time deposits" in the former category prior to that date.

3. Between July 1 and October 31, 1973, there was no ceiling for 4-year certificates with minimum denomination of $ 1,000. The amount of such certificates that a bank could issue was limited to 5 per cent of its total time and savings deposits. Sales in excess of that amount were subject to the 6½ per cent ceiling that applies to time deposits maturing in 2½ years or more. Effective Nov. 1, 1973 a ceiling rate of 7¼ per cent was imposed on certificates maturing in 4 years and over with minimum denomination of $ 1,000. There is no limitation on the amount of these certificates that banks may issue.

Source: Federal Reserve Bulletin.

restrictive periods and thereby to weaken or delay the undesirably strong restrictive impact of monetary policy on the lending activity of these institutions. At the same time, the regulation has aimed at increasing the leverage of monetary policy on larger banks' loanable funds. This second aspect of the regulation will be reviewed below in some detail.

A period of Regulation Q effectiveness (or limitation) in the latter respect may be defined as a period in which the maximum rates allowed on large deposits (CDs) are below the market rates on competing money market assets. Such a situation occurred in 1966 and 1969. In periods when commercial banks are administratively prevented from paying competitive rates, there is evidence that the high interest sensitivity of portfolio managers leads in some measure to two processes which involve a considerable degree of disintermediation:

i) a sharp run-off of CDs as portfolio managers substitute money market assets; and

ii) circumvention by financial intermediaries of administrative controls through the development of new liabilities not subject to Regulation Q control.

During the periods of Regulation Q effectiveness in 1966 and 1969, there was typically a sizeable run-off of CDs as portfolio managers shifted into market assets. This shifting meant that the banks' demand for market assets declined while that of the private sector increased. If the non-bank private sector were prepared to hold precisely those assets released by the banks, no change in relative demands or rates would result. But it seems likely that the private non-bank sector will require a portfolio somewhat more liquid than that desired by the banks, since the latter function as intermediaries to borrow short and lend long. Thus the result of disintermediation is, as argued by Tobin [98], likely to be an excess demand for short-term claims such as Treasury bills and commercial paper and an excess supply of longer-term claims such as mortgages. Thus, in themselves, the relative asset-demand changes resulting from disintermediation are deflationary in that they tend to raise long rates relative to short. If the Federal Reserve keeps money market conditions, including short-term rates, constant in the face of an excess demand for Treasury bills, it can do so only by selling bills; in this case there would be a decline in reserves associated with the process of disintermediation during the period of Regulation Q effectiveness. Indeed, such an effect was typically desired by the monetary authorities in the two phases of restraint. Clearly, the severity of the squeeze depends on the asset effect, which is likely to be quantitatively small. Nevertheless, the existence of such effects provides a rationale for the deliberate use of Regulation Q as a means of squeezing the liquidity of the banks and reducing the availability or raising the cost of bank loans to business.

These effects are, of course, mitigated or offset to the extent that the banks develop alternative means of attracting funds. This they did in 1969 by borrowing heavily in the Euro-dollar market, by issuing commercial paper through bank holding companies, and by selling loan participations; collectively these sources more than offset a $12 billion decline in CDs. Insofar as newly-developed bank liabilities are not subject to reserve requirements, the banks' demand for reserves is reduced. With a given volume of reserves, banks therefore could support a larger amount of deposits. Though it was possible for the Federal Reserve to offset such downwards shifts in the demand for reserves through open market sales, it was found desirable to reduce the incentive for banks to borrow through the newly developed markets. In 1969 reserve requirements were imposed on additional borrowing in the Euro-dollar markets. That requirement was later extended to cover increases in several other sources of bank liabilities, including single-maturity large CDs, commercial paper issued by affiliates, and sales of finance bills.[15] To further reduce borrowing incentives, the maximum rates have been suspended since June 1970 for large deposits with maturities of less than 90 days, and since May 1973 for those maturing in 90 days or more. For a time during the second half of 1973, some smaller denominations of CDs were also exempted from the ceilings.

e) VARIABLE RESERVE REQUIREMENT RATIOS

The power to vary reserve requirement ratios against the several classes of domestic deposit liabilities of member banks was established as an instrument of the Federal Reserve in 1935. The prescribed ratios, given the definition of liabilities subject to requirements, specify for any member bank a total of required reserves. Since 1960, reserves have been defined to include both balances at the Federal Reserve banks and vault cash; the latter item was formerly excluded. The definition of liabilities subject to reserve requirements has been modified in the light of commercial banking practices, as described in the preceding paragraph.

The range within which the Federal Reserve Board may vary the ratios is wide (Table 12). The ratios were near their legal maxima in the early post-war years; after a brief tightening during the Korean-war boom, they were eased on several occasions up to 1960, reflecting both a desire to eliminate the high ratios appropriate in inflationary war-time conditions and a concern that high ratios might prompt disaffiliation from the Federal Reserve System. Since 1960 the changes made have been small; in 1969 the reserve requirement was applied in a restrictive direction for the first time in 18 years. But more important effects have come about through modifications in the design of the required ratios. Differential requirements have been applied to reserve city banks and to country banks and according to the size of deposits in each of these categories. The rationale of these differences is that large banks in financial centres are likely to experience considerably greater deposit volatility than smaller banks in rural districts. But it gradually has become apparent that using only the size of the banks is a fairer way of graduating the ratios. Following some minor revisions in classification, the whole scale of ratios against demand deposits was thoroughly restructured by an amendment to the relevant Regulation D, voted by the Board on June 21st, 1972 and implemented in November 1972.[16] The new ratios depend only on bank size and range from 8 per cent for the smallest to $17\frac{1}{2}$ per cent of demand deposits for the largest banks. The direct effect of this reform was expansionary, but most of it was offset by a simultaneous tightening of

---

15. The term "finance bills" (or "working capital acceptances") refers to bank acceptances other than those which apply to specific transactions in goods.
16. See [25], 1972, pp. 626-29.

TABLE 12. **RESERVE REQUIREMENT RATIOS, 1960-1971**

Effective Date	Net Demand Deposits				Time Deposits (all classes of banks)		
	Reserve City Banks[1]		Country Banks		Savings Deposits	Other Time Deposits	
	Under $ 5 mill.	Over $ 5 mill.	Under $ 5 mill.	Over $ 5 mill.		Under $ 5 mill.	Over $ 5 mill.
In Effect:							
January 1960	16½		11		5		5
November 1960	"		12		"		"
October 1962	"		"		4		4
July 1966	"		"		"	4	5
September 1966	"		"		"	"	6
2 March 1967	"		"		3½	3½	"
16 March 1967	"		"		3	3	"
January 1968	16½	17	12	12½	"	"	"
April 1969	17	17½	12½	13	"	"	"
October 1970	"	"	"	"	"	"	5
Present legal:							
minimum	10		7		3	3	3
maximum	22		14		10	10	10

1. Prior to 28th July 1962, the Board of Governors of the Federal Reserve System classified the reserve city banks in Chicago and New York City as central reserve city banks, and reserve requirements on demand deposits at central reserve city banks were generally one or more percentage points higher than those applied to reserve city banks. See page 56 concerning recent revisions in the regulation of reserve requirements.

Source: Federal Reserve Bulletin.

Regulation J governing Federal Reserve credit through delays in cheque remittances ("float") by banks to the Federal Reserve banks.

A change in the required reserve ratio of member banks changes excess reserves and hence net free reserves. Such changes thus exert an immediate influence on all member banks' reserve position though not, of course, on their total reserves. At the same time the change in required reserve ratios modifies the volume of bank deposits that can be supported by any given volume of reserves. Moreover, any change in the percentage increases or decreases in the proportion of bank assets which must be held in the form of non-earning assets has implications for commercial bank profits. On these grounds, the variable reserve requirement ratios appear to provide a powerful way of operating on bank reserves and have the advantage of working quickly. It seems particularly useful as an instrument to achieve large changes in liquidity.

In view of these advantages it may be surprising to find that the requirement against demand deposits was modified only four times during the period under review and that against time deposits only six times. Evidently, the device is less useful to the Federal Reserve System than it might at first appear. Its main limitations may be summarised as follows:

i) In the first place the instrument is administratively asymmetrical. Member banks dislike increases in the requirement reserve ratios because these increases affect all banks in a class irrespective of their dissimilar reserve positions at the outset. Hence some member banks, despite the existence of a discount mechanism and the Federal funds market, have to make rapid portfolio adjustments which, though eased by the mechanisms mentioned, are nevertheless costly. Such adjustments appear even less acceptable when other competing banks need to make only very marginal adjustments. Thus, increases in percentages must be used rather sparingly if their incidence is not to reduce the attractions of belonging to the Federal Reserve System. For example, any large-scale use of the instrument in a restrictive direction in 1966 and 1969 might well have speeded up the process of disaffiliation from the system that has been observable since the mid-1960s.

ii) In the second place, when the ratio is changed—and particularly when it is raised—banks will adjust their positions by substantial dealings in money market assets. A large change in the reserve position may therefore have severe effects in short-term markets, which may have to be offset by the monetary authorities. This point is made more important by the fact that a change for administrative reasons is not made gradually, but takes the form of a step increase or decrease effective from a particular date.[17]

The main reason, however, why variations in required reserve ratios have not been used more frequently is that another instrument with supposedly superior features is available, *viz* open market operations. Open market operations are more flexible, can be carried out in any desired quantity, and need not be announced in advance. This instrument, therefore, has advantages over the variation in required reserve ratios which make it more useful for short-term counter-cyclical policies. The changes actually made in required reserve ratios have, in these circumstances, been prompted primarily by considerations of structure and equity. This does not mean that the instrument has not been used consistently with the aims of counter-cyclical policy, as described in Part IV. The reduction in the required ratios against demand deposits in September 1960 and the subsequent reductions (October, November 1962) in the required ratio against time deposits were both consistent with the overall stance of policy in those years; so was the increase in the demand deposit requirements in April 1969.

f) COMBINATIONS OF INSTRUMENTS AND CONSTRAINTS ON THEIR OVERALL USE

As the preceding survey shows, the most important instrument of short-term monetary policy in the United States is the purchase and sale of short-term securities in the open market. Compared with this instrument, the roles played by discount rate changes, changes in regulation Q maxima, and variations in reserve requirement ratios have been secondary.

---

17. This substantial element of discontinuity might be considerably reduced if the required ratios were to refer to increases in deposits rather than to total deposits as is the case in some other countries. Since 1969, the Federal Reserve System has begun to make limited use of marginal reserve requirements.

It is not clear whether the division of labour among the various instruments will shift significantly in the 1970s. It may, however, be noted that the use of Regulation Q was based on a theory of the strategic importance of the availability of bank credit which has met with less favour in recent years than in the mid-1960s. As noted above (page 56), the Federal Reserve has moved since 1970 to suspend some of the maximum rates; a recent Presidential Commission, moreover, suggested the removal of ceilings on large certificates of deposits entirely, while retaining them on a temporary basis for smaller deposits.[18] The abandonment of active use of Regulation Q obviously would create fewer international problems in the future by diminishing fluctuations in Euro-dollar borrowings and other forms of disintermediation. Variations in the discount rate have been of limited importance in the 1960s; recent thinking in the Federal Reserve System goes in the direction of more frequent variations. However, such a shift might not be of major significance so long as borrowing remains a small source of reserves and so long as administrative constraints (see page 51) continue to be important as a determinant of the banks' use of discount facilities even inside the narrow range where the cost of borrowing is the major consideration.

The reasons why relatively stronger emphasis is put on open market operations in the United States than is the case in most other industrial countries are not difficult to see. In all circumstances the instrument is flexible as to timing and size of operations; and its use is less likely to bring the monetary authorities up against the constraints, discussed below, on the use of certain other instruments, since the judgement of a central bank is least likely to be questioned when the instrument it applies is highly technical. But even in the use of this instrument, the Federal Reserve System is far from being able to move with the speed and strength it may find appropriate to achieve the broader aims of monetary policy agreed upon. At any given time, the actions of the authorities are subject to various kinds of constraints; these may be classified into two broad groups: political and technical.

As regards *political constraints,* it is important to recall that in the United States public opinion in general, and congressional opinion in particular, have traditionally favoured low long-term interest rates. Developments in mortgage rates have been observed with special attention. The favourable attitude to low interest rates is of long origin and reflects the strong influence of borrowers on national political affairs. It influenced the conduct of monetary policy in war-time and constrained its activation in subsequent periods. One post-war example was the resistance to the abandonment of the pegging of security prices in the early 1950s. In the 1960s it remained an objective of economic policy to keep long rates as low as possible, even after full employment had approximately been reached in 1965. The constraint has, however, clearly been weakening after the experiences of the 1966 and 1969 periods of restraint, when the remarkable relative stability of long-term rates over several decades was broken. Once significant changes in interest rates had taken place, public opinion found it more difficult to decide on a desirable level of rates. Nonetheless, the debate in 1972-73 has demonstrated the continued concern

---

18. See [29], p. 23.

in political circles, notably in Congress, at the tendency for long-term interest rates to rise. Empirical evidence of the impact of monetary policy on private expenditure (reviewed in Part IV) suggests that this concern is not without a factual basis, inasmuch as monetary policy effects are largely transmitted through changes in the long-term interest rates which have an important influence on private spending.[19]

The second important group of constraints may be regarded as *technical* in a broad sense. They will here be reviewed under three headings:

   a) the prevention of financial instability,
   b) short-term debt management problems, and
   c) external linkages.

During the long period between the 1930s and the mid-1960s there were good reasons to believe that *financial market instability* in the United States was a thing of the past. The drying-up of the mortgage market in the early summer of 1966, the short-lived crisis in the market for state and local government securities in the same year, and the liquidity squeeze leading to a crisis in the commercial paper market in 1970 tended to show that this confidence had become exaggerated. When one or more financial markets reach a crisis it becomes an important obligation of any central bank to ensure that the basic functioning of the markets continues. Although the present report looks primarily at the dynamic control functions of the monetary authorities, it is not possible to overlook the fact that the Federal Reserve System is also, as is any central bank, the lender of last resort. Its important role in the latter capacity acted as a significant constraint on the conduct of its control functions, particularly during the second half of the 1960s. On at least three occasions during this period the Federal Reserve System had to concern itself with instability in a particular market or more general financial instability. This responsibility clearly limited monetary action in 1966 and 1969-70, since it was the view of the US authorities that these limits had been reached or nearly reached in the two periods of monetary restraint (see Part IV). These experiences served to recall that monetary policy cannot carry extreme burdens of restraint, that it must not be allowed to deviate too far from a middle course, and that, in particular, violent shifts in financial conditions are undesirable.

A technical constraint in a narrower sense arises out of *Federal government debt operations*. At times when the Federal government is offering new coupon issues, or is engaged in coupon issues for conversions (refunding), the Federal Reserve pursues an open market policy known as *"even-keeling"*. Essentially this term means that, between the announcement and settlement dates of the coupon issues, the Federal Reserve does not announce policy changes or conduct open market operations in such a way as to suggest a significant change in policy. The precise span of an even-keel period can be shorter, however, or sometimes a little longer, depending on market psychology and the ease with which the financing is being absorbed. Even-keeling does not imply a pegging of rates. Indeed,

___

19. One sign that the resistance towards increases in interest rates during periods of restraint may be fading is removal of certain ceilings in recent years, e.g. the suspension of Regulation Q maxima for some categories of time deposits and of maximum coupon rates allowed on a limited issue of Treasury securities.

market rates have typically changed during such periods. Apart perhaps from the overnight Federal funds rate, interest rates and for that matter key monetary aggregates have shown no readily discernible difference in movement within as compared with outside the even-keel periods; see Axilrod [4], Appendix. It would seem that even-keel requirements have affected the timing of some policy changes, notably in the discount rate, but that in general, even-keeling has not been a significant impediment to the effective use of monetary policy.

Finally, *external* linkages may constitute a technical constraint. It was concluded above (pages 17-18) that the use of the dollar as the main international reserve asset reduced the need for open market operations by the central bank to offset impacts on domestic monetary conditions arising from the widening and highly volatile deficit on official settlements. The following three paragraphs explore whether this preliminary conclusion must be modified because of secondary effects on interest rates, bank reserves and money supply; in the process, an attempt is made to evaluate in what way the external factors have constituted a constraint or at least a complicating factor in the achievement of domestic objectives. The role of monetary policy in achieving better equilibrium in external transactions will be reviewed in Parts III and IV.

A major part of recent deficits in the US balance of payments has been settled through liability financing rather than through decreases in US reserve assets. Liability financing of an external imbalance consists of a change in the ownership of US financial assets (including bank deposits) between domestic and foreign private holders on the one hand and foreign official institutions on the other. The central question is whether these two groups of holders have approximately similar asset preferences. This depends on several factors, such as the nature of the disequilibrium to be financed—current account, long-term capital account, short-term non-monetary flows, monetary flows—and the country acquiring or losing dollar reserves. Generally speaking, asset preferences are unlikely to be similar, so that liability financing leads to a different structure of relative demand-supply conditions in financial markets. More specifically, foreign official institutions appear to have exhibited a relatively stronger preference than private holders for Treasury bills and other short-term government securities. The effect of large-scale liability financing such as occurred in 1971 would then be, other things being equal, to increase the interest rate differential between private and government money market instruments and, to a lesser extent, the differential between securities of different maturities; a large US surplus financed by a reduction of liabilities to foreign official institutions would have opposite effects. The coincidence of the 1970-71 external deficits with important deficits in the Federal government budget, according to this line of reasoning, eased the problems of debt management as foreign official institutions absorbed heavy amounts of short-term public debt; but it can hardly be inferred that it resulted in generally lower interest rates than would otherwise have been the case. Since liability financing leaves the total demand for domestic financial assets essentially unaffected, other things being equal, it has no clear-cut impact on the average level of interest rates. Ultimately, the assumption made about the course the authorities would have chosen in the absence of the external influences will determine the conclusion as to the impact of these influences on the general level of interest rates and aggregate demand. If the authorities follow a money market conditions target defined primarily in terms of the Treasury bill rate, an external liability-financed deficit is likely to result in interest rates on private debt instruments and longer-term government securities—and thus the average level of rates—being higher than otherwise would be the case; but the effect in practice is likely to have been small. Since early 1970, monetary aggregates have become important additional targets, suggesting a some-what greater reluctance on the part of the Federal Reserve to offset the impact on short-term rates from external transactions. On the other hand, this was a period of very sizeable deficits on official settlements, and the US authorities were clearly concerned about any further induce-ments to capital outflows (pages 117-118). All that may be concluded, there-fore, is that there is likely to be some impact of external influences on the domestic rate *structure,* but not much on the average *level* of rates and total expenditures.

Liability financing will have an impact on the composition of bank liabilities and thereby on required reserves if, as the available evidence suggests, foreign official institutions have a stronger preference for time deposits than foreign (and domestic) corporations and individuals. But as the size of foreign-held deposits with US commercial banks is modest, such effects on the required and net free reserves of banks have been dwarfed by the reserve impact from shifts between the time and demand deposit holdings of residents and private non-residents. The Federal Reserve has generally tended to offset any such effects on bank reserves through its open market operations, to the extent that these effects would have caused reserves and short-term interest rates to depart from target ranges. The externally-caused components of these shifts in reserves have not presented special problems in this process of neutralisation. This conclusion applies not only to the shifts arising out of liability financing, but also to the quantitatively more important shifts associated with the Euro-dollar borrowing by US banks. Prior to September 1969, these non-depository liabilities were not subject to reserve requirements (or to interest rate ceilings). As briefly mentioned above (pages 55-56) and more fully explained below [Part IV(d)], the rise of short-term market interest rates well above the maxima set in Regulation Q for rates payable on negotiable certificates of deposit caused a large-scale run-off of CDs during the periods of monetary restraint in 1966 and, particularly, in 1969. US commercial banks were able to offset this run-off by borrowing in the Euro-dollar market, mostly through their own overseas subsidiaries (Chart 12).[20] If one assumes that the offset was complete in 1969, as the chart suggests, and that the average required reserve ratio for the time deposits which were run off was unchanged, it is possible to calculate the order of magnitude of the downward shift in required reserves. Gross liabilities of US commercial banks to their foreign branches increased by $3.8 billion in the first five months of 1969 and by another $4.8 billion in the following three months; this restructuring of liabilities reduced required reserves by

---

20. While US banks were borrowing Euro-dollars, the exceptionally high interest rates in this market were attracting funds from the United States (as well as from many other countries), resulting in what is sometimes referred to as the "circular flow". See pages 85 ff for a discussion of this phenomenon from the point of view of the balance of payments.

Chart 12. INTEREST RATE DEVELOPMENTS AND US BANKS' BORROWING FROM FOREIGN BRANCHES

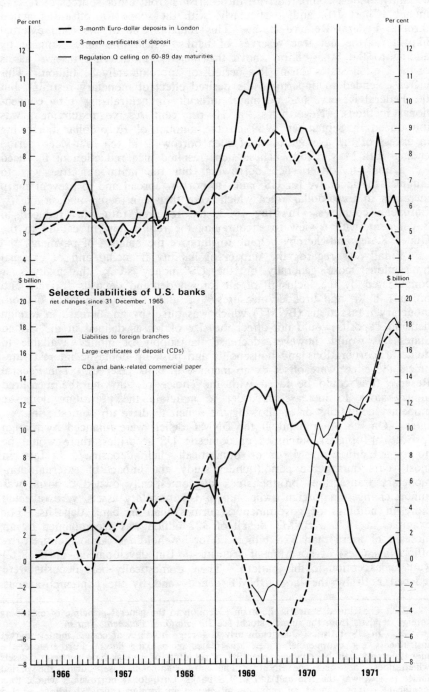

Source: Federal Reserve Bulletin.

$230 and $290 million respectively. These effects on reserve money are certainly modest compared with those arising from other sources of reserve money (Chart 10), and, particularly, with the scope for offsetting action through Federal Reserve credit. This remains true of the total external impact on the net free reserves of banks, which one may estimate by adding to the $0.5 billion above the increase in external reserve assets of the United States during this period, of approximately $1 billion. This increase tended to undermine the desired effect of monetary restraint, but the Federal Reserve had no major difficulty in neutralising it by conventional methods. Nevertheless, a 10 per cent reserve requirement was introduced in September 1969 on the amount of Euro-dollar borrowing in excess of the average level of such borrowing in the four-week period ending 28th May, 1969. These steps resulted in a reduction of the need for actions to offset such borrowing, but the main objective was to diminish the incentive for US banks to borrow abroad and to prevent sharp increases in Euro-dollar rates which were then considered undesirable by European countries. In May 1973, the required ratio was reduced to 8 per cent, with a view to encouraging the return flow of capital to the United States and thereby helping to improve the balance of payments.

Finally, as regards the impact of liability financing and of external transactions more generally on the US money stock, the analysis is complicated by the inclusion of all foreign demand deposits (private and official) in M_1 and broader measures.[21] A deficit on the balance of non-monetary transactions (BNMT) which was offset by an increase in foreign demand deposits would not affect the size of M_1 as defined in the United States. It would, however, decrease the supply of money available to domestic corporations and households and push up domestic interest rates unless the effect were offset by an increase in bank reserves. The Federal Reserve thus could be faced with the choice of allowing the measured money stock to increase in order to maintain the prevailing domestic monetary conditions or of allowing the deficit to drive up domestic interest rates. On the other hand, if the BNMT deficit were financed by foreign (private or official) purchases of domestic US securities, there would be no impact either on M_1 or on domestically held deposits.[22] In fact, in most years during the period under study, the impact of external non-monetary transactions on the stock of domestically owned deposits was minor; changes in foreign ownership of US monetary assets were reflected more in holdings of government securities than in bank deposits. For example, in 1971 a BNMT deficit of $22 billion was accompanied by an increase of more than $26 billion in foreign holdings (almost entirely by official agencies) of government securities. But developments in 1968-69 were an exception to this pattern. Then, domestically held deposits were reduced both by the large BNMT deficits and by the contemporaneous

---

21. The United States is the main exception to the general principle of excluding foreign deposits from the money stock; see *International Financial Statistics*.

22. In US statistics, changes in private foreign holdings of certain money market instruments, e.g. commercial paper, are treated as banking flows. Furthermore, the money supply can be changed even by a reshuffle of foreign-held monetary assets which does not affect the BNMT. The most significant case, during the period under review, was the rise and fall of US banks' Euro-dollar borrowings which, to a significant extent, caused an opposite movement in foreign official holdings of US Treasury bills.

surpluses on the official settlements balance. These surpluses resulted from the heavy Euro-dollar borrowing of US commercial banks; part of the consequent reduction of foreign official dollar assets took the form of sales of Treasury bills to US residents. The combined direct impact of these two developments may have been to decrease the domestically held money supply by around 3 per cent. Nonetheless, here again it must be concluded that the overall impact of external transactions on domestic monetary conditions was minor.[23] To sum up, there appears to be no reason to modify the preliminary conclusion of pages 16-18 that external factors have not played any major role in shaping monetary policy in the United States. In particular, given the size of the external factors and the instruments available to the Federal Reserve, no major constraints to the achievement of domestic objectives appear to have arisen from them.

---

23. The contractionary impacts from deposit shifts in 1968-69 were partly offset by the expansionary effects of Euro-dollar borrowing on the money stock prior to the imposition of marginal reserve requirements in September 1969 (see page 55). The net impact of external transactions in 1969 was probably rather small.

III

THE TRANSMISSION MECHANISM
OF MONETARY POLICY

a) IMPLICATIONS OF FINANCIAL BEHAVIOUR FOR THE TRANSMISSION
MECHANISM

A major question in the evaluation of the effects of monetary policy is to what extent these effects are transmitted through a rationing of particular flows of credit from financial institutions—so-called availability effects—rather than through interest rate changes. The review in Part I of the financial structure in the United States reveals three features of particular significance:

    i)   the flexibility in the composition of assets and liabilities held by both households and corporations,

   ii)   the financial innovations undertaken in recent years, and

  iii)   the relatively small share of banks in total credit flows (which is important when monetary policy is primarily directed at the commercial banks).

All three factors tend to explain why processes of disintermediation have worked particularly strongly in the United States and why availability effects are difficult to observe. One important exception is the mortgage market where, for reasons of institutional rigidity and lack of strength on the part of borrowers, funds have tended to dry up during periods of monetary restraint. For most other categories of borrowers, rationing of particular forms of credit did not seriously limit their capacity to undertake expenditure commitments because alternative sources of finance were available. This flexibility implies that financial markets have tended to exhibit a high degree of perfection in the sense that prices, i.e. interest rates, have moved in such a way as to eliminate imbalances between credit supply and demand rather quickly; each borrower is obtaining the funds which, at the ruling price, he wishes to borrow. In this case, the non-availability of particular forms of credit has no major causal significance. The main focus is on structural relations between interest rates in various sub-markets; financial flows may supply additional information as descriptive, rather than causal phenomena. This is the basic assumption that underlies the review of the transmission mechanism in the discussion which follows. It has been adopted as such in a number of large-scale econometric models, notably the FMP model, and is not rejected in others or in disaggregated empirical studies.

In adopting this basic viewpoint, one must not overlook that it remains an approximation, and possibly an unsatisfactory one in periods when the monetary brakes are suddenly applied vigorously. It may also over-simplify, more generally, the way in which monetary restraint is felt by some categories of borrowers, especially smaller non-corporate enterprises. Several observers have quoted instances from 1966 of such borrowers experiencing credit rationing of sufficient severity to delay their expenditure plans. That their access to bank credit was severely curtailed is beyond doubt; and not all of this may, in their case, have been compensated by greater reliance on non-bank borrowing, mainly through trade credits from larger firms. Unfortunately, in the macroeconomic time series used in the FMP and other models, investment expenditures by smaller enter-prises are not separately identifiable; and in the total series they are dwarfed by those of large enterprises which are not rationed in their total access to external funds. It has already been argued in the analysis of the use of Regulation Q maxima in Part II that, insofar as the total category of bank loans to industrial and commercial customers was concerned, there were few signs of any overall availability effects.

Before going on to the more specific discussion of reactions in financial markets, it may be worthwhile to note three points:

i)   "Perfection" in financial markets does not necessarily imply greater speed and effectiveness of policy than a system relying on availability; indeed the latter may work faster, as the expe-rience of housing in the United States would seem to demonstrate.

ii) A perfect capital market, in the sense described, does not imply that the best way of conducting policy is to use interest rates as the main target; this point is discussed more fully in Appen-dix II. The issue relevant to the choice of policy targets is, as already noted on page 51, whether the demand function for money is relatively more stable than the expenditure function. It would not be inconsistent to think both that this were the case and that the transmission mechanism works primarily through interest rate effects.

iii) The view that the transmission mechanism works through interest rates should not be interpreted as taking sides in the contro-versy between "monetarists" and others. There is general consensus about a transmission mechanism through interest rates; the disagreement concerns primarily the range of rates to be considered. The monetarists maintain that the money supply is useful shorthand for the rates on the wide spectrum of assets, including real assets, through which the effects of monetary policy are transmitted. Others remain unconvinced and prefer to continue the attempts to specify a transmission mechanism through a number of interest rates observable in financial markets. While the monetarist record in forecasting is not significantly worse than that of large-scale econometric models, the fact that the transmission mechanism is treated implicitly rather than explicitly is a major handicap for the purpose at hand which requires structurally specified models. Therefore references will be made only in passing to the results obtained in monetarist research.[1] It must be noted, however, that the most recent research has tended to show a certain convergence in the main conclusions about the effect of policy, notably in relation to time lags.

b) CHOICE OF MODEL AND METHOD OF QUANTITATIVE ILLUSTRATION

There is a very wide range of econometric work relevant to the assessment of how, and how strongly, monetary policy has affected components of demand in the United States during the post-war period. In view of the varied and occasionally contradictory nature of the available evidence, it may appear to be somewhat limiting to choose only one main source—the FMP model—as the basis for analysis. Nonetheless, the FMP model has proved to be of considerable usefulness, particularly because it makes possible a systematic evaluation of the widely diffused impacts of changes in the various instruments available to the monetary authorities and of the alternative courses of action available to them. In recent years, the staff of the Federal Reserve Board has begun to make regular use of the FMP model as one research tool for these purposes, modified by judgemental adjustments in assumptions and inputs as well as by the results of ongoing econometric and other current analysis.[2] Though the model provides a basis for the review of simulations of alternative policy options undertaken below, the inherent limitations of any econometric model, no matter how comprehensive and careful in its design, should be underlined here. As the authorities themselves are aware, any model will necessarily oversimplify the processes involved in the transmission of changes in monetary policy instruments through financial and commodity markets. Its conclusions will in practice have to be tempered by judgement and adjusted to special circumstances existing at any particular time. The detailed numerical results shown below should therefore be regarded as indicative rather than definitive.

This use of the FMP model as one of the tools in the policy-making process would hardly be conceivable in the absence of two important conditions:

   i) the model incorporates the main features of the US financial system noted above, notably a high degree of substitution in financial markets and, consequently a transmission mechanism

---

1. Nor will any systematic references be made to single-equation studies of individual components of demand. A discussion of a sample of such studies may be found in Fisher and Sheppard [32] Chapter 2. Differences in specification, including lag structure, as well as in estimation techniques, complicate comparisons among these studies and between them and large-scale models. Although the FMP model has to a large extent derived inspiration from successful single-equation studies, there is much additional information to be found in the latter. More extensive experimentation with complex specifications is possible, and use may be made of cross-section data; some of the latter studies will be referred to in Part IV.

2. The version of the model used has evolved gradually; it differs in some respects—apparently not essential for the results to be presented in the following—from the publicly available version. The Federal Reserve Board has used the latter in simulations which it kindly supplied for the purposes of this study. The staff of the board has also more recently developed models of the money market in the short run. Preliminary results with a monthly model have been reported by Thomson, Pierce and Parry [96].

through changes in interest rates rather than in the availability of funds (except in the mortgage market); and

ii) the numerical results are not very far from the middle of the rather wide range of results reported in econometric models.[3]

These considerations amount to saying that the FMP model is regarded as broadly realistic both in a qualitative and a quantitative sense. Not all features of the model are readily acceptable; the following review will point to some of the remaining areas of doubt: the very large role of movements in household wealth prompted by changes in stock prices, the mortgage and housing markets and the interaction between price changes, prices expectations and interest rates.

Generally, the FMP model has a satisfactory record in tracking quarterly developments in financial and other markets over the period for which it has been estimated, i.e. the mid-1950s through 1971 for the version used in the present study. More important than traditional statistical criteria is the fact that the main properties of the model during its gradual development into its present version have been thoroughly tested in dynamic and in policy simulations.[4] Dynamic simulations calculate the values of all variables by means of the combined structural relationships, starting from a particular time period and incorporating the actual values of the exogenous variables at the subsequent observation points. The purpose is to observe how the model behaves dynamically by comparing the actual and calculated values of the endogenous variables. Dynamic simulations may be confined to the period for which the model has been estimated, but a more stringent test is provided by extending them to a subsequent, but still known, period. Once such tests have demonstrated the basic reliability of the model, as has been the case for both inside and post-sample simulations with the FMP model, it is useful to proceed to the evaluation of the effects of alternative policies through policy simulations, i.e., comparisons between the dynamic—or "control"—simulation and alternatives in which one or more policy instruments are changed relative to actually observed values. For example, a particular policy variable is changed in a certain quarter and held thereafter a constant distance above or below the actually observed value of the instrument. Examples of monetary policy changes that may be studied are changes in the major instruments described in Part II: the discount rate, Federal Reserve credit (effectively, open market operations), reserve requirements ratios and Regulation Q maxima. Simulations of the effects of changing the first two of these instruments are reported in the Fisher-Sheppard study [32]. In the present study, calculations are reported on the effect of alternative courses for two variables which are not directly policy instruments: the Treasury bill rate and the money supply (M_1). While the main emphasis in the present Part is on the effects of an alternative time path for the Treasury bill rate and Federal Reserve credit, Part IV reviews a simulation of an alternative money supply.[5]

---

3. A large sample of such models is reviewed by Fisher and Sheppard [33], Chapter 3; see also Gramlich [37].

4. For a more careful statement of these procedures, see Fisher and Sheppard [32], pp. 40-48, on which this and the following paragraphs draw heavily.

5. A large number of additional simulations of changes in policy instruments, or combinations thereof, are, of course, conceivable and have been made; see [32], pp. 70-71.

The order of magnitude of the effects on real demand of a one percentage point discount rate change appears to be roughly comparable to those of a $1 billion change in Federal Reserve credit; the relative power of Federal Reserve credit and the Treasury bill rate is such that a $1 billion change in the former corresponds to a one half percentage point change in the Treasury bill rate. Thus, broadly speaking, a bill rate change of a given number of basis points is twice as powerful as a similar change in the discount rate. The policy simulations reported on changes in these two variables (Federal Reserve credit and the bill rate) are to be regarded as illustrations of what might have happened had the monetary authorities historically followed a somewhat different policy; not radically different, since the results generally are presented in terms of a change in Federal Reserve credit of $1 billion and in the bill rate of half a percentage point (50 basis points). One obvious weakness of the policy simulations is that they neglect the constraints on the manipulation of instruments outlined on pages 58-65 above. In short, the simulations are more interesting for the light they throw on the working of linkages in the financial sector and, through it, to real variables than for the precise numerical results they produce.

The rationale for putting the main emphasis on changes in Federal Reserve credit and the Treasury bill rate has already been provided by the discussions of the Federal Reserve strategy in Part II. Since the dominant instrument in the short-run is the net purchase of government securities, a natural first matter of concern would be a policy simulation illustrating what might have happened had the monetary authorities sold some amount more than they actually did in a particular quarter, and thereafter pursued policies identical to what were actually observed in the following quarters. Clearly, such a policy would have pushed up money market rates, decreased unborrowed (and net free) reserves and slowed down the growth of the monetary aggregates. Real demand would be expected to have reacted gradually to the tightening of credit, causing interest rates to ease back towards their initial level. An alternative to expressing a different policy in terms of Federal Reserve credit is to start the calculations from a change in one of the main money market variables. These variables have been used as operating targets by the authorities almost throughout the period under study and a high degree of control is achievable, in particular over money market rates. This controllability makes a strong case for studying the implications of a policy alternative formulated in terms of the main money market rate, i.e. the Treasury bill rate. Such evidence brings out clearly, without the complicating features inside the money market, the adjustments in the structure of interest rates.[6]

---

6. The possibility of starting from a strategic reserve variable among those constituting money market conditions, e.g. unborrowed reserves or net free reserves, has been studied extensively in a number of simulations with both the FMP model and other models. It is essentially a close variant of the Federal Reserve policy summarised here, the main difference being that the present simulations assume that no attempt is made to offset changes in the non-bank sector's demand for currency. For this reason, an even closer variant to the Federal Reserve credit simulation is one in which the sum of unborrowed reserves and currency, i.e. the unborrowed monetary base, is changed. The effects of a $1 billion change in unborrowed reserves are accordingly slightly stronger than those arising from a similar change in Federal Reserve credit.

Changes in monetary policy instruments do not have identical effects at all times. In particular, their impact will depend on the initial situation. A step increase in Federal Reserve credit will have a stronger expansionary effect on real aggregate demand and employment the further the economy is from any supply constraint. An illustration of the importance of initial conditions is given in the course of the review in Part IV of simulations of a less restrictive monetary policy in 1966-68 and 1969-71. It also appears to be the general experience, in the United States as elsewhere, that there are asymmetries in the effects of monetary policy in that a given absolute change in some instruments tends to have a larger impact in a restrictive than in an expansionary direction. The ultimate effects of monetary policy will depend, therefore, on both the direction of change and the general economic background. Allowance is made for some, but not all, of these asymmetries in the FMP model (pages 75-76). Since there is some presumption that simulations are more reliable when the alternative policy is more restrictive (defined by a higher Treasury bill rate) than that actually followed, the following results have aimed at illustrating the likely effects of a tightening of policy; they take as their starting point the fourth quarter of 1968, towards the end of which monetary policy was significantly tightened.[7] Generally, the results are shown for the 13 quarters following the end of 1968, i.e. up to 1971.I which was the latest quarter for which data were available when the simulations were carried out in the summer of 1972.

c) PRELIMINARY RESULTS ON RESPONSES IN THE FINANCIAL SECTOR

In evaluating the impact of monetary policy changes, it has seemed convenient to use as illustrative examples three types of simulation experiments. The first of these, to be taken up in the present section, views financial markets in isolation; i.e., no allowance is made for any impact on real variables. The purpose of such a "financial block simulation" is to display in some detail the channels through which a change in Federal Reserve credit, or in the Treasury bill rate, is related to financial variables which have an impact on real variables. Three main channels may be envisaged: measures of the cost of borrowing relevant to various categories of expenditure, the market value of securities in household-sector wealth, and the flow of funds to sectors for which the volume of credit is subject to rationing. These three main channels of influence will be referred to as the cost, wealth and availability effects of monetary policy, respectively. It is the task of the financial block simulation to illustrate the first stage of the transmission mechanism: from changes in instruments—or in variables close thereto—to financial variables relevant for spending decisions.

---

7. The FMP model shows signs of (local) instability if the simulation experiment is to keep the Treasury bill rate on a permanently lower course than actually observed. In rough terms, this feature may be seen as the result of a tendency in the model for the *real* rate of interest to continue to decline during a phase of expansionary monetary policy. The real rate falls both as a direct consequence of monetary expansion lowering nominal interest rates and as the indirect result of a faster rate of increase of prices produced by the rise in aggregate demand. Since the real rate is approximately the difference between the nominal rate and a recently observed rate of change of prices, the expansionary stimulus operating through the declining real rate is sustained. While a process somewhat like this may be at work in the real economy, it is possible that the FMP model exaggerates it.

In the following section the review of the transmission mechanism will continue to the second stage by means of two more comprehensive types of simulations.

A decrease in Federal Reserve credit generates an imbalance in the money market which is immediately reflected in a tendency for short-term rates to rise. The two most important rates in the transmission mechanism are the Treasury bill rate and the commercial paper rate, whereas the Federal funds rate, the most sensitive indicator of money market conditions in the very short run, is less relevant as an indicator of quarterly changes.[8] There is a sharp increase in rates, particularly the bill rate, in the initial quarter, which continues towards a peak in the third or fourth quarter; in the course of subsequent quarters, rates move towards an equilibrium level about mid-way between the initial level and the peak. This phenomenon, known as "overshooting" or, in the very short run, as "whipsawing" of rates, is explained by the stabilising mechanisms inside the financial sector as portfolios of Treasury bills and other financial assets are reshuffled following the initial upset from the open market sales.[9] The impact on the stock of demand deposits (and the money stock) is of the same magnitude in the initial quarter as the change in unborrowed reserves, but it rises gradually to a multiple of more than four at the end of one year and over seven by the end of two years.

Simulations which take their starting point in an alternative (higher) course for the Treasury bill rate for obvious reasons do not exhibit the features of "overshooting" in other interest rates found in the simulations with changes in Federal Reserve credit. The freezing of the bill rate to a fixed time path, in the case to be reviewed 50 basis points above the path actually observed, constrains movements in other interest rates linked to the bill rate through structural relationships. There are two such structural relationships of particular relevance for the transmission mechanism: the links from the bill rate to the commercial paper rate and from the latter to the long-term corporate bond rate. Chart 13 illustrates the response pattern over a period of thirteen quarters in these and other rates to the policy of maintaining the bill rate 50 basis points above observed values. The commercial paper rate, which, as discussed in Part I, is an important indicator of short-term marginal borrowing costs for corporations, adjusts very quickly and more than fully to the increase in the bill rate.

From the commercial paper rate, effects spread to longer-term markets through a traditional term-structure relationship. As explained in some detail in Appendix IV, long rates may be expressed as the sum of a weighted average of current and expected future short rates, plus a risk premium to overcome the possible preference of investors for short-term

---

8. The adjustment process in the financial sector is described in detail in Modigliani, Cooper and Rasche [77]; see also Modigliani [76] and Pierce and Thomson [83]. A more detailed specification of the money market, incorporating important short-run factors such as the Federal funds rate and the CD market may be found in Thomson, Pierce and Parry [96].

9. The overshooting effect is considerably stronger in simulations in which there are feed-backs from the real sector (because the dampening effect on real expenditure of the rise in interest rates slows down the demand for credit and reverses the trend of interest rates) and also in simulations in which the growth rate of the money supply is changed (see Part IV).

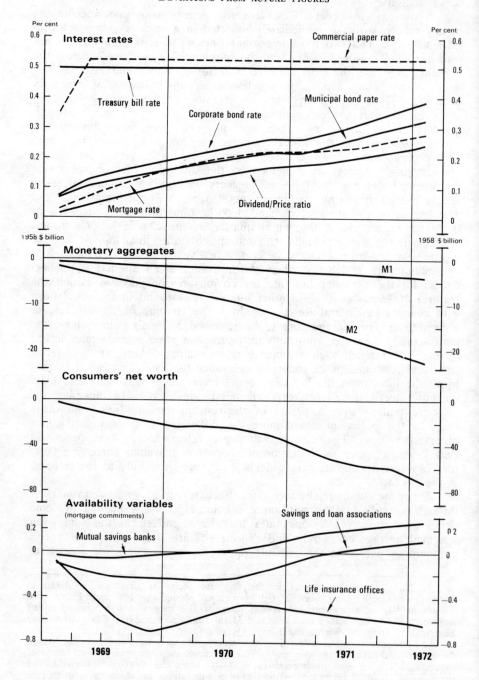

Chart 13. SIMULATIONS OF THE FINANCIAL SECTOR: RESPONSES TO AN INCREASE IN THE TREASURY BILL RATE, 1969-72

DEVIATIONS FROM ACTUAL FIGURES

Source: Simulations provided by the Federal Reserve System.

74

claims; expected future short rates may be measured as the sum of expected changes in consumer prices and the expected real rate, both of which are extrapolated in some way from recent past records. The risk premium is considered to be a constant plus a measure of the recent instability of short rates. Therefore, the most important determinants of long rates in the FMP model are recently observed changes in prices and in the commercial paper rate. The main long rate used is the market yield on corporate Aaa bonds, though this rate should preferably be replaced by the rate on new issues, which is less distorted by tax considerations.[10] Here there is a long distributed lag; the increase in the commercial paper rate causes an increase in the Aaa rate which is spread over 18 quarters; thus the effect is not terminated at the end of the three years shown in Chart 13. The rise in the long-term rate is very smooth over this long interval. At the end of four quarters the rate has risen by about one-third of the increase in the bill rate. The municipal bond rate, the mortgage rate and the dividend/price ratio show smaller absolute adjustments; e.g. the dividend ratio increases by less than 0.1 after four quarters.[11]

There are two points to be noted about the term-structure relationship which are of considerable importance in evaluating the scope for influencing long-term rates through the manipulation of short rates:

i)   The rate of change of prices may have a significant influence on interest rates. To the extent that changes in monetary policy affect the rate of change of prices, this relationship limits the extent to which long rates (but not short rates) can be changed by monetary action. This mechanism would work particularly strongly if the authorities were aiming, through a sharp lowering of the bill rate, to push long rates down; the stronger the impact of monetary expansion on prices, the earlier the downward trend in long rates will be checked by an acceleration of prices. This effect cannot be illustrated within the confines of a financial block simulation which does not allow for any financial impact on prices and a subsequent feedback to interest rates.

ii) As indicated above, the term-structure equation includes, as an additional explanatory variable, a positive effect on long-term rates from recent instability of the short rate, represented more specifically by fluctuations over the last 8 quarters of the commercial paper rate around its average for this period. This variable introduces an asymmetry between expansionary and contractionary phases of policy which accords well with experience in some recent phases of active monetary policy, such as 1971. In contractionary periods, there is a double effect from an increase in the commercial paper rate on long-term rates: the normal impact in the term-structure equation, and the increased uncertainty in financial markets arising out of the change itself. On the other

10.   Because the differential treatment of interest income and capital gains is relevant to the expected holding period, yields for outstanding issues depend on the tax system. For a discussion of this point, see *inter alia,* Eckstein and Feldstein [20].
11.   The chart does not show what happens to long-term government bond rates or the rates charged to commercial bank borrowers, because it has not yet been possible to link movements in these rates to aggregate demand in the model. This is clearly a weakness in view of the important roles of these financial instruments among the assets and liabilities of the private sector.

75

hand, in expansionary periods, a fall in long rates reflecting the normal adjustment to a decline in short rates is partly offset by the increased risk premium arising from the instability of short rates. This formulation supplies a rationale for the difficulties of reducing long-term interest rates through sharp declines in short-term rates.

The cost-of-capital measures relevant to decision makers in various sectors are not directly observable. Non-financial borrowers will be facing different supply-of-funds schedules according to whether they are engaged in the markets for producers durables or structures, consumer durables or housing. Therefore most empirical work on investment functions in recent years has found it useful to construct weighted averages of various interest rates; in the present case, this usage permits a judgement as to how fast the cost-of-capital measures of individual sectors are influenced by changes in the Treasury bill rate via the commercial paper rate, the long-term Aaa rate and other relevant observable rates. The strongest response is on the cost of borrowing for consumer durables, then for producers durables, and finally for structures; the time pattern is approximately similar and obviously reflects, rather closely, the pattern for the rates in Chart 13 from which the cost-of-capital measures have been derived. The rates shown are nominal, and they have to be adjusted for expected rates of change of prices to arrive at the real cost of capital.

The other channel through which changes in interest rates are seen to influence spending is through changes in the market valuation of securities held by the household sector. Holdings of securities, mainly shares, constitute approximately one-third of the new worth of the household sector, the remaining two-thirds consisting largely of houses, consumer durables and net equity in unincorporated enterprises. Changes in interest rates, through changes in the price/dividend ratio, influence the former of these components.[12] Dividends are unchanged, because all the real variables which determine them are held fixed in a financial sector simulation; but share prices decline, since the rate at which future earnings of firms are capitalized rises. Following the increase in the bill rate of 50 basis points, the simulations suggest a decline in the net wealth of households by about one half of one per cent in the course of four quarters and a little more than three times as much over a three-year period. While this impact may not appear to be very significant, the absolute amounts involved are large, consumer net wealth constituting about $3,000 billion towards the end of 1968. Even with a modest sensitivity in the flow of consumption expenditures to variations in wealth, there is scope for a sizeable impact on real expenditure through this channel. Indeed, as the simulations in the following section suggest, the wealth effect seems to be quantitatively the most significant of the three channels through which policy effects are transmitted.

The reactions of fund flows in the mortgage market give an indication of the availability effects of monetary restraint. In addition to two different measures of the cost of capital to house builders—for multi- and one- or two-family dwellings—the mortgage commitments of the three

_____

12. Interest rate changes presumably also affect the other components of wealth, but it has not yet proved feasible to give a quantitative illustration of this impact.

principal financial lenders (savings and loan associations, mutual savings banks and life insurance offices) provide operational measures of funds made available for housing. Commitments by the first two categories of institutions at first decline, but then rise back to or beyond original levels, as these non-bank financial intermediaries react to the rising interest rates elsewhere by adjusting upwards the rates they themselves offer to compete for funds. Thus, over time, rationing effects in these markets should tend to diminish. This pattern of a reversal following a relatively quick initial impact presumes that the mortgage lenders are able to compete; to the extent that they are not due to the institutional factors discussed in Part I, availability effects are likely to be more permanent. Generally, empirical knowledge about reactions in the mortgage market remains weak. For that reason, simulations are often undertaken which regard the housing market and the financial flows associated with it as exogenous.[13]

The contractionary impact on the money stock arising from the policy of maintaining the Treasury bill rate 50 basis points above the actual path increases gradually over the simulation period. The effect on the narrowly defined money stock (currency and demand deposits, M_1) rises smoothly by about $0.3 billion each quarter; thus, starting from the final quarter of 1968 the financial simulation suggests that the higher bill rate would have reduced M_1 by about $\frac{1}{2}$ per cent after one year. Almost all of this decline is observed in the demand deposit component, since currency demand is largely unaffected so long as income is not allowed to vary. The rise in interest rates on market instruments competing with time deposits is such that the contractionary impact of the assumed policy change on quasi-money is much stronger than on demand deposits. In terms of percentage deviations from the actual path, the effect on the broadly defined stock (which includes time deposits together with demand deposits and currency) rises gradually from -0.4 in the initial quarter to -4.4 by the end of the three years.

d) EVIDENCE FROM PARTIAL AND FULL SIMULATIONS WITH THE FMP MODEL: DEMAND, OUTPUT, PRICES AND THE CURRENT BALANCE

The results of two additional kinds of simulations are presented in this section. The first, introduced primarily for expository reasons, may be termed "partial" in the sense that, while it does focus on the direct impact of financial variables on real expenditures, it disregards the structural relations in the real sector and the feed-back to financial markets.[14] The purpose of presenting these amputated simulations is to illustrate how the various channels through which policy effects are transmitted combine to produce an overall effect, notably on private consumption and housing. The actual numerical results of the partial simulation of a

---

13. For a more detailed survey of the housing and mortgage markets, see Appendix III and the references given therein, notably Kalchbrenner's contributions to [38].

14. Thus, when the impact on, say, private investment and state and local government expenditure is studied, the identity defining GNP as the sum of a number of expenditure components is suppressed, so that there is no accelerator effect operating on investment nor any effect on state and local government expenditure through changes in tax revenues linked to GNP.

50 basis-point increase in the bill rate from the end of 1968 are less interesting than those of the corresponding full simulation to be reviewed subsequently. For what they are worth, they suggest (Chart 14) that the increase in the bill rate would, through its direct impact on individual expenditure components, have reduced real aggregate demand (in 1958 dollars) by a quarter of one per cent by the fourth quarter and a little more than double that by the eighth; by the thirteenth quarter the response is roughly one per cent of GNP. These calculations indicate that even without the complications of the responses inside the real sector, the repercussions of discretionary monetary actions take a long time to die down.

Perhaps more interesting than the impact on aggregate demand is the distribution of this impact over the major demand components. Somewhat less than half shows up in consumption and a little more than one quarter in private fixed investment; the effects on state and local government expenditure and residential construction are rather small, the proportions depending somewhat on the number of quarters elapsed since the start of the simulation. As regards *consumption,* not only spending on durables, but also that on non-durables is affected by monetary policy. There are two transmission mechanisms at work, one through the wealth effect with an impact on consumption of both durables and non-durables and another through a cost of capital effect, which is operating only on durables. The cost effect is the larger of the two operating on durables, but the weight of non-durables in total consumption is so considerable that the wealth effect accounts for 70-80 per cent of the calculated decline in total consumption. The decline in consumption appears to continue for a very long time, even beyond the three-year span illustrated in the simulations.

Turning to *private fixed non-residential investments,* only cost effects can be shown to have been at work.[15] The separate series for producers structures and durables suggest a smooth response which has not been completed by the end of the thirteenth quarter. The percentage change of corporate investment associated with a 50 basis-point change in the Treasury bill rate is of the order of slightly less than 0.4 at the end of four quarters and about 1.8 after eight quarters. It may be noted that there is no response in *inventory investment;* this finding is consistent with a number of disaggregated studies which have found no direct sensitivity in this demand component to either cost or availability factors. Nevertheless, the understanding of what determines inventory investment remains disappointing, and it is possible that disaggregation by type (and better data) would be required to arrive at more definite conclusions. As regards *state and local government expenditures* the sensitivity to financial changes is far smaller than for the other expenditure components, though it is not entirely negligible. Finally, as regards *residential investment* a combination of cost of capital and availability effects is at work. As the review of the mortgage market on pages 76-77 suggests, the availability effect is relatively quick to operate; but it declines after some quarters as savings and loan associations and mutual savings banks gradually adopt more competitive rates. Up to the eighth quarter, the availability effect accounts for slightly more than half the total housing response; subsequently, its relative importance declines and presumably would continue to do so after the thirteenth

---

15. The investment functions estimated are of the neoclassical variety inspired by the work of Jorgenson and associates [56]-[59] and Bischoff [5].

Chart 14. AGGREGATE DEMAND: PARTIAL SIMULATION, 1969-72

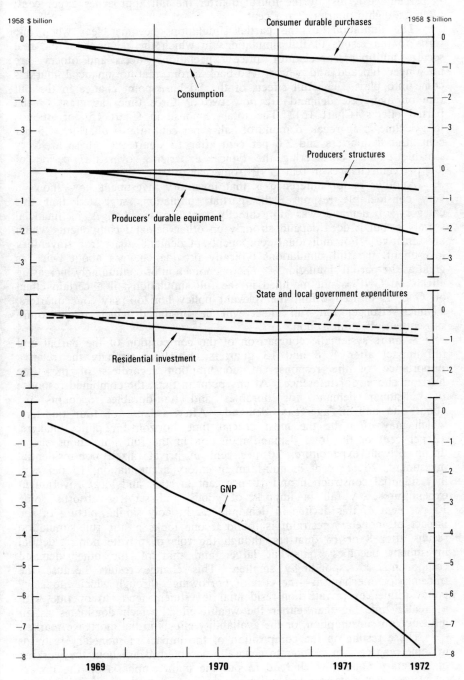

Source: Simulations provided by the Federal Reserve System.

quarter. Overall, the response of residential investment is relatively large in percentage terms; by the fourth quarter the fall approaches 2 per cent; after the eighth quarter, 3 per cent.

The limitations of the partial simulations become clear when one turns to the results of full simulations in which the relations of the real sector—multiplier, accelerator, price expectations effects and others—are no longer blocked and where feed-backs from real to financial markets come into play. The full effects of the 50 basis-point change in the bill rate on aggregate demand are now two or three times as great as the partial effects (Chart 15). The total response in Chart 15 corresponds to a decline in aggregate demand of half a per cent after 4 quarters, 1.3 per cent after 8 quarters and 2.6 per cent after 13 quarters. These are very sizeable effects, considering the typical experience over this period of 4-5 per cent changes in real GNP from year to year.

Another major difference is that inventory investment now shows a very considerable response; the partial simulations suggested that this category of demand was not directly sensitive to changes in financial variables, but it does depend strongly on other demand components which are sensitive. For individual components of demand apart from inventory investment, the full simulations typically provide changes about twice as great as the partial simulations. The phenomenon of continuingly increasing effects on GNP is not modified in the full simulations; if a certain effect on GNP is desired within the relevant policy horizon, say four quarters, a much stronger long-run effect will be produced which may require subsequent offsetting action.

A more systematic comparison of the composition of the partial and full impact after 4, 8 and 13 quarters underlines strongly the relative importance of the response of consumption regardless of the time horizon chosen for reference. At any point in time, the combined response of consumer demand for durables and non-durables accounts for about one half of aggregate demand. After a lapse of four quarters, which may often be the most crucial time horizon for policy makers, 42 per cent of the total demand reduction in the full simulations shows up in private expenditure, 20 per cent in private fixed non-residential investment, 26 per cent in non-farm inventory accumulation, 17 per cent in residential construction and 10 per cent in state and local government expenditures. A fall in imports of goods and services absorbs some 15 per cent of this decline in demand. A broadly similar picture of the impact of monetary restraint is found if one looks at the full simulation results after 8 or 13 quarters, though the role of private non-residential investment becomes somewhat larger and that of the other demand components correspondingly smaller. This change results because the transmission mechanism—the cost of borrowing—through which monetary policy influences private non-residential investment tends to operate with a greater time lag than either the wealth effect, which dominates as an influence on consumption, or the availability effects in the mortgage market.

These results on the composition of the impact of monetary restraint in some respects run counter to generally accepted ideas about the working of monetary policy, which tend to put the main emphasis on the impact on private sector capital expenditures (excluding inventories) as defined in Part I. The dominant role of the effects on consumption is repeated, though in a slightly weaker form, in the partial simulations (Table 13); it is not, therefore, primarily a result of particular features in those parts of the real sector of the model which are activated only in the full simulations, but rather the consequence of the strength of the direct transmission mechanism through which household wealth changes in response to changes in interest rates. This aspect of the FMP model, possibly its main distinguishing characteristic vis-à-vis other models, merits further critical review.

It is possible to bring out even more clearly the role of the wealth effect which, though novel in the framework of a large-scale model, has considerable empirical support in the specialised literature on the consumption function. In a recent study by Modigliani [76], simulations similar to those considered in the present study of an increase in the Treasury bill rate are run to illustrate the magnitude of the wealth effect in the full model, but also to investigate one particular aspect for its apparent strength, *viz* the role of price expectations.[16] The latter play a role on the stock market via the dividend-price ratio, in fixed investment and consumer durables expenditures and in the determination of long-term interest rates. However, on the stock market there is no evidence of any significant effect of price expectations prior to 1966; commodity prices of course rose much more slowly before than after the mid-1960s. Consequently their role cannot yet be said to have been firmly established, and it seems worthwhile to explore the functioning of the system in the absence of price expectations effects. The simulations carried out by Modigliani study the impact of various monetary changes on GNP with and without a wealth effect and, for both cases, with and without price expectations effects. The main conclusions are that

i) in the absence of the wealth effect, the inclusion of price expectations effects, i.e. in real demand and the formation of long-term interest rates, makes little difference;

ii) in the presence of the wealth effect, the inclusion of expectations effects increases the total impact on GNP by about 50 per cent; and

iii) in the presence of expectations effects, the inclusion of the wealth effect nearly doubles the total impact of the monetary change, while in the absence of expectations effects, it makes a much smaller difference to the total effect whether the wealth effect is included or not.

It therefore appears that the particularly strong impact of monetary changes in the FMP model is linked to the powerful mixture of wealth and expectations effects; if both were absent, the impact would be reduced to around one-third of that reported in the full simulation in Chart 15 (and Table 13).

There are indications from other research that the time response is likely to lie much closer to the full simulation results than to those produced when wealth or expectational effects are excluded. In the first place, there is considerable support for the presence of a wealth effect in studies of consumption expenditures for the United States. Second, the size of monetary responses and the length of the time lags involved in the

16. The simulations reviewed in [76] take their starting point in 1967.I but are otherwise similar to the simulations supplied by the Federal Reserve Board for the purpose of the present study. For a summary of the wealth effect, price expectations, etc., see also Fisher and Sheppard [32], pp. 78 ff.

Chart 15. AGGREGATE DEMAND: FULL SIMULATION, 1969-72

DEVIATIONS FROM ACTUAL FIGURES

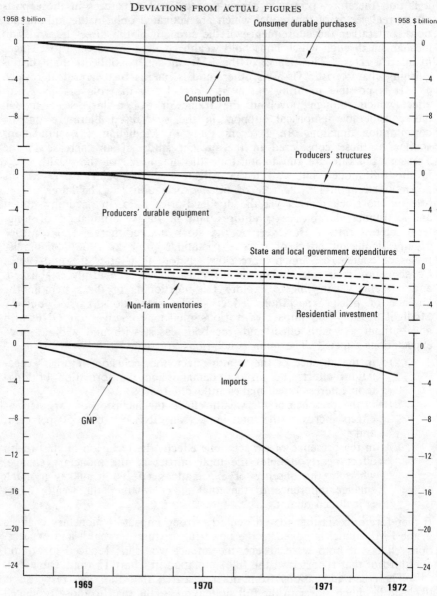

Source: Simulations provided by the Federal Reserve System.

transmission mechanism of most large-scale models incorporating a detailed specification of the financial sector have been in some conflict with both the views of informed observers and the results of research of a "monetarist" variety, which tended to find a somewhat stronger and quicker impact on real demand from changes in the money stock or the monetary base. While there is reason to believe that the simpler monetarist models

82

TABLE 13. PARTIAL AND FULL SIMULATIONS[1] OF THE EFFECTS
ON REAL DEMAND OF ADDITIONAL MONETARY RESTRAINT, 1969-71

	After 4 quarters		After 8 quarters		After 12 quarters	
	As % of initial value 1968. IV	As % of GNP 1968. IV	As % of initial value 1968. IV	As % of GNP 1968. IV	As % of initial value 1968. IV	As % of GNP 1968. IV
PARTIAL						
Consumption of Non-durable Goods and Services	−0.06	−0.03	−0.13	−0.07	−0.38	−0.20
Consumer Durable Purchases	−0.47	−0.05	−0.71	−0.08	−0.97	−0.11
Private Fixed Non-residential Investment	−0.43	−0.05	−1.83	−0.20	−3.31	−0.35
Residential Investment	−0.86	−0.03	−1.32	−0.04	−2.22	−0.07
State and Local Government Expenditures	−0.29	−0.03	−0.49	−0.05	−0.81	−0.08
GNP	−0.19	−0.19	−0.44	−0.44	−0.82	−0.81
FULL						
Consumption of Non-durable Goods and Services	−0.14	−0.07	−0.44	−0.23	−1.23	−0.64
Consumer Durable Purchases	−0.92	−0.11	−1.86	−0.22	−3.58	−0.42
Private Fixed Non-residential Investment	−0.83	−0.09	−4.00	−0.43	−8.75	−0.93
Residential Investment	−2.14	−0.07	−4.45	−0.15	−8.22	−0.27
Inventory Investment	−10.78	−0.11	−24.59	−0.25	−42.36	−0.44
State and Local Government Expenditures	−0.43	−0.04	−0.82	−0.08	−1.58	−0.16
Total Demand	−0.46	−0.49	−1.28	−1.36	−2.69	−2.86
Imports	−1.00	−0.06	−2.56	−0.16	−5.35	−0.34
GNP	−0.42	−0.42	−1.20	−1.20	−2.52	−2.52

1. The simulations measure the impact on real demand (in 1958 dollars) of keeping the Treasury bill rate 50 basis points above its actual level from the end of 1968. The " partial " results refer to simulations with no feed-backs from the real sector, while the " full " simulations include such feed-back effects.

Source: Simulations provided by the Federal Reserve System.

overstate the impact of monetary changes, it is noteworthy that the speedier responses in recent versions of the FMP model have tended nearly to close the gap between the two sets of results.[17]   While the particular form of the transmission mechanism incorporated in the FMP model requires intensive further work both theoretically and empirically before it can be regarded as well established, the broad conclusions on the magnitude of the total impact are supported by a fair amount of other evidence.

In conclusion, the apparent magnitude of the wealth effect is presently the least settled feature of the FMP model. While it has long been recognised both in economic theory and among policy makers that a rise in interest rates is bound to have some restraining impact on consumer spending, the apparent magnitude of the impact does raise considerable doubts.   It is possible that the observed association between wealth and consumption could be produced by a third set of factors, broadly labelled "the economic outlook" or "consumer sentiment"; an improved outlook would lead both to rising share prices (and thereby private wealth) and

17. See notably Modigliani [76] epilogue, and Hamburger [40].   But very significant differences persist in the assessment of fiscal effects.

to increased consumer spending, but the relationship between the latter two might display considerable instability. The possibilities for quantifying this hypothesis are obviously limited; but to the extent that existing survey data on consumer sentiments have been incorporated directly into consumption functions, they have not performed as well as the wealth measures used in the FMP model; see [76]. In the second place, it is somewhat disturbing that wealth changes due to capital gains from the stock market affect consumption in the same way as wealth changes due to the steady accumulation of savings. Research is currently under way in which allowance is made for somewhat longer time lags in the adjustment of consumption to capital gains than to wealth additions through saving. Such work has been prompted by the observation that the model does not perform reliably when large swings occur in equity prices. Preliminary results suggest that some modification of the FMP model along these lines may be justified, though the propensity to consume out of the two types of wealth change appears to be nearly identical over a one-year horizon.[18] Finally, it must be pointed out that even if the magnitude of the wealth effect turns out not to be overestimated in the FMP model, this powerful element in the transmission mechanism may give policy-makers little cause for comfort, because it will necessarily be particularly difficult in any specific situation to predict how strongly it will work. While the pressure of large wealth effects on consumption increases the scope for monetary policy, it also makes its overall impact more capricious.

The present discussion has concentrated on illustrating the effects of increasing the Treasury bill rate by 50 basis points. Broadly similar conclusions would have been reached had the starting point been an increase in the discount rate of one percentage point, i.e. twice the change in the bill rate, or a $1 billion decrease in Federal Reserve credit. There are interesting, though rather small, differences between the effects of these three ways of formulating roughly equivalent doses of additional monetary restraint, notably in relation to the money stock, but these do not affect the general picture conveyed by the full simulations of the change in the bill rate. More interesting differences emerge from simulations in which the starting point is an alternative course for the money stock (M_1). Such simulations have attracted much attention in the controversy surrounding the "monetarist" position, which accords a central role in the transmission mechanism to the money stock. The simulations have usually aimed to show what difference it would have made to real demand and prices if some variant of a monetary rule had been followed, i.e. a steady growth rate of the money stock, or an "adaptive control rule"[19] which takes into account deviations in ultimate target variables from supposedly desired levels. Such simulations mark a more radical departure from actual experiences and therefore a greater lack of realism than those surveyed above. This is so, not only because one cannot be confident that the economic structure would remain unaffected if some monetary rule were to be applied consistently over a longer period, but also because it is difficult for the monetary authorities to control the money stock accurately from quarter to quarter, as discussed in Part II and Appendix II. As noted there, it is much more difficult to control a monetary aggregate

18. Private communication from Professor Franco Modigliani.
19. For a survey of experiments with the latter, see Cooper and Fisher [14].

in the short run than to keep the Treasury bill rate on a prescribed course. Nevertheless, the simulations of alternative money supply time paths are interesting as crude indications of what could have happened under a different monetary policy stance. In Part IV some such experiments will be supplied as another illustration of the impact of the change in monetary policy during the two periods of restraint in 1966 and 1969.

It is possible to take the quantitative illustrations of policy effects beyond the components of aggregate demand to the ultimate targets of policy, notably the percentage of unemployed, the rate of change of prices and the balance of payments. An important part of the latter has already been shown in Chart 15 and Table 13. Since US exports do not respond in the model to changes in the domestic demand situation, the sole impact on the current account is on imports; they were shown to decline moderately in response to the increase in the bill rate, improving the current account by about $500 million during the first four quarters and by around $800 million after eight quarters. The manner and degree to which the capital account is likely to be improved by a more restrictive monetary policy is discussed further below. The two main domestic variables which have figured among ultimate targets, the rate of change of the GNP deflator and the unemployment rate, show a modest response to the increase in the bill rate (Chart 16). Over the first four quarters the simulations do not indicate any change in the rate of price change, but after eight and thirteen quarters there is a deceleration by .1 and .2 percentage points respectively. The percentage of unemployed might have been .1, .2 and .6 percentage points higher in the similar observation quarters. There is no evident mechanism whereby monetary or financial variables could directly affect these ultimate target variables;[20] the impact on them is transmitted through changes in aggregate demand relative to productive capacity. This conclusion does not exclude the possibility that the impacts of monetary instruments on ultimate targets have characteristics that distinguish them from those of other instruments, notably fiscal policy changes. To the extent that:

   i)   the unemployment and price effects depend not only on aggregate demand but also on its composition, and

   ii) monetary and other economic policies have a differential impact on these components,

it will make a difference to the achievement of ultimate policy objectives whether a given change in aggregate demand is brought about through monetary or other means. However, the issue of the optimal policy mix falls outside the scope of the present study of monetary policy.

e) INTERNATIONAL CAPITAL MOVEMENTS

Large-scale econometric models typically do not attempt to explain capital flows in and out of the United States. This omission has not been serious because, as already indicated above (pages 17-18 and 62-65), the consequences of such flows for US monetary developments have been sharply

---

20. Some monetarist research has included the rate of growth of a monetary aggregate directly as a determinant of price expectations or of stock market prices; see e.g. Sprinkel [93] and Homa and Jaffee [51]. But such features have not been incorporated in large-scale econometric models.

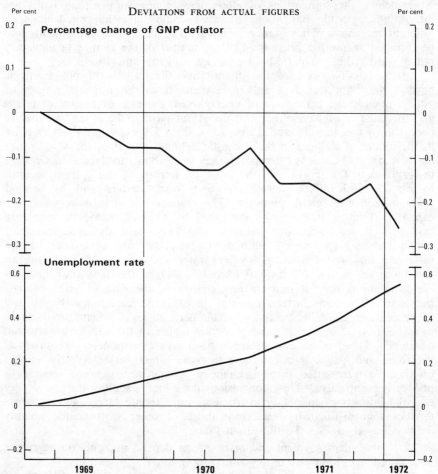

DEVIATIONS FROM ACTUAL FIGURES

Source: Simulations provided by the Federal Reserve System.

limited by the reserve position of the dollar; and, to the extent that this role did not effectively insulate the domestic money market, the Federal Reserve has had the technical means of sterilising undesired impacts on bank reserves or, alternatively, interest rates. But the greater prominence given to external aims during the period under study, combined with the vastly increased scope for capital flows in recent years, make it unsatisfactory not to try to evaluate the scope of monetary policy for achieving external aims. This is a task even more difficult than the assessment of the domestic impact. The institutional framework in which these flows take place has evolved very considerably since 1960, partly because of financial innovations in international transactions (notably the growth of Euro-currency markets) and partly because of changing regulations in the United States and elsewhere. The US authorities tightened such regulations on several occasions during the period under review (see below); the programmes subsequently were eased and were completely removed by early 1974. Furthermore, widespread expectations of a realignment of important parities have on occasions, mainly in 1971, given rise to massive flows. None of these factors is readily quantifiable for the purposes of econometric work; and since demand and supply functions for internationally held financial assets undoubtedly would be unstable even in their absence, it is not surprising that empirical estimates generally have been less successful than empirical work on domestic relationships. Nevertheless, some results are worth reporting and are reviewed below, following a very brief mention of the main restrictions used by the US authorities. More detailed comments are made on one important study, that of Branson and Hill.[9] 21

The first important selective instrument used to influence the capital account was the Interest Equalisation Tax (IET) on foreign long-term securities, introduced in July 1963. The IET stopped but did not, except for a short period of initial portfolio shifting, reverse the rapid growth of outflows related to long-term portfolio claims on foreigners. The limited effectiveness of the IET was mainly due to the exemption of Canadian issues. More disturbing overall, however, was the surge in short-term portfolio claims and long-term banking claims on foreigners which followed the introduction of the IET. This disturbance prompted the authorities to extend the control to these flows through the voluntary foreign credit restraint programme (VFCR) of 1965 which was repeatedly strengthened and was made mandatory in 1968. Along with bank credit, foreign direct investments also were subjected to control, on a voluntary basis from 1965 to 1968 and on a mandatory basis thereafter. The aim of this last facet of the balance of payments programme was less to curb foreign direct investment than to encourage US corporations and their foreign subsidiaries to finance such investment through foreign borrowing rather than from domestic sources. As a result, the ever-growing outflow related to foreign direct investment was mitigated after 1968 as foreign subsidiaries of US corporations borrowed heavily on the Euro-bond and Euro-currency markets. Generally, the selective controls have been effective in curbing the flows at which they were specifically aimed, but the substitution effects which the controls have induced in the rest of the capital account raise doubts about their net effectiveness. Since 1967 they have tended to be swamped by changes in capital inflows and by the response of unregulated short-term outflows to the sharp swings in monetary policy.

The striking feature of the US capital account during the period 1966-71 was the progressive dominance of short-term flows and the sharp increase in their magnitude. As shown in Chart 17, both the size and the variations of total capital, private non-direct (or financial) capital and short-term capital were remarkably close; and the relative importance of direct investment and long-term flows in general declined rapidly. The correlation between changes in interest rates and financial capital movements

---

21. While the Branson and Hill study is the most comprehensive and proceeds at a fairly high level of aggregation, other research has aimed at disaggregating US capital flows by country. For a major attempt along these lines see Bryant and Hendershott [13].

in general and short-term flows in particular has been shown to be high in a number of econometric studies. During the period under review, there was a tendency for interest rates around the world to follow monetary developments in the United States, largely through the intermediation of the Euro-dollar market. But this response was far from immediate and complete, especially in the case of the sharp tightening of US monetary conditions in 1968-69 when interest differentials between Euro-dollar rates and rates in most other countries reached exceptionally high levels. As a result, the tidal flow and reflow of funds across the Atlantic in these years can be explained largely in terms of monetary variables. On the other hand, no interest rate variable can come close to explaining the explosive capital outflows of 1971 when speculative expectations outweighed all other factors. The following paragraphs discuss each one of the six components of financial flows: short- and long-term liabilities to foreigners, errors and omissions, short- and long-term portfolio claims on foreigners, and long-term banking claims on foreigners. The purpose in each case is to ascertain the responsiveness of these flows to monetary variables. Given the paramount importance of short-term liabilities to foreigners, the discussion below emphasizes that component of total financial flows.

Short-term liabilities to foreigners include liabilities of banks and non-banking concerns. The former can be divided into liabilities to banks' foreign branches and liabilities to other foreign banks and the non-banking public. While all these liabilities show some elasticity with respect to interest rates and other monetary variables, it is primarily bank liabilities to their foreign branches (representing Euro-dollar borrowing) which have shown an impressive responsiveness to changing monetary conditions in the United States. Euro-dollar borrowing started practically from zero in the credit crunch of 1966 and soon dominated not only bank liabilities to foreigners (see Chart 12 and page 62) but the entire short-term capital account, at least until the spring of 1971 when it was eclipsed by speculative flows. The liabilities of US banks to their foreign branches, being legally defined as non-depositary liabilities, initially were subject neither to interest rate ceilings nor to reserve requirements; the latter were introduced in September 1969. The exemption from rate ceilings meant that in periods when Regulation Q was not effective, Euro-dollar borrowing represented merely an alternative to CDs as a major source of loanable funds; according to relative costs, banks would either increase or decrease Euro-dollar borrowing. But when Regulation Q was effective, as in 1966 and in 1968-70, banks could hardly issue new CDs and the most important alternative to Euro-dollar borrowing was thereby nullified.[22] Generally speaking, banks then would compare the cost of Euro-dollar borrowing with the return on loans and investments. Considerations of customer goodwill may also have played a role and may explain why banks at times were borrowing Euro-dollars at rates apparently higher than those on their loans. Thus in 1969 the massive

22. Other alternative sources of loanable funds remained viable. The major money market banks sharply increased their net purchases of Federal funds during these periods. After the introduction of reserve requirements on Euro-dollar borrowing in 1969, banks also made increasing use of the commercial paper market. Commercial paper remained free of interest rate ceilings and, until September 1970, of reserve requirements; Federal funds purchases remain free of both types of regulations.

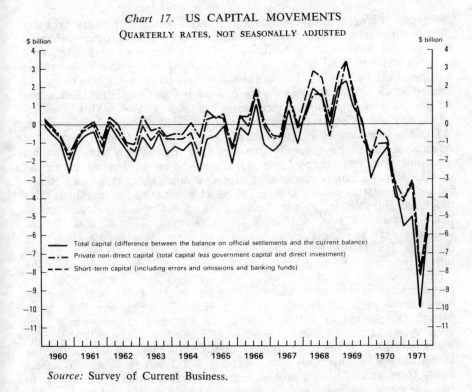

Chart 17. US CAPITAL MOVEMENTS

QUARTERLY RATES, NOT SEASONALLY ADJUSTED

Total capital (difference between the balance on official settlements and the current balance)
Private non-direct capital (total capital *less* government capital and direct investment)
Short-term capital (including errors and omissions and banking funds)

Source: Survey of Current Business.

run-off of CDs was accompanied by an equally impressive increase in Euro-dollar borrowing at interest rates at times exceeding 10 per cent. To the extent that a "circular flow" was involved, the substitution of Euro-dollar borrowing for CDs was essentially an accounting operation leaving the balance on official settlements unaffected. The outflows of capital related to the circular flow being difficult to identify, they were largely included in the errors and omissions item. The bulk of these Euro-dollar borrowings probably represented a net inflow of foreign funds attracted by straightforward interest considerations.

Because of the United States dominance of the demand for Euro-dollars and the widely diffused origin of these funds, up to 1971 Euro-dollar rates closely reflected US monetary developments.[23] But the interest

---

23. In an early investigation using monthly data for 1957-64, Hendershott [46] found the Treasury bill rate to be the primary determinant of the Euro-dollar rate, with the latter adjusting completely to changes in the former within a period of about a year. However, about three-quarters of the explanatory power came from seasonal dummies. Broadly similar conclusions were reached by Black [6], using weekly data for 1966-68. A one percentage point change in the Treasury bill rate generated a change of nearly 0.8 in the Euro-dollar rate, with about 75 per cent of the effect taking place in the first period. Lags were much shorter here and all the explanatory power came from economic variables. Using quarterly data for the 1960-70 period, Branson and Hill [9] also found the coefficient on changes in the US bill rate to be close to one. The existence of an interest differential in favour of the Euro-dollar market may be due, among other factors, to lower transaction costs of Euro-banks,

differential between Euro-dollar rates and US rates (either on Treasury bills or commercial paper) fluctuated sharply after 1965, following primarily the ups and downs of US banks' Euro-dollar borrowing and reaching a peak in 1969. Thus among its other functions, the Euro-dollar market has provided the rest of the world with short-term dollar investment at interest rates significantly above those available in the United States, the differential widening with the increase in the level of rates. This consideration may be relevant for an accurate analysis of capital movements. While the direction of the huge flows and reflows of capital across the Atlantic seems to be generally explicable by interest rate considerations, a complete understanding of the magnitudes or of the interest elasticities of these flows requires recognition of the institutional background to the Euro-dollar market at that time. US banks were willing to pay high rates to obtain Euro-dollars in part because the effectiveness of Regulation Q had restricted the availability of substitute sources of funds; thus foreign investors were reacting to rates which were rising much more than were domestic US rates. Simple estimates of relationships between capital movements and US and foreign interest rates would thereby overstate the interest elasticity of these flows. The difficult question of what the magnitude of capital flows and the state of the US balance of payments would have been in the absence of policies favouring the Euro-dollar market (Regulation Q and exemption from reserve requirements) is of some relevance for the future conduct of monetary policy. Without the given incentive to mobilise foreign funds, financial institutions in the United States would likely have developed other techniques to attract funds from abroad. Also, the increase in domestic rates resulting from the absence of the Euro-dollar market would have provided some incentive for non-residents' placements of funds in the US domestic market. Nonetheless, there seems to be little doubt that the flow of funds to the United States in 1968-69 would have been somewhat smaller without the Euro-dollar market.

In addition to Euro-dollar borrowing from overseas branches, bank short-term liabilities include those to other foreign banks and to other foreigners. The liabilities to foreign banks showed a rising and accelerating trend through 1969, a small drop in 1970 and a much larger drop in 1971. Some of these accounts (totalling about $9.5 billion at the end of 1971) probably include working balances for trade and financial transaction, while the rest may represent roughly the "reserve base" of the Euro-dollar market. In any case, these balances have changed generally in the same direction as liabilities to foreign branches (i.e. in the direction indicated by interest differentials), but the magnitudes of the reflows during 1970-71 were substantially smaller in this category. The last type of liability (to foreign non-banking concerns) increased steadily but moderately until the end of 1968; the trend was then reversed, presumably because of the attraction of higher interest rates in the Euro-dollar market and, beginning

---

as well as to a higher degree of risk. But the sharp rise in the differential after 1965 would probably not have been possible without the United States' balance of payments programme, which prevented domestic investors from freely arbitrating between the two markets. In a forthcoming article, based on monthly data 1961-71, Argy and Hodjera [3] show speculation to be an additional significant factor in explaining the differential.

in 1971, exchange rate considerations. But the small size of the 1971 decline may indicate that these liabilities (amounting to some $3.75 billion at the end of 1971) largely consist of working balances that react only marginally to changes in relative monetary conditions.

As for short-term liabilities of US corporations, which have increasingly reflected changes in the foreign direct investment programme and conditions in the international money market relative to the international capital market, there is evidence that during periods of high interest rates in capital markets, short- and medium-term foreign borrowing was substituted for new issues of securities sold abroad as a source of finance.

Long-term liabilities to foreigners. The capital flow originating from changes in these liabilities may be divided, somewhat arbitrarily, into three components: changes in US securities other than Treasury issues, changes in long-term liabilities reported by non-banking concerns, and changes in long-term liabilities reported by US banks. The latter two flows remained rather marginal throughout the period under review, except for the sharp increase in non-bank liabilities beginning in 1968, which apparently resulted from the tightening of the foreign direct investment programme. The first and by far the dominant category, US securities held by foreigners, includes new issues sold abroad by US corporations (Euro-bonds) and foreign purchases of existing US stocks and bonds. Not surprisingly, new issues sold abroad by US corporations gained in importance after the introduction of the foreign direct investment programme in 1965 and even more after this programme was made mandatory in 1968. Foreign investment in US stocks exhibits a clear association with the performance of Wall Street, especially during the 1967-70 period. Since stock prices have been shown to be influenceable through changes in monetary policy (page 76), such changes have some impact on long-term capital flows, although the lags may be important. The sharp increase in foreign investment in US stocks in the late 1960s may also have owed much to the proliferation of investment funds around the world (mainly off-shore funds) specialising in investment in the United States. Similarly, the drastic drop in net foreign purchases in the following years may have been in part a consequence of general disenchantment with off-shore funds and the imposition in several countries of strict legal limitations on their operations. Finally, some foreign purchases of US stocks and bonds may have reflected the desire of investors abroad to keep a steady or even rising proportion of their growing wealth in US assets.

Errors and omissions. Especially in the last years of the period considered, the errors and omissions item seems to have represented unrecorded financial capital transactions. Its exceptionally large negative values in 1968-69 are probably an indication of the magnitude of the unrecorded flow of US funds to the Euro-dollar market as part of the so-called circular flow. And a very large proportion (perhaps as much as one-third) of the massive outflows in 1971 are to be found in the $10 billion of errors and omissions. Consequently, this item is to be explained essentially in terms of monetary variables and speculative factors; given its typically negative values during the 1960-71 period, it may be treated together with changes in US claims on foreigners.

United States claims on foreigners. Compared to flows resulting from changes in US liabilities to foreigners and errors and omissions, capital flows related to (identified) changes in US claims on foreigners were rather small. As mentioned above, short- and long-term portfolio claims were significantly affected by the IET and the foreign credit restraint programme, especially during the initial periods of portfolio adjustment which followed the imposition of these programmes. But the impact of the VFCR programme on US claims on foreigners, while certainly noticeable, affected only a minor portion of the total flow since export credit, an important part of the banking component of short-term claims, was exempted. Thus, reasonably stable equations largely based on monetary variables have been fitted to this type of capital movement. On the other hand, long-term banking claims have been so affected, either directly or through substitution effects, by the various measures to improve the US balance of payments, and notably by the constantly changing foreign credit restraint programme, that the estimation of a stable equation has seemed impossible to Branson and Hill [9] and others.

From this brief analysis, it would seem that monetary policy, especially in the second part of the period under review, had a powerful impact on US capital movements. This impact, however, was highly concentrated on certain short-term flows which, because of institutional factors and the peculiar implementation of monetary policy, were largely channelled through the Euro-dollar market. The best estimates available of this impact are probably those by Branson and Hill [9] which suggest that an increase in the US Treasury bill rate by one percentage point tended around 1969 to be associated with an inflow of $1.5 billion, mainly in the first two quarters after the change; these calculations allow for the impact of the change on the Euro-dollar rate. But in 1971, conditions changed drastically, and considerations of cost and availability of credit were outweighed by speculative forces. The connection between monetary variables and long-term capital flows would seem to have been more tenuous and indirect and to have operated with longer lags. Several other factors, such as internationally marketed mutual funds and growing foreign wealth, may also have played a primary role. Moreover, the impact of the various selective measures to improve the US capital account was more important on long-term than on short-term flows.

IV

THE DATING OF PHASES OF MONETARY POLICY
AND THE CONDUCT OF POLICY
IN SELECTED PHASES

a) INDICATORS OF THE STRENGTH OF MONETARY POLICY: "EX POST"
DATING

There are, essentially, two ways of identifying phases of monetary policy. The first of these *(ex ante* dating) focuses on the actions of the monetary authorities, i.e. major changes in policy instruments or in the main operating target, notably money market conditions in the case of the United States policy throughout most of the period under study. The second *(ex post* dating) classifies periods by reference to some measurable indicator of monetary thrust. There is no reason why the two should yield identical qualitative or quantitative characterisations of policy periods. Furthermore, neither of the two gives unambiguous results. The choice of an indicator is not a simple and straightforward matter, since it reflects a prior view of the origin of demand fluctuations and of the transmission mechanism connecting the instruments to aggregate demand and thence to the ultimate targets of policy. The following paragraphs will review these issues in the light of the results of the transmission mechanism from Part III, while an outline of the somewhat more clear-cut dating of policy phases based on the actions of the Federal Reserve (or on the more immediate consequences of such actions) is offered in the following section.

There is a very considerable literature, both theoretical and empirical, on the selection of an appropriate indicator of monetary policy thrust.[1] A number of possible indicators have been proposed to measure the *ex post* impact of Federal Reserve actions on aggregate demand. The leading candidates are the nominal money supply and a nominal interest rate (other than those short-term rates which define money market conditions); in the following paragraphs, these two concepts are represented by the narrow money supply (M_1) and the corporate Aaa rate. Both of these variables are clearly subject to influences in addition to those of the monetary instruments: they depend on the current and lagged values of all the exogenous variables in the system.[2] The scope for offsetting these other

---

1. Among the better known references are Brunner [11], Brunner and Meltzer [12], Hendershott [44], [45], Keran [63], Tobin [97] and Saving [90].
2. The money supply is endogenous in that it depends not only on Federal Reserve actions but also on other endogenous variables, notably interest rates. Furthermore, the variables controlled by the Federal Reserve may also display endo-

influences in the short run is limited. Given the complicated lag structure in the financial linkages, it is obvious that one will get different answers depending on the precise variable chosen as an indicator. It must be pointed out that the corporate bond rate is an indicator of past, rather than present, monetary action, given the long lags involved in the term-structure relationships (page 75).

In a complex economic system in which none of the underlying structural relationships is exact, it is intuitively obvious that no endogenous variable can be an unambiguously correct indicator. It is, indeed, a simple matter to devise illustrative examples of situations in which either or both indicators can give incorrect information. Consider, for example, a situation in which political or other uncertainties generate an increase in the demand for money. Interest rates will rise, and the corporate Aaa rate indicator therefore will suggest that monetary action is tightening. But the rise in interest rates typically will reduce the demand for free reserves and generate an expansion in the money supply. Hence the money supply indicator will suggest that policy is easing. Experiences in April-July 1971 provide an illustration of conflicting indicators; both M_1 and most interest rates rose during this period (see the detailed review in Appendix II). Alternatively, consider a situation in which investment plans are revised upwards because of an improved outlook for profits. Again interest rates will rise, inducing an expansion of the money supply and leading to the same contradictory signals from the two indicators as in the first case. The interest rate indicator suggests a tightening in both cases and is correct in the first case; the money supply indicator suggests an easing in both cases and is correct in the second case.

Before proceeding to the general conclusion which may be inferred from this discussion, it should be noted that a measure of Federal Reserve actions, such as adjusted unborrowed reserves, may well characterise a particular period in a way which conflicts with both indicators. If unborrowed reserves during the phases described above remain unchanged, a straight-forward interpretation based on Federal Reserve actions suggests that both indicators are in error in suggesting that an active policy is being pursued, though they disagree about its qualitative nature. The semantic possibilities here are considerable and have been well explored in the literature. It is also conceivable that the unborrowed reserves measure will side with one or other of the indicators. Thus, if reserves increase in the two phases described, but insufficiently to prevent interest rates from rising, there will be agreement with the M_1 indicator in suggesting easing; if reserves decline, but insufficiently to halt fully the growth in M_1, the reserves measure will agree with the corporate bond rate indicator in suggesting tightening.

Neglecting the complications arising out of time lags, the general conclusion to the indicator discussion above is that the interest rate is superior as an indicator where the typical source of unpredictability in the economic system is in the demand for money, while the money supply indicator is superior where the typical form of instability lies in unpre-

geneity via the systematic reactions of the authorities to observed or projected developments in the ultimate target variables of policy. This second aspect of endogeneity is neglected in the present discussion. For empirical evidence on the reaction function, see notably Teigen [95], Wood [100] and Keran and Babb [64].

dictable shifts in investment (or saving). As briefly stated on page 51 and further explained in Appendix II, a similar conclusion, formulated initially by Poole [85] and refined by Pierce and Thomson [83] holds in regard to the choice of the optimal policy target. The indicator/target problems are identical in the sense that the information required to form a judgement on either of them is the same. But the terms "instability" or "unpredictability" have meaning only in relation to a definite period of calendar time. One might typically think of a policy horizon of about four quarters. It is then a matter of judgement whether the predictability of the demand for money is greater or smaller than that of investment (or saving), in the sense that the probability of error is significantly changed by adopting a money stock rather than an interest rate indicator.[3] Most empirical studies in recent years have tended to the view that the money supply in some form, usually M_1, is a more reliable indicator.[4]

Some of the observed changes in M_1 are due to factors other than Federal Reserve actions; to that extent M_1 does not meet the first of the criteria mentioned above (page 93). This inspires the idea that it must be possible to construct a money supply indicator superior to observed M_1 by eliminating from the latter those changes which can be explained by cyclical swings in economic activity. Hendershott [45] has developed such a purified indicator in the form of a "neutralised" money stock, a concept analogous to the high employment surplus, changes in which are designed precisely to reflect Federal Reserve actions.[5] Since Hendershott's data are not available beyond 1964, a crude approximation to his procedure is adopted here; it eliminates from observed changes in the seasonally adjusted (monthly and quarterly) M_1 that part which is statistically explained by the industrial production index and a price index of industrial output. The time pattern of this series—the "approximately neutralised money stock"—naturally gives an impression of monetary action somewhat different from that of M_1 (Chart 18). For example, periods with steady but moderate growth in observed M_1, which would be classified as accommodating by an M_1 indicator, reveal a clearly decelerating neutralised money stock because the demand for money has outgrown the supply; the clearest instance of this is in the 1960-61 expansion.

An *ex post* classification of policy phases based upon an M_1 indicator reveals some important differences with the *ex ante* classification which emerges from Federal Reserve actions. Chart 18 shows quarterly growth at

---

3. Even if the probability of error is significantly reduced by such a change, it is quite possible for the interest rate indicator to perform more reliably than the money supply in a particular period or in a shorter sequence of such periods. Furthermore, a careful statement of the problem really requires that the errors associated with the two indicators be weighted. For example, it is conceivable that watching a money supply indicator leads to more infrequent but larger errors.

4. Apart from the references already cited in footnote 1 page 93, single-equation studies suggesting that (*i*) changes in M_1 are dominated by Federal Reserve action, and (*ii*) changes in M_1 explain much of observed changes in nominal income (with or without a distributed lag) are relevant. A number of studies from the Federal Reserve Bank of St. Louis, surveyed in Fisher and Sheppard [32] Chapter 4, discuss these issues.

5. Since information on the current economic situation is unlikely to be fully up to date, considerable uncertainty would surround any attempt to estimate the current value of the neutralised money stock. The series is therefore more useful in a retrospective analysis than in the design of policy.

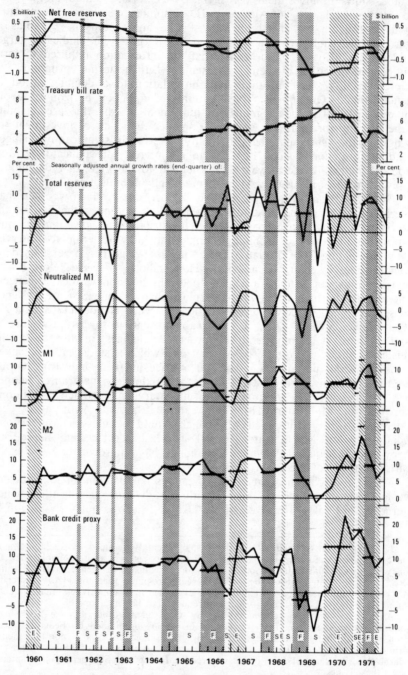

Chart 18. POLICY PHASES FROM FOMC RECORDS

Policy phases: E=ease; S=stable; F=firming.
The averages given for the policy phases are based on monthly data.
Source: Data supplied by the Federal Reserve System.

annual rates for M_1 (and the "approximately neutralised money stock") and other monetary aggregates during each of the *ex ante* phases to be defined in section *(b)*. There are a number of cases in which expansionary (or restrictive) action is unaccompanied by faster (slower) growth in M_1; for example, in 1960-61 M_1 growth accelerated while Federal Reserve actions became gradually less expansionary. Similar discrepancies occurred in 1967-68, and in 1971, during a temporary firming of policy, the growth of M_1 accelerated. These and other discrepancies have been the basis for considerable academic criticism of the Federal Reserve (see notably Brunner [11] and Brunner and Meltzer [12]). Nevertheless, from the viewpoint of reviewing phases of active monetary policy, the usefulness of the M_1 and other indicators is mainly as a supplement and possible corrective to the more clear-cut characterisation derived from Federal Reserve actions to be reviewed in the next section. In section *(d)* some policy simulations are reviewed in which alternative policies are formulated in terms of a different time path for M_1.

b) FEDERAL OPEN MARKET COMMITTEE ACTIONS: "EX ANTE" DATING

There are two main documentary sources which can be used for the purpose of *ex ante* dating. The first of these consists of the directives (see pages 46 ff and records of the FOMC. Following a method developed by Poole [85], these can be classified by whether they imply an "easing", "stable" or "firming" open market policy.[6] FOMC meetings occur at intervals of 3 or 4 weeks; it follows that this method gives a rather fine classification which, over longer periods of time such as 3 or 6 months, is not always easy to interpret (Table 14). A somewhat cruder classification can be obtained by examining the Annual Reports of the Board of Governors or of the Federal Reserve Bank of New York. Combining these two, it is possible to identify, at least approximately, periods which can be classified broadly as characterised by intended monetary ease or restraint. Furthermore, it is possible, by comparing the starting and ending dates of such periods with the cyclical pattern of economic activity, as represented most conveniently by the NBER reference cycles, to draw some inferences regarding the timing of policy changes, that is, regarding the so-called inside or recognition lag in the design of monetary policy.[7]

For most of the period under review the operations of the Desk in carrying out FOMC directives were based upon instructions relating to an operating target described as money market conditions. An interpretation of this term and the gradual decline in its dominance in recent years are examined on pages 47-51 and in Appendix II. At this stage money market conditions are assumed to be defined by the Federal funds rate, the net

---

6. Poole's classification has been extended to cover 1969-71. Any interpretation is, of course, open to objection, and it is not suggested that Poole would necessarily accept the interpretations made in this report.

7. Strictly speaking, what the comparison measures is the lapse of time between a "need for action", as indicated by the NBER turning points, and monetary action. In addition, to recognising a need to act, the authorities must of course decide to act, typically in an FOMC meeting. In practice the action lag may be assumed to be short.

TABLE 14. DATES OF PRINCIPAL MONETARY POLICY DECISIONS
AND OF BUSINESS CYCLE PEAKS AND TROUGHS

Business Cycle		FOMC Policy Decisions	
Turning point	Date	Policy	Starting date
Peak	1960, May	Easing	1960 - Mar. 1
		Stable	Aug. 16
Trough	1961, February	Firming	1961 - Oct. 24
		Stable	Nov. 14
		Firming	1962 - June 19
		Stable	July 10
		Firming	Dec. 18
		Stable	1963 - Jan. 8
		Firming	May 7
		Stable	Aug. 20
		Firming	1964 - Aug. 18
		Stable	1965 - Mar. 2
		Firming	Dec. 14
		Stable	1966 - Sept. 13
		Easing	Nov. 1
		Stable	1967 - May 2
		Firming	Nov. 27
		Stable	1968 - Apr. 30
		Easing	July 16
		Stable	Aug. 13
		Firming	Dec. 17
Peak	1969, November	Stable	1969 - June 24[1]
		Easing	Dec. 14
Trough	1970, November	Stable	1970 - Dec. 15
		Firming	1971 - Jan. 12
		Easing	Apr. 6
		Stable	Aug. 24
		Easing	Oct. 19
		Stable	1972 - Feb. 15

1. Poole [85] dates the beginning of the " stable " period from the FOMC meeting held on 14th April 1969.
The present study follows a different interpretation of the minutes of the two subsequent meetings of the FOMC
and uses the later date, 24th June.

Source: Federal Reserve Bulletin.

free reserves of member banks and the Treasury bill rate. Both rates
should decline in periods of ease and rise in periods of firming, and net
free reserves should rise in periods of ease and fall in periods of firming;
though it is conceivable that a constant level of reserves could be consistent
with either policy, depending on the initial situation. The behaviour of
these immediate operating targets thus serves as a check on the time
classification derived from the qualitative tabulation of directives supplemented by the broader classifications of the Annual Reports. There is no
implication that the movements in the two key interest rates referred to
are in any sense a quantitative indicator of policy thrust.

A comparison of the "easing", "stable", "firming" classification with
quarterly movements in two strategic money market variables, net free
reserves and the bill rate, reveals a high degree of correspondance (Chart 18).
The same is broadly the case with the growth rate of total reserves, though
the more erratic behaviour of this variable masks the relationship. As

already mentioned, it is of particular interest to place changes in policy in their cyclical context. Measured by the NBER method, cyclical peaks in economic activity occurred in May 1960 and November 1969. In the former case, policy was shifted to ease in March when open market operations began to supply reserve money; relevant measures of reserves moved up and the bill rate declined, though less than in earlier comparable phases. The inside lag was thus approximately *minus* two months. In the latter case the dating of the policy shift is less sure. A move towards ease took place in December 1969, or at the latest in January 1970; the turning point in the quarterly observations of money market conditions was clearly the fourth quarter of 1969. In this case, the inside lag was 1 to 2 months. This finding does not suggest any significant failure to forecast turning points or to modify policy on the basis of such forecasts. This very short inside lag is in contrast with the criticism developed by academic economists of Federal Reserve procedures in earlier periods. In particular, Kareken and Solow [62] found that the policy actions of the 1950s displayed rather longer lags and asymmetry between the speed of reaction in modifying monetary policy after peaks and troughs in economic activity; a similar criticism was raised in a report of the Joint Economic Committee of Congress [55], Chapter 9. It would appear therefore that the speed of reaction to the authorities has increased considerably relative to periods before 1960.

This impression is broadly confirmed if one looks at the timing of policy changes around the growth recession of 1966-67. The economy became overheated towards the end of 1965, as suggested, for example, by the relationship between actual and potential GNP (Chart 1); at the same time, fiscal policy changes were stimulative because of increased defence expenditures. Monetary policy was firming from December 1965, when the discount rate was increased, and it remained restrictive through September 1966. Policy was modified to stable slightly before the peak in industrial production and the sharp fall in the rate of inventory accumulation which came in the fourth quarter. A further movement towards ease came in December 1966 when it seemed likely that 1967 would begin with too slow a rate of demand expansion. Even with the full benefit of hindsight, these policy shifts appear to indicate a negligible inside lag, suggesting that Federal Reserve forecasting is sufficiently developed to allow the direction of policy to be appropriately adjusted by the FOMC. However, this conclusion would not be universally accepted; economic activity was particularly difficult to forecast in 1966-67 and there is no evidence that the changes in late 1966 had been accurately foreseen.[8] It must also be pointed out that the longer the time lags in the transmission of policy effects, the greater the premium on forecasting for the monetary authorities; if, as the FMP model and experience generally suggest, policy effects require a few quarters to build up to a significant level and only

8. The timing of policy changes in relation to cyclical troughs is not examined in the present study. While it typically makes sense to move in the direction of monetary ease at, or slightly before, a business cycle peak, it may make little sense to move to restraint at, or slightly before, a cycle trough. This is because the level of capacity utilisation is a relevant consideration in the determining of the appropriate moment at which to move towards restraint. For example, it would have made litte sense to modify the expansionary policy stance around the February 1961 trough, because the economy was then operating at far from full capacity utilisation.

reach their maximum impact much later, policy adjustments based on an ability to forecast only imminent turning points in economic activity can hardly be expected to be fully offsetting.

The following two sections review in detail some selected phases of active monetary policy. In two of these phases, the view of the authorities was clearly that the economy needed a monetary stimulus. Using quarterly observations these phases may be defined as 1960.I to 1962.IV and 1970.I to 1971.IV.[9] The decade separating these two major instances of expansionary policies make the two phases somewhat different both in the monetary techniques employed and in the responses in financial and other markets; they are therefore—in contrast to their treatment in the FMP and other models which estimate average responses over a longer span, such as the late 1950s up to 1971—regarded as qualitatively different and are treated separately. Two brief periods of rather vigorous monetary restraint—1965.IV to 1966.III and 1968.IV to 1969.IV—are also reviewed. These two periods, much closer to each other in time and background than the two expansionary phases, are in many respects comparable, and special emphasis is put on bringing out their common features. They are further analysed and compared in the section (d) of the present Part by means of alternative policy simulations, which assume, in a necessarily arbitrary way, an absence of restraint in 1966 and 1969. The particular selection of policy phases studied in the present section thus covers somewhat more than half of the 12-year period 1960-71; it leaves out most references to the years 1963-65 and 1967-68 which were, from a monetary viewpoint, less eventful years than the selected phases. Policy during those five years did not aim to change the course of the economy in any major way. It must therefore be recalled that the sample of phases included in the following sections is biased in the direction of active policy; there has, for the period as a whole, been a larger role for a relatively accommodating policy stance than the discussion suggests.

c) TWO PERIODS OF EXPANSION: 1960.I-1962.IV AND 1970.I-1971.IV

1960-62. The early period of expansionary monetary policy was designed to mitigate the 1960-61 recession and prompt the subsequent recovery. According to the dating of the National Bureau of Economic Research, the recession lasted from May 1960 to February 1961. Measured by most indicators, the 10-month recession was not only the shortest, but also the mildest of the post-war recessions up to that time; the decline in real output was marginal. But the facts that the peak from which it started in the second quarter of 1960 represented a level of activity well below capacity and that the increase in the percentage of unemployed was substantial—roughly from 5 to 7 per cent of the civilian labour force—made it desirable not only to take vigorous expansionary measures in the recession itself, but also to continue them well beyond the trough in economic activity in early 1961. Thus it appears legitimate to regard the whole period as a phase during which monetary expansion was appropriate for domestic objectives. The major complication was the external position. After a temporary deterioration in 1959 of the trade

---

9. Expansionary policies continued throughout 1972, beyond the period here under study.

balance, a substantial surplus of nearly $5 billion was restored in 1960, mainly because of the relatively low activity level in the United States, and was maintained more or less steadily in the following two years. However, private capital outflows, particularly in short-term form, rose sharply from 1959 to 1960, leaving a deficit on official settlements of close to $3.5 billion, even larger than those recorded in the two previous—and initial—years of external deficit. This outflow posed a policy dilemma for the monetary authorities: the current account was bound to worsen as expansion got underway, so the need to contain capital outflows, notably by bringing about monetary expansion without any significant further widening of the excess of foreign over US interest rates, was becoming extremely pressing.

This combination of domestic and external factors defines a situation in which most economists would have recommended an expansionist fiscal policy, buttressed by an accommodating, rather than an actively expansionist, monetary policy. Such a policy mix might have moderated the recession and promoted expansion without an externally awkward decline in interest rates. But fiscal policy only slowly and gradually came to play an active counter-cyclical role. Indeed, the high-employment surplus (see pages 18-22 and Chart 3) indicates that fiscal policy became increasingly restrictive through 1959-60 and was only modified in an expansionist direction in 1961. This indication accords with the estimate by Bent Hansen[10] that discretionary Federal budget effects were deflationary by about 1 per cent of GNP in 1960 and increased demand by about 2 per cent fo GNP in 1961. A somewhat similar picture is found if one looks at the actual surplus or deficit on a national accounts basis. Here the budget, which was in deficit in 1959, moved sharply into surplus in the first half of 1960 and did not return to deficit until 1961. From the first quarter of that year until mid-1962, fiscal policy became increasingly expansionary on both definitions, reflecting mainly a number of measures taken by the new administration to speed up expenditures. From mid-1962, expenditures levelled off, and the overall expansionary fiscal impact disappeared. Although it was in 1962 that Congress enacted an investment tax credit programme which, together with more liberal depreciation schedules, stimulated domestic investment, a more general tax cut did not obtain Congressional approval until 1964.

The presence of a Federal budget surplus not only removed a possible expansionist fiscal element, but potentially increased the downward pressure on the Treasury bill rate, since the surplus may be assumed to have reduced the bill issue. In these circumstances the objective of monetary policy, viz to promote a necessary degree of monetary ease while minimising private capital outflows, became very difficult to achieve. From early 1961 the fiscal position became more favourable from a monetary viewpoint, and it left more scope for active debt-management policies. An expansionary stance of the monetary authorities is assumed from March 1960, and it is arguable that it was maintained until late 1962. The beginning of the phase may be dated from the switch in open market operations from substantial net sales in the three months prior to March 1960 to net purchases of a similar order of magnitude over the following year. This shift to "ease" in the terminology of the FOMC suggests, as already noted,

---

10. [43], pp. 494-515.

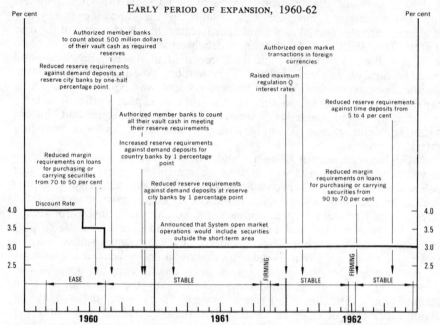

Source: Annual Report of the Board of Governors of the Federal Reserve System.

that the Federal Reserve successfully forecast the turning point of the cycle, since, if one adopts the NBER dating, the monetary authorities appear to have forecast the peak about two months in advance. No important change in policy was made in the months surrounding the trough; a stable accommodating posture prevailed between the late summer of 1960 and the final months of 1961. Although it was then—and again in mid-1962—briefly interrupted by short periods of firming, a basically expansionary stance was maintained until the end of 1962. A chronology of the measures taken is shown in Chart 19.

A dating of policy phases by means of the use of FOMC records or the use of other monetary instruments may not, as already argued above, be uncontroversial. In the case of the 1960-62 expansionary phase, the results obtained by looking at either short-run operating targets or monetary aggregates are not, however, very different (Charts 20 and 21). Thus, the movement in unborrowed reserves was steadily upwards between April 1960 and the final quarter of 1962. During 1960, member banks reduced their borrowing at the Federal Reserve to a minimum and kept it negligible throughout the rest of the expansionary phase. Finally, net free reserves rose steadily from a negative level in the first quarter of 1960 to a plateau of about $500 million where they remained for the following two years. Short-term interest rates fell rather sharply during the first half of 1960; the Treasury bill rate reached 2.3 per cent in mid-1960, remained very stable for more than a year and then edged up very gradually towards 3 per cent. The amplitude of cyclical fluctuations in rates was much more

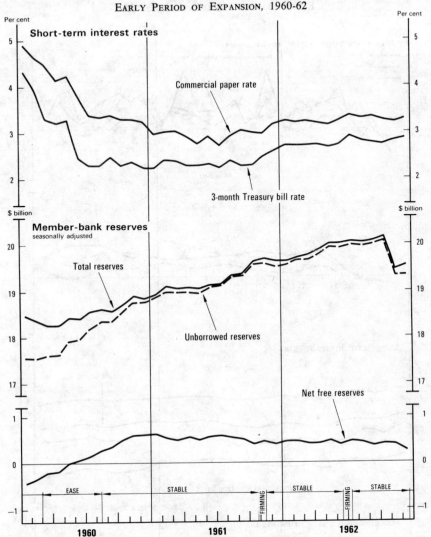

Chart 20. MONEY MARKET VARIABLES

EARLY PERIOD OF EXPANSION, 1960-62

Source: Federal Reserve Bulletin.

limited in 1960-61 than in earlier recessions; the bill rate never came near the very low levels—around 1 per cent—observed in the 1954 and 1958 recessions, and the subsequent rise was much gentler than in comparable phases of earlier upswings. Long-term interest rates remained remarkably stable throughout the three-year period, while the decline in the main monetary aggregates was replaced from the second quarter of 1960 by moderate growth in M_1 and somewhat faster growth in M_2; Regulation Q ceilings were raised towards the end of 1961, and banks responded by introducing negotiable certificates of deposit. In the case of both aggregates,

103

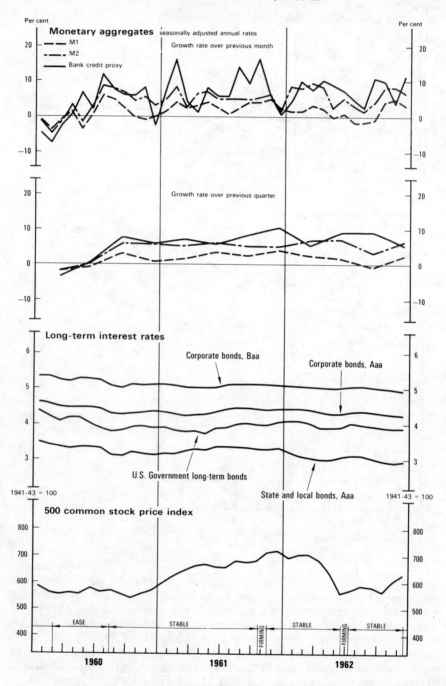

Chart 21. MONETARY AGGREGATES AND LONG-TERM INTEREST RATES
EARLY PERIOD OF EXPANSION, 1960-62

Source: Federal Reserve Bulletin.

there were no major fluctuations up to the end of 1962. Thus observed behaviour both of money market variables, which constituted the main operating target for policy at the time, and of the monetary aggregates fits well into the dating suggested by FOMC records; the period between the second quarter of 1960 and the first quarter of 1961 was one of clear monetary expansion, and the subsequent seven or eight quarters preserved an accommodating stance with relatively low and stable rates. From the viewpoint of the transmission mechanism, it is highly significant that long-term rates remained stable after the upswing got underway. This did not assure, however, that the wealth effect was positive or at worst neutral throughout the expansionary phase. In May-June 1962, stock market prices, which had been declining gently since end-1961, fell sharply. This break had no major identifiable reason; it reflected a weakening confidence in economic prospects and in turn contributed to making these prospects worse, directly through a wealth effect and indirectly through a negative impact on expectations.

These developments in money and capital markets partly reflect the effects of policies designed to mitigate the dilemma between external and internal policy objectives. It was attempted in 1960 to take strong expansionary action while minimising downward pressures on short-term interest rates. This effect was achieved by diminishing in two ways the reliance on the traditional main weapon of monetary expansion, open market purchases of Treasury bills (Chart 19):

i)   by redefining, in two stages, member banks' reserves to include vault cash, thereby adding more than $2 billion to member bank reserves;

ii)   by shifting, from the final quarter of 1960, some of the purchases from the bill market to longer-term markets, thus modifying if not abandoning the doctrine of "bills only".

In these two ways, banks were supplied with additional reserves without any direct impact on the bill rate. The attempts of the monetary authorities to modify the term structure of interest rates so as to raise short-term relative to long-term rates were reinforced by the debt-management operations of the Treasury. From mid-1960 to the end of 1962, the share of the public's holdings of marketable securities held in maturities of less than one year rose from 32 to 41 per cent (see Table C in Appendix IV), with a corresponding decline in the category of 1-5 year maturities. This shift in the debt structure was the result of the so-called "Operation Twist", which apparently remained in effect until 1964 though its clearest impact could probably be observed in 1961. Its effects have been the subject of intensive debate, some of which is reviewed in Appendix IV. The general conclusion emerging from this debate is that the effects were modest; more specifically, empirical work suggests that Operation Twist made the bill rate only 15 basis points higher than it would otherwise have been. If so, this particular policy would only have improved the US capital account by about $160 million in 1961, an amount corresponding to less than 8 per cent of the deficit on official settlements in that year. Though this conclusion may represent a minimum estimate of the effects of Operation Twist, it is clear that this interesting innovation had a much smaller impact on the interest-rate structure than was generally thought at the time, and less than a more casual inspection of the time series would suggest.

In summary, monetary policy during the 1960-62 expansionary phase appears to have achieved some of its declared proximate objectives. The easing of bank reserve positions was accompanied by a resumption of satisfactory growth rates in the monetary aggregates. But on the asset side of bank balance sheets, holdings of securities rather than direct lending increased, the demand for loans showing obvious signs of slack reflecting near-stagnant fixed investment and declining inventories until late 1961 (Table 15). However, the flow of mortgage finance rose very sharply, mainly because of exceptionally large acquisitions by commercial banks (Table 16). The increase in the supply of mortgage finance even outstripped the sharp rise in housing starts from the first quarter of 1961, so that mortgage rates declined slightly.

Data for GNP and its main components indicate that the slowdown in total demand during the year starting from the first quarter of 1960 was initiated by a sharp decline in inventory investment and a deceleration of residential investment and consumers' expenditure on durables. A reversal of the course of these demand components, together with a strong rise in Federal government expenditure, was the most important factor contributing to a pick-up of economic activity in 1962 (Table 17). But demand was still well below sustainable levels (Chart 1). The interest-rate structure was modified by Operation Twist, but the relatively small effects coupled with long time lags in the transmission mechanism through cost effects tended to minimise both the external and internal impact. The failure to reach satisfactory levels for the ultimate policy objectives—with the exception of the rate of increase in the price level, which never gave much cause for concern—could hardly be blamed on the monetary authorities. Fiscal policy contributed importantly to bringing about the 1960-61 recession, and its expansionary effects disappointingly faded in mid-1962. In the absence of policy simulations for this period, it is not possible to give any numerical illustration of the extent to which the change to expansionary monetary policies was responsible for the shallowness of the recession and the upswing that followed.[11] All that can safely be said is that monetary policy was alone in moving counter-cyclically prior to 1961.II.

1970-71. A second period of expansionary monetary policy began around the end of 1969 and continued through the end of the period here under study. Initially the aim of policy was to control the severity of the downswing which began after the peak in activity in November 1969; later the purpose was to promote recovery from the trough of November 1970 (Chart 1). By then unemployment had risen from the level of around 3.5 per cent prevailing throughout most of 1969 to 6.1 per cent, a rise of more than two-thirds. While the deteriorating balance of payments position, as in the first expansionary phase, may have exerted some influence on policy, the dominant objectives remained the domestic ones of securing higher employment while reducing the rate of price change. Reconciling these objectives led to an apparent wavering of the expansionary policy stance in mid-1971. In August of that year, a recognition of the inadequacy of existing policies for price stabilisation led to the introduction of the New Economic Policy including an initial three-month price-wage freeze.

11. The basic policy simulations presented in Part III take their starting point in restrictive action undertaken in 1968.IV. It would be more than hazardous to attempt to apply them to expansionary action undertaken nine years earlier.

TABLE 15. CREDIT MARKET TRANSACTIONS: EARLY PERIOD OF EXPANSION, 1960-62
$ BILLION, AT SEASONALLY ADJUSTED ANNUAL RATES

	1960				1961				1962			
	I	II	III	IV	I	II	III	IV	I	II	III	IV
Total Funds Raised (Non-financial Sector) by:	41.9	38.8	34.9	32.7	32.0	45.4	59.0	50.7	55.9	57.6	44.6	54.8
US Government	-5.2	-0.2	-1.4	-1.3	-0.3	7.6	17.9	3.7	10.2	9.9	-0.7	8.6
Private Non-financial Sectors	47.1	39.0	36.3	34.0	32.4	37.8	41.2	47.0	45.6	47.7	45.3	46.2
Funds Supplied Directly by:												
Federal Reserve System	-1.9	2.9	2.4	-0.4	0.3	0.2	2.7	2.8	3.7	0.7	0.9	2.7
Commercial Banks, net	0.6	6.3	12.8	15.7	13.0	8.8	27.7	9.7	16.2	24.8	15.3	20.1
Private Non-bank Financial Institutions	24.8	23.2	23.9	20.1	18.4	21.1	23.5	28.5	28.8	26.5	29.0	31.6
Private Domestic Non-financial Sectors	17.3	5.4	-7.0	-4.9	-7.4	10.1	2.4	12.2	5.2	3.0	3.1	0.1
of which:												
Households	13.8	11.0	-2.3	-2.1	-3.9	7.7	3.0	9.1	-2.7	-1.2	-0.5	-6.1
MEMORANDUM ITEMS:												
Percentage ratio of:												
Commercial Banks to Private Non-financial Sectors	1.3	16.2	35.3	46.2	40.1	23.3	67.2	20.6	35.5	52.0	33.8	43.5
Commercial Banks and Private Non-bank Financial to Private Non-financial Sectors	53.9	75.6	101.1	105.3	96.9	79.1	124.3	81.3	98.7	107.5	97.8	111.9
Private Domestic Non-financial Sectors to Private Non-financial Sectors	36.7	13.8	-19.3	-14.4	-22.8	26.7	5.8	26.0	11.4	6.3	6.8	0.2

Source: Data supplied by the Federal Reserve System.

TABLE 16. TRANSACTIONS IN THE MORTGAGE MARKET: EARLY PERIOD OF EXPANSION, 1960-62

$ BILLION, SEASONALLY ADJUSTED AT ANNUAL RATES

	1960				1961				1962			
	I	II	III	IV	I	II	III	IV	I	II	III	IV
Total Mortgage Credit	16.964	15.188	16.136	14.628	17.300	17.924	18.668	21.296	20.100	21.476	21.828	23.332
of which:												
Federal Sponsored Credit Agencies	1.468	1.552	0.928	0.280	-0.244	-0.260	0.440	0.996	0.840	0.056	-0.020	-0.084
Total Main Private Intermediaries	12.928	11.324	12.328	11.812	13.959	14.740	14.836	16.524	17.328	19.500	20.112	22.168
Savings and Loans Associations	6.812	6.564	7.032	7.308	7.932	8.552	8.800	9.772	9.636	9.676	9.816	10.616
Mutual Savings Banks	1.648	1.780	2.324	2.020	2.048	2.272	2.296	2.224	2.752	3.220	3.384	3.344
Commercial Banks	1.512	0.172	0.428	0.496	1.567	1.092	1.584	2.192	3.028	4.200	4.240	4.400
Life Insurance Companies	2.956	2.808	2.544	1.988	2.412	2.824	2.156	2.336	1.912	2.404	2.672	3.808
Flow of Funds into Main Intermediaries	7.480	8.196	9.536	9.876	11.060	11.136	11.172	12.060	11.640	13.088	13.736	14.436
Savings and Loans Associations (Savings Shares)	6.944	7.196	8.160	7.936	8.380	8.672	8.616	3.300	8.140	9.300	9.636	10.320
Savings and Loans Associations (FHLB Advances)	-0.148	-0.016	-0.408	-0.040	0.636	0.336	0.700	1.052	0.900	1.012	0.728	0.628
Mutual Savings Banks (Savings Deposits)	0.684	1.016	1.784	1.980	2.044	2.128	1.856	1.708	2.600	2.776	3.372	3.488

Source: Data supplied by the Federal Reserve System.

TABLE 17. REAL AGGREGATE DEMAND
EARLY PERIOD OF EXPANSION, 1960-62

BASED ON SEASONALLY ADJUSTED QUARTERLY FIGURES AT 1958 PRICES

	Change 1960. I to 1961. I		Change 1961. I to 1962. IV	
	$ billion	% at annual rate	$ billion	% at annual rate
Consumer Durables	−7.6	−1.6	55.7	6.4
Consumer Non-durables	6.1	2.3	10.3	3.4
Private Gross Fixed Investment				
Non-residential	−1.7	−3.7	5.8	7.2
Residential	−2.8	−11.8	2.9	8.2
Inventory Change	−13.0	..	9.6	..
Federal Government Expenditure	1.0	1.9	8.4	8.9
State and Local Government Expenditure	2.8	6.6	2.6	2.8
Net exports	3.8	..	−2.0	..
GNP	−7.6	−1.6	55.7	6.4

Percentage changes are not meaningful for inventory changes or net exports and are omitted here.
Source: Survey of Current Business.

However, despite the temporary tightening of policy, the period had sufficient unity of purpose to be treated as a whole from the viewpoint of
monetary policy. Typically, fiscal changes were expansionary during 1970-
71; the high employment surplus, which had been running at an annual
rate of $15 billion towards the end of 1969, gradually vanished. Adjusting
for the bias towards restriction of this measure of the fiscal impact, the
stimulating effects of the Federal budget may have been of the order of
½ per cent of GNP in 1970 and slightly less in 1971.[12]

From the viewpoint of the monetary instruments used, the phase may
be divided into two parts (Chart 22). Broadly speaking, during most of
1970 the main expansionary thrust was supplied by open market purchases
and relaxation of Regulation Q. To bring about a recovery of intermediation,
the Q maxima were revised in January and suspended in June on large
deposits with 30-89 day maturities. The latter move had the special purpose
of preventing a serious short-term liquidity crisis from developing in the wake
of the Penn Central bankruptcy. By enabling the banks to compete freely
for large CDs, the authorities encouraged bank lending to firms unable to
roll over their borrowing in the commercial paper market. A further
consequence of this suspension and the concurrent decline in interest rates
was to prompt massive repayments of bank borrowing in the Euro-dollar
market, thus worsening sharply the deficit on official settlements. To
dampen this outflow, the Federal Reserve sought, by modifying Regulations D and M, to limit such repayments. These steps were supported by
a relaxation of margin requirements in May and a reduction in reserve
requirements in August. From November, while open market operations

12. The measure of the full employment surplus given in the Economic Report
of the President is slightly different from that used here. It suggests a somewhat
different time pattern but does not disturb the general qualitative conclusion.

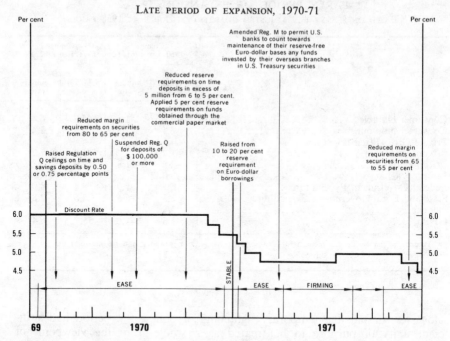

Chart 22. PRINCIPAL FEDERAL RESERVE ACTIONS

LATE PERIOD OF EXPANSION, 1970-71

Source: Annual Report of the Board of Governors of the Federal Reserve System; Federal Reserve Bulletin.

continued to be expansionary, the emphasis shifted towards lowering the discount rate. No less than eight changes—seven in a downward and one (July 1971) in an upward direction—were made between November 1970 and December 1971. In a sense, therefore, 1971 saw a return to a more traditional instrument mix.

The operating targets of monetary policy were modified during this period in the sense that the FOMC became progressively more concerned to attain target rates of growth in monetary aggregates, while money market conditions came to play a more subordinate role.[13] Over the two years there was a major improvement in the net free reserve position as the inevitable consequence of the rapid rate of expansion of unborrowed reserves—7 per cent in 1970 and 8 per cent in 1971 (Chart 23). But while the change in net free reserves in 1970 was, in absolute terms, as large as in the comparable phase of the 1960-61 expansion, the level of free reserves remained substantially lower—indeed it was negative throughout. Moreover, the rise took place mainly in the second half of 1970; the behaviour of this variable in 1971 reflected the minor firming of the summer

---

13. Nevertheless, the FOMC directives continued to employ the concept; the Desk was in effect instructed to obtain money market conditions consistent with targets of monetary aggregates. It therefore seems legitimate to follow the same form of presentation in reviewing this policy phase as for other phases rather than starting with the aggregates.

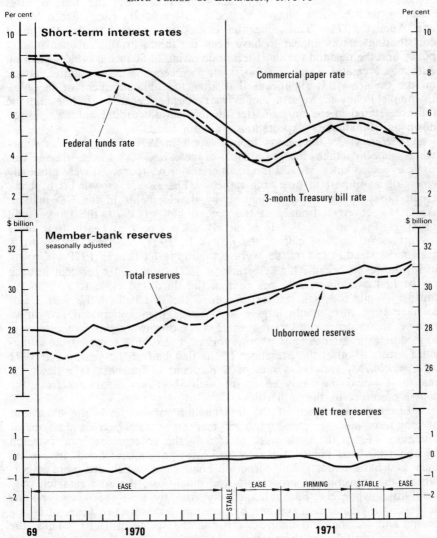

Chart 23. MONEY MARKET VARIABLES
LATE PERIOD OF EXPANSION, 1970-71

Source: Federal Reserve Bulletin.

of 1971. The Federal funds rate fell by more than 4 percentage points and the Treasury bill and commercial paper rates by around 3 per cent, declines much larger than in the first expansionary phase. The rate of decline over the year 1970 was uneven; the sharp downward trend was interrupted in the spring and summer reflecting the financial nervousness at the time of the Cambodian invasion, the failure of policy in curbing

111

rising prices and the fears that the financial failure of the Penn Central railroad might not be an isolated instance of strain in the commercial paper market. Once these temporary factors had receded, the fall in rates resumed, until it was again interrupted by a temporary rise between March and August 1971. This time the causes were less specific; the main contributing factors appear to have been the minor firming in open market policy and the demand for short-term borrowing to finance a rapidly growing outflow of capital which was increasingly becoming a speculative attack on the dollar. It is significant that after the announcement of the New Economic Policy in August, money market rates began to decline and the fall accelerated in the final quarter; in this period, capital outflows slowed down and inflationary expectations were modified.

The growth of the narrow money supply in 1970 (Chart 24) was somewhat smoother than the behaviour of reserves. This smoothness was to be expected since M_1 and the bank credit proxy (page 49) were gradually emerging as important operating targets. The rise of growth in the bank credit proxy was strongly influenced by developments in the CD market. As CDs recovered strongly in the second half of 1970, the bank credit proxy grew at an annual rate of nearly 13 per cent or nearly four times as fast as in the first half of the year. In 1971, the bank credit proxy grew more steadily and on the average slightly faster than in 1970. Growth in M_1, however, became highly erratic in 1971: around 10 per cent in each of the first two quarters, 4 per cent in the third and close to zero in the fourth. While the high rate of growth in the first half of the year seems to have been attributable largely to a faster than anticipated growth of income, the evidence suggests that there was a downward shift in the money-to-income ratio after August, though this may also have reflected the authorities' effort to offset the overshoot of the first half of the year. For 1971 as a whole, M_1 grew at a rate of 6 per cent. Appendix II reviews the reasons for and the likely effects of such short-run departures from the course preferred by the authorities.

From the viewpoint of the transmission process, it is the behaviour of long-term interest rates and stock market prices which demand major attention. From the cycle peak to trough, the government bond rate fell by about 80 basis points, and state and local government bonds by no less than 140 basis points. But corporate bond rates, which are more important in the transmission process, moved much less; the Aaa rate fell only very little, while the Baa rate actually rose by nearly 50 basis points, suggesting a greater risk aversion by investors following two years of falling profits and the incipient financial crisis in the spring of 1970. Thus, the very sharp decline in short-term rates during 1970 was not effectively transmitted to the cost of borrowing. It is likely that the main explanation for this is to be found in the spreading of inflationary expectations, though the volatility of short rates may also have complicated the task of lowering long rates (pages 75-76). In 1971, long-term rates typically fell by about 40 basis points. The corporate Baa rate declined by twice this amount, but retained a considerably greater margin over the Aaa rate than at end-1969. Over the two years as a whole, the Aaa rate fell by 47 and the Baa rate by 27 basis points as against the declines of around 400 basis points in the Treasury bill and commercial paper rates, an unusual illustration of weakness or long time lags in the transmission through cost effects. The stimulus provided through wealth effects in the form of rising share prices

112

Chart 24. MONETARY AGGREGATES AND LONG-TERM INTEREST RATES

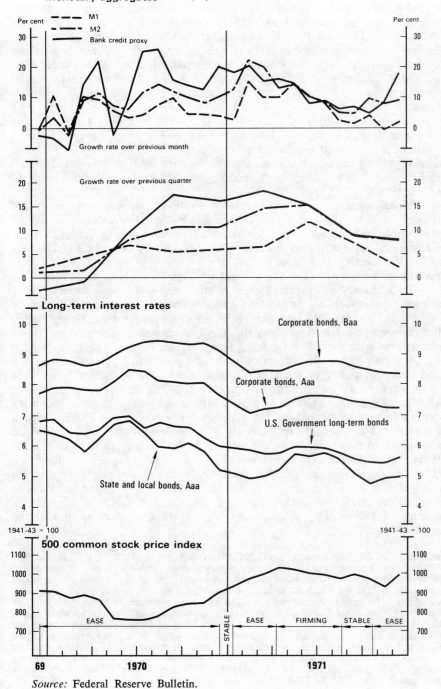

Source: Federal Reserve Bulletin.

113

was more in line with experiences from earlier recessions. Equity prices reached a trough in June 1970, some 5 months prior to the cycle trough, and the wealth effect was thereafter positive, though somewhat uneven.

Apart from interest rates and equity prices, the principal transmission variables are the cost and availability of funds in the mortgage market (Table 19). Between 1969.IV and 1970.IV, the rate of mortgage purchases by the principal intermediaries increased by about 60 per cent, and those by savings and loan associations more than doubled. Mortgage rates peaked in December 1969 and subsequently followed a time pattern similar to that of the bill rate; their decline was barely interrupted by the incipient financial crisis of 1970. Thus, throughout the expansionary phase both the cost and availability of mortgage funds moved in a direction favourable to a recovery in residential construction expenditures. There was also a substantial change in the extent of intermediation in other credit markets. The supply of credit by commercial banks rose sharply between 1969.IV and 1970.IV, while the direct lending by non-financial sectors declined (Table 18).

Housing starts turned up in March 1970, and expenditures recovered strongly from the third quarter of that year, a behaviour which is qualitatively compatible with the account of the transmission mechanism given in Part III. Consumers' expenditure on durables also rose sharply between 1970.IV and 1971.IV. During the same period, the recovery of non-residential fixed investment was slow, while stock-building declined slightly (Table 20).

In summary, the experiences of the 1970-71 expansionary phase suggest that parts of the transmission mechanism, notably the cost of borrowing, but possibly also the wealth effects, operate more slowly within the relevant policy horizon than the average responses suggested by policy simulations with the FMP model. This difference might be accounted for by an asymmetry in the effects of monetary policy in phases of expansion and restraint; policy is generally thought to work less strongly when used in an expansionary direction. It may nevertheless be of some interest to attempt to calculate by means of the FMP model what difference monetary expansion may have made to the course of the economy in 1970. Such a calculation has unavoidable elements of arbitrariness, notably because an alternative to observed policy can not be defined in any unambiguous way. If one measures the expansionary shift in monetary policy as the difference between observed quarterly changes in unborrowed reserves (adjusted for changes in reserve requirement ratios) in 1970 and 1969,[14] the calculations suggest that the shift added about 1 per cent to GNP by the fourth quarter of 1970. This estimate may be regarded as a maximum in the

14. Denoting adjusted unborrowed reserves by ΔUR^*, the expansionary shift in policy in the first quarter of 1970 is then defined as ΔUR^* (1970-.I) - ΔUR^* (1969.I); and correspondingly for the subsequent three quarters. One may note that the information supplied by such calculations is different from the policy simulations presented in Part III which presented the possible consequences of a policy alternative in which some policy instrument is held a constant distance from the path actually observed. The present method of calculation is designed to measure to what extent the shift in policy was expansionary. The measure is broadly analogous with the changes in the marginal high employment surplus which is a rough measure not of fiscal policy, but of changes in it. Finally it must be noted that ΔUR^* is a measure of only two elements in the complex of actions undertaken by the Federal Reserve; notably it includes no estimate of the effect of the significant change in discount rate policy from 1969 to 1970.

TABLE 18. CREDIT MARKET TRANSACTIONS: LATE PERIOD OF EXPANSION, 1970-71

$ BILLION, AT SEASONALLY ADJUSTED ANNUAL RATES

	1969	1970				1971			
	IV	I	II	III	IV	I	II	III	IV
Total Funds Raised (Non-financial Sector) by	89.0	87.1	100.5	101.1	118.3	115.8	170.0	173.7	164.1
US Government	-0.4	7.1	9.4	16.8	18.0	3.9	40.6	25.9	31.4
Private Non-financial Sectors	89.4	80.1	91.1	84.4	100.3	112.0	129.3	147.9	132.7
Funds Supplied Directly by:									
Federal Reserve System	8.7	-0.3	5.9	9.7	4.6	14.1	2.7	8.8	9.8
Commercial Banks, net	18.1	15.6	27.6	45.0	38.0	43.7	55.1	43.7	56.3
Private Non-bank Financial Institutions	28.3	25.8	39.7	50.8	38.3	56.5	56.5	48.3	62.3
Private Domestic Non-financial Sectors	39.6	42.5	16.6	-27.9	-2.1	-37.1	10.4	29.0	13.3
MEMORANDUM ITEMS:									
Percentage ratio of:									
Commercial Banks to Private Non-financial Sectors	21.1	19.5	30.3	53.3	37.9	39.0	42.6	29.5	42.4
Commercial Banks and Private Non-bank Financial to Private Non-financial Sectors	54.1	51.7	73.9	113.5	76.1	89.5	86.3	62.2	89.4
Private Domestic Non-financial Sectors to Private Non-financial Sectors	46.2	53.1	18.2	-33.1	-2.1	-33.1	8.0	19.6	10.0

Source: Data supplied by the Federal Reserve System.

TABLE 19. TRANSACTIONS IN THE MORTGAGE MARKET: LATE PERIOD OF EXPANSION, 1970-71

$ BILLION, SEASONALLY ADJUSTED AT ANNUAL RATES

	1969	1970				1971			
	IV	I	II	III	IV	I	II	III	IV
Total Mortgage Credit	25.932	22.672	22.760	28.260	29.688	6.852	11.661	14.195	14.248
of which:									
Federal Sponsored Credit Agencies	6.900	6.472	5.924	6.416	4.524	0.631	1.577	2.178	1.942
Total Main Private Intermediaries	15.204	11.088	11.396	19.008	24.424	5.864	10.880	12.788	10.868
Savings and Loans Associations	7.048	5.088	7.168	12.008	16.428	3.868	7.010	7.024	6.258
Mutual Savings Banks	3.116	0.732	1.944	2.088	2.616	0.732	0.963	0.982	1.261
Commercial Banks	3.568	2.460	0.624	2.964	3.404	1.123	2.888	3.270	2.552
Life Insurance Companies	1.472	2.808	2.660	1.948	1.976	0.141	0.019	1.512	0.797
Flow of Funds into Main Intermediaries	7.448	6.860	15.016	21.220	23.412	11.603	7.708	7.266	8.673
Savings and Loans Associations (Savings Shares)	0.920	1.492	9.404	15.236	17.336	9.106	7.476	5.317	6.169
Savings and Loans Associations (FHLB Advances)	4.444	3.732	1.832	0.480	-0.740	-0.925	-2.449	0.396	0.299
Mutual Savings Banks (Savings Deposits)	2.084	1.636	3.780	5.504	6.816	3.422	2.681	1.553	2.205

Source: Data supplied by the Federal Reserve System.

TABLE 20. REAL AGGREGATE DEMAND: LATE PERIOD OF EXPANSION, 1970-71

BASED ON SEASONALLY ADJUSTED QUARTERLY FIGURES AT 1958 PRICES

	Change 1969.IV to 1970.IV		Change 1970.IV to 1971.IV	
	$ billion	% at annual rate	$ billion	% at annual rate
Consumer Durables	−7.8	−9.2	16.4	21.4
Consumer Non-durables	9.4	2.4	8.3	2.1
Private Gross Fixed Investment:				
Non-residential	6.2	−7.6	6.0	7.9
Residential	1.0	4.6	6.4	28.3
Inventory Change	−1.8	..	−0.7	..
Federal Government Expenditure	−8.4	−11.7	0.8	1.3
State and Local Government Expenditure ...	3.0	4.2	3.4	4.5
Net Exports	1.5	..	−5.1	..
GNP	−9.3	−1.3	35.4	4.9

Percentage changes are not meaningful for inventory changes or net exports and are omitted here.
Source: Survey of Current Business.

sense that it measures the impact of a full swing from the firm restraint throughout 1969 to the active expansion of 1970. But a continuation of restraint into 1970 was hardly a realistic alternative to the policy actually followed. Nevertheless, the calculations confirm the ability of changes in Federal Reserve actions to extend a quantitatively significant influence on key variables even within the relatively short horizon of one year. Moreover, since the underlying dynamic multipliers are increasing over time, calculations for later quarters would typically show a larger impact than prior to end-1970.

While there is evidence to suggest that the recession was modified and the upturn strengthened by the expansionary monetary policies, it is obvious that the aims of external balance became more difficult, indeed impossible, to achieve in 1970-71. There was some strengthening early in 1970 of the trade balance in response to the lower level of activity in the United States relative to the rest of the world, but in the second half of the year anti-inflationary policies abroad began to bite more, checking the growth of US exports. The deterioration continued in 1971, when for the first time the trade balance swung into deficit. To the extent that an expansionary monetary policy was successful in stimulating US demand, it aggravated the current balance, though this was undoubtedly a minor factor among those that produced the drastic worsening which started in 1970 and continued in 1971.[15] And the shift in monetary policy was the major cause of the worsening of the capital account in 1970. The expansionary

15. Following the very rough method of calculation outlined on page 114, imports may have been running at an annual rate of approximately $0.5 billion higher towards the end of 1970 than one would have expected in the absence of restraint.

policy at a time when other countries were, if anything, moving in the opposite direction, prompted a return flow to foreign commercial banks of borrowed funds; though the Federal Reserve took steps to slow down the rate of repayment through special measures, the outflow reached more than $6 billion for the year. If one assumes that short-term interest rates, especially the bill rate, had been kept constant at the end-1969 level instead of falling by 3 percentage points, the results of some econometric studies, notably Branson and Hill [9], imply that the partly policy-induced[16] decline in rates had increased the outflow of short-term capital by as much as $5 billion by early or mid-1971.[17] There was a deterioration also in other parts of the capital account, though they were less clearly related to US monetary policy.

In 1971, both the current and the capital account worsened dramatically. Judging from the simple type of calculation referred to above, the continuation of expansionary monetary policy had little to do with either. The deceleration in economic activity in Europe caused a downturn in US exports of machinery and industrial materials, and the increasing likelihood of changes in currency values was the main factor behind the swelling outflow of capital. Only a modest part of the $15 billion increase in the net deficit on capital account could have been checked by putting an end to monetary expansion,[18] and this policy change would have dampened a domestic upswing that remained weak until late in the year. The measures of August 15 demonstrated a recognition by the United States authorities that even sizeable adjustments in conventional fiscal and monetary instruments could no longer be expected to deal with this acute policy dilemma.

d)   TWO PERIODS OF RESTRAINT: 1965.IV-1966.III AND 1968.IV-1969.IV

The present section will review, in much the same way as above for the expansionary phases, two rather brief periods of monetary restraint. According to the method of *ex ante* dating outlined in section *(b)* above, these periods may be dated 1965.IV-1966.III and 1968.IV-1969.IV. Since the two phases of restraint exhibit many similarities, particularly in the techniques employed by the monetary authorities, they are treated together. This treatment also seems justified by the common elements in the economic background which prompted monetary restraint (Table 21). In both cases

---

16. It is not suggested that the full decline in the bill rate was policy-induced; some of it was due to demand factors.

17. This result is obtained in the following way: the direct impact on the US capital account of a one percentage point increase in the bill rate is, *ceteris paribus,* to induce an inflow of $2.5 billion, mostly in the course of two quarters. If allowance is made for the tendency of the Euro-dollar rate to move parallel to the US bill rate, this estimate reduces to around $1.5 billion. The bill rate dropped by more than 3 percentage points between end-1969 and early 1971.

18. If one compares the spread between long- and short-term rates in, say, mid-1971 to that prevailing at the comparable point in time of the 1960-62 expansion, i.e. late 1971, it will appear that the relationship was less "favourable" for the resolution of the external/internal policy dilemma in the later phase. The two interest rates in transmitting monetary policy changes to external and internal objectives are, respectively, the bill rate and the corporate Aaa rate. As measured between these two rates, the spread was 2.5 percentage points in late 1961 and 3.5 in mid-1971. Thus if the same rate structure had prevailed as in 1961, the external deficit would have been smaller or domestic activity higher.

PERCENTAGE RATE OF CHANGE

	1965. IV to 1966. IV	1968. IV to 1969. IV
Interest rates:		
Treasury bills	21.2	30.4
Commercial paper (4 to 6 months)	34.2	44.6
Corporate Aaa bonds	16.2	19.7
Monetary aggregates:		
Money supply (M1)	4.2	4.2
Broad money supply (M2)	6.5	3.4
Bank credit proxy	4.0	−3.3
Components of aggregate demand (constant prices):		
Consumer durables	3.6	1.3
Consumer non-durables	2.6	2.9
Private fixed non-residential investment	7.3	6.7
Residential investment	−21.8	−8.9
Federal government expenditure	15.1	−8.3
State and local government expenditure	7.3	1.8
Gross National Product	4.9	1.2

actual GNP was running above its estimated long-run potential; the unemployment percentage was low by historical standards; the rate of change of prices accelerated; and the balance of payments was in deficit—though the symptoms of demand pressure were somewhat more strongly in evidence in late 1968. With respect to the stance of fiscal policy there was, however, an important difference between the two phases.

For the first two of the four quarters which made up the earlier of the two phases—1966.I and II—fiscal policy was mildly restrictive. The high employment surplus rose by about $2 billion in each of these quarters, adding up to a dampening impact—when corrected for the restrictive bias of the surplus measure—of around half a per cent of GNP. But in the third quarter there was a marked decline in the surplus offsetting approximately the fiscal restraint of the first half year. Thus fiscal policy gave rather minimal support to the efforts of the monetary authorities in the first two quarters and rather more than minimal hindrance in the third quarter. It was only towards the end of 1966 when monetary restraint was abandoned that the two main methods of demand management were moving in step. In 1968, fiscal restraint, marked by the enactment of the surcharge in 1968.II, preceded the first stages of monetary restraint by about six months. The high employment surplus rose by no less than $14 billion in 1968.III and continued to rise through 1969.II; in the next two quarters it had little net impact on demand. At the end of 1969, the surplus declined sharply, coinciding with or leading slightly the Federal Reserve's own move towards expansion. Thus fiscal policy was moving counter-cyclically in the first half of 1969; roughly adjusting for the bias, the cumulative thrust of fiscal policy was a bit in excess of 1 per cent of GNP. This was the period when the monetary authorities were looking to fiscal policy for support. Generally the changes in fiscal policy between mid-1968 and end-1969 were stabilising and not insignificant in magnitude, though it has been argued that the enactment of the surcharge was long overdue. Nevertheless, fiscal policy was more helpful to the monetary authorities in 1968-69 than in 1965-66, when monetary policy had to do most of the running. Indeed, when the monetary brakes were first put on near the end of 1965 in the form of a discount rate increase, the Federal Reserve was openly critical of the rapid growth of Government expenditures which had been accelerating for at least half a year, although the full extent of this trend had not been appreciated at the time.[19]

In both restrictive phases the discount rate and reserve requirements were raised and net sales were undertaken in the open market (Chart 25). Furthermore, Regulation Q maxima played an important role in both phases; in 1966 they were reduced, while in 1969 the ceilings became effective without any action as the sharp rise in market rates pushed these well beyond existing Q maxima. Indeed, the "margin", i.e. the difference between the secondary market yield and Regulation Q maxima for large CDs became much larger in 1969, and it is therefore arguable that Q effectiveness was more severe in the later period (see Chart 25). In general, therefore, the main instruments used in both periods were open market operations and Regulation Q. An interesting difference was that "moral suasion" was employed in 1966; commercial banks were asked to moderate their rate of loan expansion, particularly to business, and were warned that their access to the discount window might depend on the extent to which they observed this request. Another difference between the two phases is that the former was marked by severe difficulties in two financial sub-markets: a so-called mortgage market crunch occurred in April-June, and another crunch in the market for state and local government securities in mid-August to early September. By contrast, 1969 was free from crunches, though in May-June 1970, six months after a change of policy towards ease had taken place, the Federal Reserve had to take special steps to deal with an incipient crisis in the commercial paper market (page 109).[20] One possible interpretation of this contrast is that monetary restraint was pushed nearer to the constraint of maintaining existing financial institutions in 1966, whereas in 1969 active support by Federal agencies tended to cushion the mortgage market to a greater extent (see page 128). A second and more plausible interpretation is that the degree of restraint was about equally severe in both phases, but that the capacity of the business and financial community to learn from the experiences of 1966 had the effect of slowing the system's response; an important

19. The discussion at the November 2 and 23, 1965 meetings of the FOMC reveals some hesitation in assessing the need for a firmer policy stance. This attitude reflected (i) the unavailability at that time of detailed information on the Federal government budget; and (ii) a reluctance to see a sharp rise in interest rates. See Annual Report [25] for 1965, pp. 141-148.

20. In March 1970 the Board of Governors had extended authorisation for the Federal Reserve banks to provide emergency credit facilities to non-member depository institutions, notably savings and loan associations. Though this authorisation was not used, it probably played a role in preventing a repetition of the credit crunch of 1966.

Chart 25. PRINCIPAL FEDERAL RESERVE ACTIONS

TWO PERIODS OF RESTRAINT, 1966 AND 1969
DEVIATIONS FROM ACTUAL FIGURES

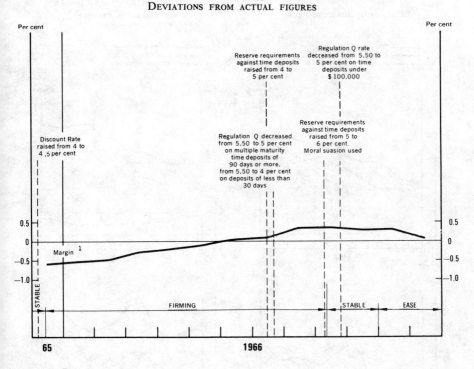

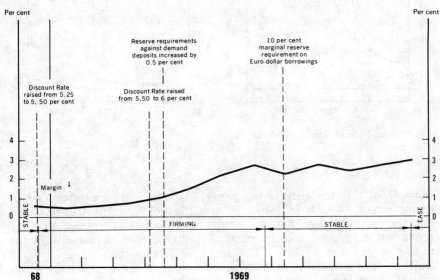

1.   Margin calculated as Secondary Market yield on large CDs *minus* Regulation Q maxima on large CDs.

Source: Annual Report of the Board of Governors of the Federal Reserve System.

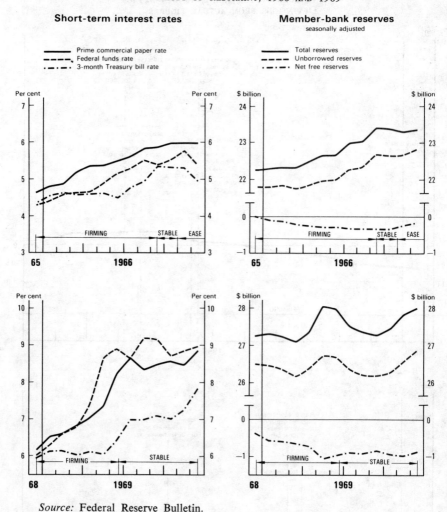

Chart 26. MONEY MARKET VARIABLES
Two periods of restraint, 1966 and 1969

Short-term interest rates

— Prime commercial paper rate
- - - Federal funds rate
-·-·- 3-month Treasury bill rate

Member-bank reserves
seasonally adjusted

— Total reserves
- - - Unborrowed reserves
-·-·- Net free reserves

Source: Federal Reserve Bulletin.

example of this tendency is the better adaptation by commercial banks to the run-off of CDs in 1969. A tentative conclusion is therefore that the two periods were broadly similar not only with respect to their economic background and the range of instruments used, but also in the degree of restraint applied. The speed of interest-rate changes and of shifts in fund flows was in both periods close to the limit within which market participants could adjust themselves without incipient crises appearing in one or more financial sub-markets.

The immediate operating target of the monetary authorities in the first period and probably also in the second, despite the introduction of

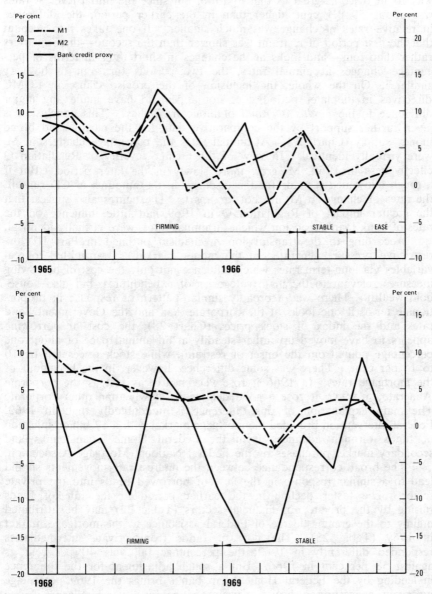

Chart 27. MONETARY AGGREGATES
Two Periods of Restraint, 1966 and 1969
Seasonally adjusted annual growth rates over previous month

Source: Federal Reserve Bulletin.

the *proviso clause* and the emerging emphasis on aggregates, was money market conditions, defined as usual by the Federal funds rate, the net free reserves of member banks and the Treasury bill rate.   In both periods

123

short-term rates rose while net free reserves declined and reached sizeable negative values (Chart 26). In absolute terms the rise in rates in 1969 was about twice as great as that in 1966, but since the initial level of rates was about 50 per cent higher than in the earlier period, the difference in relative rates of change was much smaller. If one takes into account that the first period of restraint was shorter than the second—three quarters rather than four—and looks at the changes in short rates in terms of percentage changes at annual rates, the two periods turn out to be very similar.[21] On the whole, the inclusion of the proviso clause in FOMC directives in the later period does not appear to have made any major difference to the *modus operandi* of monetary policy. This conclusion is given further support by the comparative data for the narrow and broad money supply (Chart 27). At annual rates the percentage changes in M_1 were virtually identical. In view of the greater severity of Regulation Q effectiveness in 1969, M_2 grew more slowly in the later period. But if a rough allowance is made for the disparity in the amounts of CD run-off, the rates of change in M_2 are not far apart. The figures also suggest that the greater impact of Regulation Q in 1969 had little influence on the rates of bank loan expansion which, at annual rates, were virtually identical.

According to the transmission mechanism outlined in Part III, the restrictive pressure generated in the money market is transmitted to real variables via long-term rates which influence not only the cost of borrowing measures relevant to the main categories of expenditures, but also household wealth. There was a broadly similar pattern of response in proportionate terms if one looks at the corporate Aaa and the Government bond rates and the index of stock prices (Chart 28); the cost of borrowing appears to have moved up rather steadily at an annual pace of about one percentage point from the onset of restraint, while stock prices fell by 10 to 15 per cent. There was some difference, however, in the behaviour of the mortgage rate. In 1966 it rose very nearly as fast as the corporate Aaa rate; in 1969, it rose a good deal more slowly than other corporate The main explanation of this difference is undoubtedly that, in 1969, Federal intervention provided the mortgage market with a $7 billion injection of funds through advances from the Federal Home Loan banks and secondary market purchases by the Federal National Mortgage Association.

The broad correspondance between the interest rate movements should lead to a similar response in the flow of borrowed funds into the private sector. The faster decline in the earlier period in the rate of funds raising by the private non-financial sectors (Table 22) may be attributed mainly to the greater degree of Federal assistance to the mortgage market in 1969 (Table 23). The flow of funds from private intermediaries responded differently in 1969: the percentage fall was 40 per cent as against 58 per cent in 1966. But a rough adjustment for the difference in lending by the Federal Home Loan banks brings the 1969 percentage up again suggesting a broad measure of conformity. Similarly, if one adjusts the figures of total mortgage lending for the Federal intervention in 1969, the two percentage changes are of the same order. It thus appears

---

21. This impression is confirmed by an analysis of percentage changes at an annual rate in unborrowed, total and net free reserves. The analysis is complicated by the fact that the seasonally adjusted and unadjusted figures yield rather different results for 1969. The conclusion indicated is based on seasonally unadjusted data.

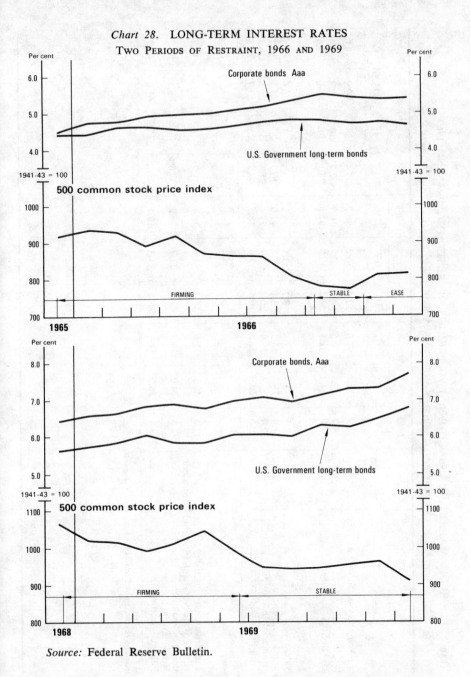

Chart 28. LONG-TERM INTEREST RATES
TWO PERIODS OF RESTRAINT, 1966 AND 1969

Source: Federal Reserve Bulletin.

that the private-sector element on the supply side of the mortgage market responded to monetary restraint—and the influence of other exogenous variables—in much the same way, quantitatively as well as qualitatively, in 1966 and 1969. More broadly it may be concluded that, despite the differences in the stance of fiscal policy and possibly in initial conditions,

125

TABLE 22. CREDIT MARKET TRANSACTIONS: TWO PERIODS OF RESTRAINT, 1966 AND 1969
$ BILLION. AT SEASONALLY ADJUSTED ANNUAL RATES

	1965	1966				1968	1969			
	IV	I	II	III	IV	IV	I	II	III	IV
Total Funds Raised (Non-financial Sector) by	75.6	74.7	90.6	52.4	56.2	90.7	95.4	88.8	92.9	89.0
US Government	6.7	0.5	9.5	-4.8	9.3	-6.9	-2.7	-10.1	-0.7	-0.4
Private Non-financial Sectors	69.0	74.2	81.1	57.2	46.8	97.6	98.1	98.9	93.6	89.4
Funds Supplied Directly by:										
Federal Reserve System	2.5	3.7	3.6	3.2	3.5	-4.9	3.3	4.0	0.9	8.7
Commercial Banks, net	31.4	18.5	34.3	8.1	7.1	47.0	20.7	25.7	11.1	18.1
Private Non-bank Financial Institutions	32.4	36.4	26.4	20.2	27.4	27.4	31.1	48.0	29.6	28.3
Private Domestic Non-financial Sectors	9.5	20.9	22.2	16.5	15.6	18.7	47.2	25.6	57.7	39.6
MEMORANDUM ITEMS:										
Percentage ratio of:										
Commercial Banks to Private Non-financial Sectors	47.0	49.1	32.6	35.3	58.5	28.1	31.7	48.5	31.6	31.7
Commercial Banks and Private Non-bank Financial Institutions to Private Non-financial Sectors	92.5	74.0	74.8	49.5	73.7	76.2	52.8	74.5	43.5	51.9
Private Domestic Non-financial Sector to Private Non-financial Sectors	13.8	28.2	27.4	28.8	33.3	19.2	48.1	25.9	61.6	44.3

Source: Data supplied by the Board of Governors of the Federal Reserve System.

TABLE 23. TRANSACTIONS IN THE MORTGAGE: MARKET TWO PERIODS OF RESTRAINT, 1966 AND 1969

$ BILLION, SEASONALLY ADJUSTED AT ANNUAL RATES

	1965	1966				1968	1969			
	IV	I	II	III	IV	IV	I	II	III	IV
Total Mortgage Credit	26.012	27.864	25.552	19.860	15.908	29.352	29.196	29.396	27.132	25.932
of which:										
Federal Sponsored Credit Agencies	1.784	3.544	2.884	2.108	1.670	1.412	2.576	3.372	5.036	6.900
Total Main Private Intermediaries	23.424	22.708	17.660	12.568	9.972	25.464	23.680	20.088	16.564	15.204
Savings and Loans Associations	8.480	8.680	4.752	0.688	0.936	10.660	11.248	11.412	8.252	7.048
Mutual Savings Banks	4.312	3.012	2.052	2.956	2.860	3.840	2.888	2.664	2.060	3.116
Commercial Banks	5.488	5.796	5.400	4.168	3.224	7.864	7.680	6.012	3.688	3.568
Life Insurance Companies	5.144	5.220	5.456	4.756	2.952	3.100	1.864	2.308	2.564	1.472
Flow of Funds into Main Intermediaries	12.424	9.856	5.444	5.296	7.740	12.760	14.052	10.248	10.352	7.448
Savings and Loans Associations (Savings Shares)	8.828	5.740	1.808	1.016	5.768	8.252	7.868	4.008	2.868	0.920
Savings and Loans Associations (FHLB Advances)	-0.032	1.680	2.708	1.008	-1.644	0.156	2.332	3.884	5.460	4.444
Mutual Savings Banks (Savings Deposits)	3.628	2.436	0.928	3.272	3.616	4.352	3.852	2.356	2.024	2.084

Source: Data supplied by the Federal Reserve System.

127

the two phases of restraint suggest a pattern of response sufficiently similar to be regarded as relatively stable.[22]

In both phases of restraint the monetary authorities were aiming to dampen an excessive expansion of demand and thereby to improve the price and balance of payments performance. Both were examples of action by the authorities nearly one year before a peak in economic activity; such peaks occurred in the fourth quarters of 1966 and 1969 around the time when monetary policy was once more relaxed. Data for GNP and its main components over the two periods of restraint point out that the slow-down in total demand was much sharper in 1969 but that this difference is mainly explained by the course of Federal government expenditure, which accelerated in 1966 but decelerated in 1969 (Table 24). Among the variables most directly influenced by monetary policy, residential invest-ment expenditure fell in both periods but much more sharply in 1966. The main reason for this difference was not in the transmission mechanism, but in the change of attitude of the Federal government. The effects of the 1966 phase of restraint had hit the housing sector more severely than was desirable on social grounds and had shaken the institutions involved in its financing in such a way as to create a financial crisis. It was therefore decided to take offsetting action through direct Federal intervention in 1969. The growth of expenditures on consumer durables was reduced in both periods of restraint, sharply below the rate for the previous years and well below its long-term trends. The time pattern of fixed non-residential investment may suggest a longer time lag in the effects of restraint in 1969;[23] the percentage changes in investment from beginning to end of the two phases are quite similar. The impact on state and local govern-ment expenditures was probably greater in 1969; the time series suggest that the differential impact came mainly in the third and fourth quarters of 1969.[24] Inventory investment turned negative in 1969, whereas expen-ditures continued to rise strongly in 1966. The reversal in 1966 of the secular downward trend in inventories was at least partly due to a rapid defence build-up connected with the escalation of the Vietnam War, and, since there is only limited evidence that inventories are directly influenced by monetary variables, it would be inappropriate to draw any inferences about changes in the transmission mechanism. Finally, the worsening of

---

22. Furthermore, there is nothing in the observed behaviour of aggregates, other financial flows and interest rates to suggest that the introduction of the proviso clause made any substantial difference to the working of monetary policy in these two periods of restraint, both of which were characterised by sharp changes in the extent of intermediation and the associated changes in the direct lending by private non-financial sectors (Table 22).

23. A cross-section study by Crockett, Friend and Shavell [15] finds the response of corporate investment to have been weak even to the severe monetary stringency of 1966; investment intentions were scaled down by .8 per cent in 1966 and 1.2 per cent in 1967 because of rising interest rates, reduced availability of bank loans and falling stock prices—in that order of importance. It should be noted that a complete interpretation of investment in 1966-67 must also note the fiscal changes introduced at the time. In September 1966 the investment tax credit was suspended with effects similar to those of an increase in interest rates.

24. Evidence on state and local government expenditures in the two phases of restraint may be found in two cross-section studies by McGouldrick and Peterson [74] and Peterson [81]. The former finds that state and local governments postponed 20 per cent of their planned long-term debt issues in 1966 and a further 7 per cent in 1967. However, the effects on planned expenditures were relatively small, *viz* 1-1½ per cent over the two years. The second study shows a much larger response: 4-5 times in value terms that of 1966-67.

	Change 1965. IV-1966. IV		Change 1968. IV-1969. IV	
	$ billion	% at annual rate	$ billion	% at annual rate
Consumer Durables	2.5	3.6	1.1	1.3
Consumer Non-durables	9.1	2.6	11.3	2.9
Private Gross Fixed Investment:				
Non-residential	5.1	7.3	5.1	6.7
Residential	−5.2	−21.8	−2.1	−8.9
Inventory Change	9.2	..	−2.5	..
Federal Government Expenditure	9.0	15.1	−6.5	−8.3
State and Local Government Expenditure	4.3	7.3	1.3	1.8
Net Exports	−2.4	..	0.9	..
GNP	31.5	4.9	8.7	1.2

Percentage changes are not meaningful for inventory changes or net exports and are omitted here.

Source: Survey of Current Business.

the current account of the balance of payments was not arrested in either of the two restrictive phases, but the capital account improved significantly in both, as private capital flows responded to the shift in interest-rate differentials in 1966 and 1969. Measured on an official settlements basis, the US balance of payments was near balance in 1966 and registered a surplus of $3 billion in 1969.

As already argued above, the question of what difference monetary policy made to the course of the economy in any particular phase of active policy is answerable only on an explicit assumption of what the alternative was to the policy followed. Such an assumption is necessarily arbitrary; there is a wide range of possibilities from which to choose. These possibilities attempt to define the alternative policy as either unchanged or neutral. The following results have the aim of illustrating a change in policy. They focus on the two periods of restraint and compare the observed situation with an illustration of the effects of an alternative higher time path for the narrow money supply (M_1) over a three-year horizon. As before, policy simulations with the FMP model supply the illustrations.

The assumed alternative policy in the two phases is one of "no restraint", defined in the following sense: M_1 grows quarter by quarter in 1966 and 1969 at the average rate of growth observed over the previous year, i.e. 1965 and 1968. Thereafter, from 1967.I and 1970.I respectively, M_1 grows at the actually observed rate for these quarters.[25] The "no

25. Note that the earlier of the two phases of restraint is here seen to extend through 1966.IV, whereas in the discussion in sections (b) and (d) above, restraint was dated to have ended in 1966.III. If one looks at the behaviour of M_1 there was a small decline from the third to the fourth quarter; it was only from 1967.I that policy ease was reflected in M_1.

129

Chart 29. ABSENCE OF RESTRAINT: THE BASIC ASSUMPTION
UNDERLYING POLICY SIMULATIONS FOR 1966-68 AND 1969-71

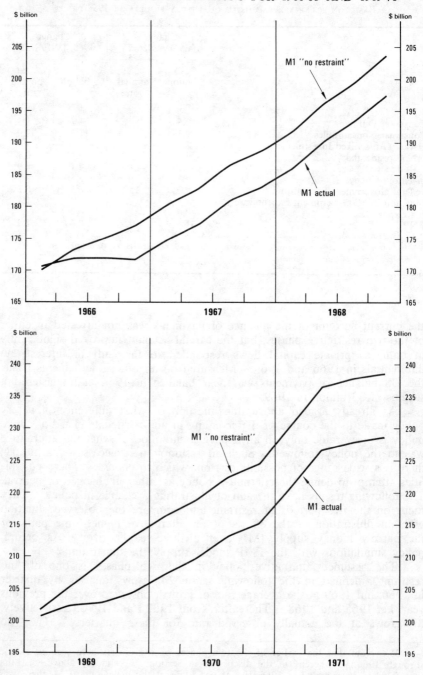

Source: Simulations provided by the Federal Reserve System.

130

restraint" policy is accordingly not one of maintaining a constant rate of growth of M_1, though it is much closer to such a policy than the course actually followed. As shown in Chart 29, the alternative for M_1 is a good deal above the actually observed level—more than $5 billion by 1966.IV and $9 billion by 1969.IV. Restraint, on the present definition, may then be characterised as having removed 3 to 4 per cent of M_1 at the end of four quarters; and, again according to the present arbitrary assumption, this shortfall was not made up subsequently.

This way of defining restraint does not imply that the Federal Reserve could have achieved the "no restraint" time path, had it considered such a policy with respect to M_1 desirable. There remains considerable doubt as to the feasibility of controlling the monetary aggregates accurately over shorter periods (see for example the review of the 1971 experience in Appendix II), though, for quarterly averages, the degree of control may be such as to justify the assumption as a rough approximation.[26] Nor does the procedure imply that the authorities were aiming for a specific time path for M_1; it has been argued above that policy continued to be formulated in terms of money market conditions despite the addition from 1966 of the proviso clause to the directive. The possible justification for describing monetary policy by movements in an M_1 indicator was reviewed in section (a); it is that the main source of instability may be found in the investment and saving functions rather than in the demand for money. Although this appears generally to be the case, it may not be true for a shorter time span. Finally, it must be pointed out that the "no restraint" path for M_1 cannot be considered a realistic policy alternative in either period. In both December 1965 and December 1968 the question was how sharply restraint was to be applied, not whether there was a need for modifying the basically accommodating policies.

The results of the simulations indicate very substantial effects on demand (Chart 30). Though the composition of the impact is not very different from that surveyed in Part III (page 80) from additional restraint —with consumer non-durables accounting for around 40 per cent of the total—its size is much larger. In principle, using M_1 rather than Federal Reserve credit or the bill rates as the policy "instrument" tends to speed up initial responses, since the lags in the money supply function are eliminated. At the same time the alternative is a more drastic departure from actual policy than was the case for the unit changes in the bill rate of 50 basis points illustrated earlier. The calculated effect of the "no restraint" policy is, in broad terms, to allow for a real GNP approximately 1 per cent higher than observed towards the end of 1966 and about 2 per cent higher than observed towards the end of 1969. After the end of the 4-quarter horizon the simulations indicate steadily widening effects of the larger money stock. The total magnitude of the impact becomes very large over the 3-year horizon shown in the charts—close to 5 per cent of real GNP in 1968.IV and near 9 per cent in 1971.IV. If the calculation could be regarded as realistic, it would imply a real GNP

26. In more technical terms, the money supply is an endogenous variable in the FMP model. It is conceptually unsatisfactory to regard it as an instrument, i.e. an exogenous variable, as the simulations here do. It would have been more satisfactory to add random errors (with limits derived from experience) to the 6 per cent growth.

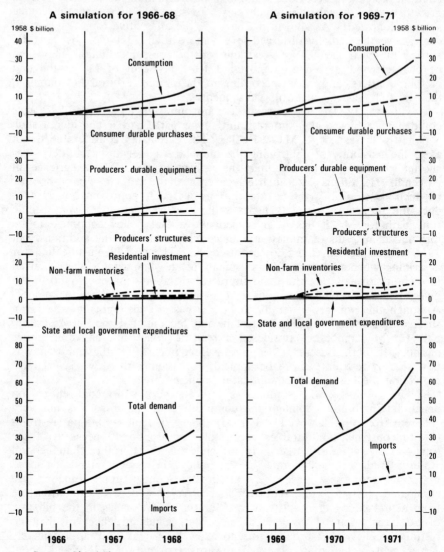

Chart 30. THE IMPACT OF RESTRAINT ON AGGREGATE DEMAND:

A simulation for 1966-68   A simulation for 1969-71

Source: Simulations provided by the Federal Reserve System.

running above its long-term potential throughout 1966-68 and very near its potential in 1969-71. In terms of the unemployment rate, the implication is a gradual fall to about 2½ per cent in late 1968, and for the second simulation a rise to only a little over 4 per cent instead of the 5½-6 per cent observed (Chart 31).

It was argued at pages 124-128 that the two phases of restraint were similar in many respects and of about the same degree of severity. The simulations bring out that, although this may be true from a financial viewpoint, the economic background during and following the two phases

132

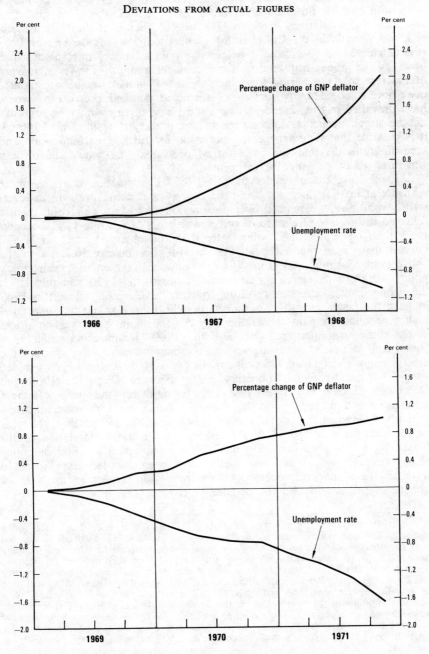

Chart 31. THE IMPACT OF MONETARY RESTRAINT ON INFLATION
AND UNEMPLOYMENT RATES: SIMULATIONS FOR 1966-68 AND 1979-71[1]

DEVIATIONS FROM ACTUAL FIGURES

1. The chart shows changes produced by simulations which remove the monetary restraint actually observed over the periods shown; see pages 129-130.
Source: Simulations provided by the Federal Reserve System.

133

was different. During 1966-68 a gap between actual and potential GNP did not emerge at any time; the mini-recession of 1966-67 was indeed very mild and left little scope for increases in real GNP and possibly even less than the simulations suggest. The rate of change of the GNP deflator picks up strongly in the "no restraint" simulation; towards the end of 1968 it is calculated to be around 2 percentage points (annual rate) higher than observed, i.e. about 6 instead of 4 per cent per annum. However, in view of the fact that the period for which the FMP model has been estimated does not include lengthy periods of sustained demand pressure as would have prevailed in the absence of the 1966 phase of restraint, it is advisable not to attach particular importance to the numerical results for 1966-68; it is possible that they exaggerate the scope for further real expansion and accordingly understate the inflationary pressures that would have been generated in the absence of restraint.

In this light the results of the 1969-71 simulation may be more realistic; at least it does not bring the degree of demand pressure to levels well beyond any experienced over the previous decade. This result is also reflected in the rate of change of prices which only from mid-1971 becomes more than one percentage point faster than the observed rate. It is also interesting to note that although the rate of price change is faster in the "no restraint" simulation from 1969.IV onwards, the more expansionary policy works to decelerate price trends between mid-1970 and mid-1971; the strong demand pressure resulting from the absence of restraint in 1969 induced the faster growth of output with some time lag, and the associated higher productivity gains offset the impact of demand pressures on prices in the subsequent quarters. But still the 1969-71 simulation produces a conclusion so strong as to inspire doubts about its credibility, *viz* that the emergence of slack in the US economy in 1969-71 could have been avoided simply by not tightening monetary policy between December 1968 and December 1969. The most that can be said on the basis of these simulations is that they suggest that monetary policy is a very powerful determinant of demand, particularly over a time horizon longer than the year or so usually considered by policy-makers. Even if the simulation results pertaining to 1969-71 had been available and accepted in 1969, a policy of no restraint would not necessarily have been adopted since it could have led to a markedly worse performance with respect to the rate of change of prices and also the balance of payments.[27]

---

27. It may, therefore, be of interest to simulate not only the effects of a radically different policy such as the "no restraint" alternative outlined above, but also of other policies somewhat closer in their average stance to what was actually done. Two such simulations were run for 1969-71 but will not be reported in detail here. The first of these reviewed the effects of maintaining the narrow money stock on a growth path corresponding, on the average, to the observed annual rate of growth between end-1968 and end-1971. The second simulated the effects of a policy of smoothing the fluctuations in the Treasury bill rate; arbitrarily the bill rate was allowed to change in each quarter by only half the change which actually occurred in any quarter. Both of these simulations illustrate the effects of smaller shifts in policy stance than actually occurred; both are on balance expansionary over the three years because they imply a much milder degree of restraint in 1969, the first part of the three-year period. While more in the nature of genuine policy alternatives than the "no restraint" simulations, they could hardly be regarded as realistic. Their primary purpose is to study the technical consequences of moderate modifications in policy stance and design.

V

CONCLUDING OBSERVATIONS

The United States economy has shown less internal cyclical instability in the period 1960-71 than before. There were two downturns in activity. Both were to some extent policy-induced; in 1960 by a swing to restrictive fiscal policy and in 1969 by a sharp tightening of both fiscal and monetary instruments. Between these two mild recessions, each of which lasted less than a year and led only to a marginal decline in GNP, there was a strong upswing of unprecedented duration in US economic history. The upswing was interrupted briefly by the mini-recession of 1966-67. Discretionary fiscal changes were made on many occasions, but far from always in a counter-cyclical way; the main examples of pro-cyclical changes were in 1960 and 1965. In other instances fiscal policy was moving in the right direction, but not very strongly; for example, it gave only modest support in the cooling-off of the 1965 boom. In these circumstances monetary policy was used actively, and the changes in policy stance do not appear to be open to the criticism of long time lags, levelled at the Federal Reserve prior to 1960. Significant policy adjustments were made shortly before and just after the two peaks in economic activity in May 1960 and November 1969.

The policy objectives, shared by the administration and the Federal Reserve, were to aim for maximum employment consistent with a high degree of price stability and a reduction of the external deficit. In the first half of the 1960s, when prices continued to rise only moderately and the external deficit was shrinking, there was heavy emphasis on the reduction of the unemployment percentage towards a long-term target level around four. Though unemployment continued to fall until 1969, more concern was provoked by an acceleration of prices and a renewed widening of the external deficit from 1965; but disillusionment with the impact of traditional demand management policies on either of these two targets prompted the adoption in 1971 of a package of new measures including a price/wage freeze, a suspension of dollar convertibility, and a *de facto* devaluation of the dollar vis-à-vis a majority of other currencies. Prior to 1971, the aim of external balance had influenced the design of monetary policy in some cyclical phases, notably by prompting Operation Twist to allow US short-term interest rates to rise relative to long term rates; some special measures (the Interest Equalisation Tax and a balance of payments programme relying increasingly on mandatory elements) also had been introduced. But the external aim had remained subsidiary to the two domestic objectives. The deficit on official settlements was financed largely by an increase in US short-term liabilities to overseas official institutions and only to a minor extent by decreases in gold and other reserve assets. This minimised the direct external impact on reserve money in the United States; the indirect effects also appear to have been modest. Given the size of domestic financial markets, even larger external deficits could, however, have been offset by the open market operations of the Federal Reserve; the external impact that did arise was in fact offset.

The structure of a financial system determines both the nature of the transmission process and the choice of main instruments of that policy. In the United States, financial markets and institutions are highly developed. The possibilities of substitution between short-term and long-term markets and between the assets and liabilities of various financial institutions are large and heavily exploited by both lenders and borrowers. Financial sophistication extends beyond banks, non-bank intermediaries and non-financial firms to households. These characteristics imply that the transmission effects work through changes in interest rates more than through changes in the availability of particular flows of credit, because it typically will be possible for a prospective borrower to find alternative sources of funds. The only important exception to the high degree of perfection in US financial markets is the market for housing finance where the borrowers typically lack strength, and where the supply of funds is rationed by financial institutions in reflection of the institutional rigidity of interest rates.

Among the instruments used, open market operations have dominated throughout the period under study. They have been supplemented in most phases of active policy by variations in the maximum interest rates that banks (and more recently non-bank intermediaries) may pay on various categories of deposits, according to the so-called Regulation Q. Discount rate changes, though more frequent since 1970, have played a minor role; bank borrowing at the Federal Reserve has always been very short-run and minimal by international standards; and there has been no major cyclical use of variations in the quantity of central bank credit available. Much of the offsetting of short-run fluctuations in the creation of the monetary base, effected in other countries through variations in central bank lending, takes place through open market operations. Finally, changes in reserve requirement ratios have also occurred, but rather infrequently. The motives for using changes in Regulation Q maxima have been two-fold:

> i) to protect non-bank financial intermediaries who were less able than the banks to compete for longer-term funds by offering higher returns on deposits in periods of monetary tightness; and
> ii) to dampen the lending potential of banks.

Experiences in 1966 and 1969-70 suggest that the brunt of the adjustment in bank assets that took place in periods when Q maxima were effective and the public was running off its holdings of certificates of deposits was concentrated in banks' holdings of securities rather than in loans to business. Some of the effect was offset through bank borrowing in the Euro-dollar market or the issue of commercial paper through bank holding companies. Non-financial firms were therefore able to maintain much of their borrowing from the banks; to the extent that this was impossible, there were alternative sources of funds, notably the commercial paper market. The suspension of Regulation Q maxima for large CDs in the spring of 1970 is an indication that the second motive for using this

136

instrument may be given less weight in the future, since the availability mechanism, i.e. a sharper rationing of bank loans, which it had been designed to promote did not work efficiently.

The design of operating targets for open market operations has evolved considerably during the period under study. Up to 1969 the main emphasis was on "money market conditions", a term referring primarily to selected short-term interest rates and the net free reserves of banks. These variables are of no immediate significance for spending decisions, but they take on greater importance as summary characteristics of changing forces in the national money market and hence as a guide to conditions in financial markets more generally. Another practical justification for using money market conditions as a short-run operating target is that information about the main variables is available almost continuously and that these variables are influenceable with a minimal time lag. These features make it possible for the main policy-making body, the Federal Open Market Committee (FOMC), to delegate the implementation of its decisions in an unambiguous way.

From 1966 through early 1970 the directives of the FOMC contained a so-called proviso clause, stipulating that the instructions for money market conditions were conditional upon the continuation of selected monetary aggregates near their projected course. The range of permissible variation in these growth rates may have been too wide and the scope for conflict among various aggregates too great; in any case there is no evidence to suggest that the addition of the proviso clause was a substantial modification of open market strategy. But such a change did come about in 1970 when monetary aggregates became an operating target of policy, though not in the very short run, because reliable up-to-date information is not available; nor can the aggregates be closely controlled by the authorities over short periods. The FOMC had great difficulties in keeping M_1 and other aggregates on their preferred course during 1970 and, parti- cularly, 1971. It would appear that changes in the demand for money were accommodated to a larger extent than the wording of the directive suggests, though technical difficulties in implementing these directives also played a role. The justification for moving to an open market strategy formulated in terms of monetary aggregates is that the demand function for money is, on the average, likely to be more accurately predictable than investment (and savings) functions quarter by quarter. But in parti- cular periods where uncertainties in financial markets are important, the demand for money may become so unstable that adhering to a target growth rate of a monetary aggregate is no longer useful. In recognition of this, the Federal Reserve has adopted a pragmatic and eclectic attitude to the formulation of operating targets; this attitude also applies to recent modifications to the statement of targets for money market conditions in the FOMC directives. Although short-term interest rates have been de- emphasised somewhat, they are still reviewed as a constraint on policy in the short run; it is generally realised that they may at times convey information essential to policy formulation.

Whatever formulation is chosen for operating targets, there may be difficulties in adjusting such targets quickly in the light of a changing economic outlook. There is reason to believe that these difficulties were on occasion in the past aggravated by the emphasis on money market conditions and, particularly, the interest rate variables involved. Sudden shifts in interest rates, especially in an upward direction, were harder to bring about, since they led to interpretations of financial instability and attracted criticism because of preferences for low nominal interest rates. It is arguable that on at least one important occasion, late 1965, a move towards restraint was delayed by an attachment to relatively low and stable interest rates. There were also possible technical conflicts with debt management considerations during periods of "even-keeling". There is accordingly some reason to believe that the monetary authorities, by de-emphasising a money market conditions target and accepting somewhat wider fluctuations in short-term rates, have eased somewhat a constraint on their operations. But there are obviously other constraints, notably the need to avoid crises in financial sub-markets such as those which threatened the mortgage market in 1966 and the commercial paper market in 1970. In such situations the Federal Reserve has had to rely on an even wider and more complicated set of operating targets than the previous discussion suggests.

The transmission mechanism by which changes in monetary policy instruments make themselves felt proceeds through three main channels, two of which are linked to interest rate changes. When short-term rates change, there is an impact on the cost of borrowing for major non-financial sectors; elements in these costs are the commercial paper rate, the corporate Aaa bond rate and the price of equities. With rather lengthy time lags these changes in borrowing costs help to modify plant and equipment expenditures. But there is also an impact on private consumption particularly because of the change in equity prices. The relative importance of these two effects remains a subject for dispute, but recent econometric research, including that incorporated into the FMP model, suggests that the role of the wealth effect is very substantial, particularly in an environment of inflationary expectations. These results would make the response of consumption quantitatively the most important impact of monetary policy; according to the FMP model it accounts for nearly 40 per cent of the total response of GNP. The third channel in the transmission mechanism is the availability of funds in the mortgage market, which affects housing starts (and expenditures) with a relatively short time lag. The result of research on the response pattern to a change in monetary policy indicates that the most important effects during four quarters or so (the normal time horizon for policy makers) are predominantly to be found in consumption expenditures and residential investment and only to a smaller extent in fixed non-residential investment and inventories, which traditionally are considered the demand components most responsive to monetary policy changes. Although the impact on consumption may be overstated in the empirical work referred to, significant revisions of the traditional views of the sectoral impact of monetary policy appear warranted in the case of the United States.

The scope for influencing aggregate demand appears very considerable, from inspection of both individual time series and simulations with the FMP model. The latter indicate, for example, that the impact of keeping the key money market rate, the three-month Treasury bill rate, 50 basis points above its actually observed level during the final three years of the period under study, i.e. 1969-71, might have been to reduce real GNP by .5, 1.3 and 2.7 per cent at the end of one, two and three years. Broadly similar effects would have been produced by keeping the level of unborrowed reserves $1 billion below actually observed levels from the end of 1968 onwards. These illustrative simulations underline the strong build-up over long time periods of monetary effects. Put differently, if a significant policy impact is desired within a relatively short horizon such as a year, the impact in subsequent quarters is likely to become excessively strong unless opposite exogenous changes occur in commodity markets or policy is changed again. This tendency for monetary policy to have its maximum effect after the typical horizon in policy-making raises serious questions about its prospects for carrying a very major burden of economic stabilisation, as was the case in the United States throughout most of the period under study. It is, however, equally clear that discretionary monetary actions can be an important stabilising influence in the shorter run, provided the ability of the authorities to assess correctly underlying trends in the economy is as good as was the case for the Federal Reserve over the years since 1960.

Four phases in which monetary policy has been used actively are reviewed in some detail. In two of them—1960.I to 1962.IV and 1970.I to 1971.IV—the stance was expansionary; a downturn in activity was checked and upturn facilitated. But in both, the recovery remained rather weak despite the success of the authorities in pushing up flows of credit and keeping borrowing costs steady or lower. During both phases, the balance of payments deficit made it desirable to prevent US short-term interest rates from falling sharply. This policy dilemma was not resolved in a satisfactory way; in the early phase, the attempts to raise short rates relative to long had only a minor effect on the capital account, and in 1970 a sharp swing in short-term interest rate differentials in favour of other countries helped to increase the outflow of capital dramatically despite a number of special measures.

The two phases of restraint—1965.IV to 1966.III and 1968.IV to 1969.IV—were designed to cool off the persistent boom in the 1965-69 period. Monetary policy was a factor in bringing about the mini-recession of 1966-67 and the downturn of 1969-70; policy was eased in both cases around the peak in economic activity. The two phases of restraint have much in common in duration and degree of severity; but there is evidence in the later phase that both participants in financial markets and the public authorities had learned from the experiences of the earlier phase: market participants became even more flexible in adjusting to monetary restraint, and the Federal authorities intervened to avert a repetition of the 1966 crisis in the mortgage market. Illustrative simulations suggest that monetary policy had significant effects on the course of aggregate demand in and particularly following the two phases of restraint.

The main emphasis throughout the study has been on the domestic impact of monetary policy. It is not meant to imply thereby that external motivations or consequences of the actions taken were unimportant; at times they were important. But the position of the dollar as the main international reserve asset and the size of US financial markets relative even to the large external disequilibria of recent years made such disequilibria more manageable from a monetary viewpoint than in any other country. However, concern with the tendency towards rising outflows of capital prompted a series of specific measures, starting with the Interest Equalisation Tax in 1963 and supplemented by the gradually extended Foreign Credit Restraint Programme from 1965. Moreover, the desirability

139

of not lowering short-term interest rates and thereby adding to the outflow of funds during the 1960-62 expansionary phase clearly influenced the choice of instruments in that phase. The available evidence suggests, however, that this particular experiment—the so-called Operation Twist—did not have important effects, not because capital flows were insensitive to interest rate changes, but because the debt management and open market operations pursued had only a marginal impact on the relationship between short- and long-term interest rates. That capital flows were indeed sensitive to changes in interest rate differentials was demonstrated particularly clearly in 1969-70 when relative monetary conditions in the United States and Europe changed sharply. Subsequently, capital flows appear to have been dominated by exchange rate uncertainties and shifting regulations; the impact of changes in United States monetary policy has become even more difficult to assess. In the light of the potentially important domestic contribution from monetary policy in the expansionary phase which started at the beginning of 1970, it is not surprising that external considerations do not appear to have significantly influenced the design of policy.

APPENDICES

Appendix I

CHRONOLOGY OF PRINCIPAL MONETARY MEASURES

1960

June

Reduced discount rates from 4 to 3½ per cent at all Reserve Banks.

July

Reduced margin requirements on loans for purchasing or carrying listed securities from 90 to 70 per cent of market value of securities.

August

Authorised member banks to count about $500 million of their vault cash as required reserves, effective for country banks August 25 and for central reserve and reserve city banks September 1.

Reduced reserve requirements against net demand deposits at central reserve city banks from 18 to 17½ per cent, effective September 1, thereby releasing about $125 million of reserves.

August-September

Reduced discount rates from 3½ to 3 per cent at all Reserve Banks.

Late November-December

Authorised member banks to count all their vault cash in meeting their reserve requirements and increased reserve requirements against net demand deposits for country banks from 11 to 12 per cent.

Reduced reserve requirements against net demand deposits at central reserve city banks from 17½ to 16½ per cent, effective December 1.

1961

February

Announced that System open market operations would include securities outside the short-term area.

December

Raised, effective January 1, 1962, maximum interest rates payable by member banks on any savings deposit from 3 to 3½ per cent, and to 4 per cent on those left in the bank for 1 year or more; also raised maximum rates on time deposits with a maturity of 6 months to 1 year from 3 to 3½ per cent, and to 4 per cent on those deposits with a maturity of a year or longer.

1962

February

Authorised open market transactions in foreign currencies.

July

Reduced margin requirements on loans for purchasing or carrying listed securities from 70 to 50 per cent of market value of securities.

October

Reduced reserve requirements against time deposits from 5 to 4 per cent, effective October 25 for reserve city banks and November 1 for other member banks, thereby releasing about $780 million of reserves.

1963

Mid-July

Raised the discount rate from 3 to 3½ per cent.

Raised maximum interest rates payable by member banks on time deposits (other than savings) and certificates of deposit with maturities of 90 days to 6 months from 2½ to 4 per cent and with maturities of 6 months to 1 year from 3½ to 4 per cent.

November

Raised margin requirements on loans for purchasing or carrying listed securities from 50 to 70 per cent of market value of securities. Also increased retention requirements on proceeds of sales from under-margined accounts from 50 to 70 per cent.

1964

Late November

Raised the discount rate from 3½ to 4 per cent. Raised maximum interest rates payable on savings deposits held for less than 1 year from 3½ to 4 per cent and those on other time deposits from 4 to 4½ per cent for maturities of 90 days or more and from 1 to 4 per cent for maturities of 30-89 days.

1965

February

Introduced a programme, at the request of the President and in co-operation with the Treasury, under which financial institutions were asked to limit voluntarily their expansion of foreign loans and investments.

Early December

Raised the discount rate from 4 to 4½ per cent.

Raised maximum interest rates payable by member banks on time deposits (other than savings deposits) from 4 to 5½ per cent for maturities of 30-89 days and from 4½ to 5½ per cent for longer maturities.

1966

June

Raised from 4 to 5 per cent the reserve requirements against time deposits, other than savings deposits, in excess of $5 million at each member bank, effective July 14 and 21 for reserve city and country member banks, respectively, thereby increasing required reserves by about $420 million.

Made shorter-term bank promissory notes and similar instruments issued after June 26, 1966 subject to regulations governing reserve requirements and payment of interest on deposits, effective September 1, 1966.

July

Lowered from 5½ to 5 per cent the maximum rate payable by member banks on new multiple-maturity time deposits of 90 days or more, and from 5½ to 4 per cent the maximum rate payable on such deposits with maturities of less than 90 days.

Granted temporary authority to the Federal Reserve Banks to provide emergency credit facilities, under certain conditions, to non-member depositary-type institutions, including mutual savings banks and savings and loan associations. No lending was necessary under this authority.

August

Raised reserve requirements from 5 to 6 per cent against time deposits, other than savings deposits, in excess of $5 million at each member bank, effective September 8 and 15 for reserve city and country banks, respectively, thereby increasing required reserves by about $450 million.

September

Requested member banks to moderate their rate of expansion of loans, particularly business loans; indicated that bank use of Reserve Bank discount facilities would be expected to be in a manner consistent with this objective; and noted the continuing availability of discount facilities to cushion deposit shrinkages.

September

In exercise of authority given by new temporary legislation, reduced from 5½ to 5 per cent the maximum interest rate payable on any time deposit under $100,000 other than savings deposits, effective September 26.

December

Issued new 1967 guidelines for banks and other financial institutions as part of broader governmental programme of voluntary foreign credit restraint.

Terminated special discount arrangements announced on September 1 when member banks were asked to curtail their business loan expansion.

1967

February

Reduced from 4 to 3 per cent reserve requirements on savings deposits, Christmas and vacation club accounts and the first $5 million of other time deposits at each member bank, in two steps: from 4 to 3½ per cent, effective March 2; and from 3½ to 3 per cent, effective March 16.

April

Reduced discount rates at 10 Reserve Banks from 4½ to 4 per cent, effective April 7. (Reductions at the two remaining Reserve Banks were effective April 10 and 14.)

November

Increased discount rates at 10 Reserve Banks from 4 to 4½ per cent, effective November 20. (Increases at the two remaining Reserve Banks were effective November 21 and 27.)

December

Increased reserve requirements against demand deposits in excess of $5 million per bank from 16½ to 17 per cent for reserve city banks, effective January 11, 1968; and from 12 to 12½ per cent for other member banks, effective January 18, 1968.

1968

January

Issued revised and substantially more restrictive guidelines for banks and other financial institutions for restraint of foreign credits as a part of the President's balance of payments programme.

March

Imposed a new margin requirement of 70 per cent on loans made by "other lenders" (i.e. other than banks, brokers, and dealers) for the purpose of purchasing or carrying registered equity securities.

Imposed a new margin requirement of 50 per cent on such loans made by banks or "other lenders" against securities convertible into registered equity securities. Lowered the margin requirement on such loans by brokers and dealers to 50 per cent.

Announced revisions in the guidelines for banks and non-bank financial institutions issued under the President's balance of payments programme.

Increased discount rates from $4\frac{1}{2}$ to 5 per cent at 9 Reserve Banks, effective March 15. (By March 22, the 5 per cent rate was in effect at all Reserve Banks.)

April

Increased discount rates from 5 to $5\frac{1}{2}$ per cent at 3 Reserve Banks, effective April 19. (By April 26, the $5\frac{1}{2}$ per cent rate was in effect at all Reserve Banks.)

Revised maximum interest rates payable by member banks on single-maturity time deposits of $100,000 or more, effective April 19, 1968, from $5\frac{1}{2}$ per cent on all maturities to:

Per cent	Maturity group
$5\frac{1}{2}$	30-59 days
$5\frac{3}{4}$	60-89 days
6	90-179 days
$6\frac{1}{4}$	180 days and over

June

Increased the margin requirement on loans by banks, brokers and dealers, and other lenders for the purpose of purchasing or carrying registered equity securities from 70 to 80 per cent.

Increased the margin requirement on such loans by these lenders against securities convertible into registered equity securities from 50 to 60 per cent.

August

Reduced the discount rate from $5\frac{1}{2}$ to $5\frac{1}{4}$ per cent at one Reserve Bank, effective August 16 (By August 30, the $5\frac{1}{4}$ per cent rate was in effect at all Reserve Banks.)

December

Raised discount rates from 5¼ to 5½ per cent at 9 Reserve Banks, effective December 18. (By December 20, the 5½ per cent rate was in effect at all Reserve Banks.)

Announced revised guidelines for restraint of foreign credits by banks and other financial institutions.

1969

April

Raised discount rates from 5½ to 6 per cent at 11 Reserve Banks, effective April 4. (By April 8, the 6 per cent rate was in effect at all Reserve Banks.)

Increased reserve requirements against net demand deposits at all member banks—from 16½ to 17 per cent on deposits under $5 million, and from 17 to 17½ per cent on deposits over $5 million at each reserve city bank; from 12 to 12½ per cent on deposits under $5 million and from 12½ to 13 per cent on deposits over $5 million at each country bank—effective in the reserve computation period beginning April 17 and applicable to average deposits in the period April 3-9 inclusive.

Issued revised 1969 guidelines, effective immediately, covering foreign credits and investment by US banks and other financial institutions, representing a modification of guidelines announced December 23, 1968.

July

Amended rules governing member-bank reserves (Regulation D), effective July 31, to assure that certain officers' cheques issued in connection with transactions with foreign branches were included as deposits for purposes of computing reserve requirements.

Amended rules governing member-bank reserves (Regulation D) and payment of interest on deposits (Regulation Q), effective July 25, to bring certain member bank liabilities on repurchase agreements within the coverage of such rules.

August

Amended rules governing member-bank reserves (Regulation D) and foreign branches of member banks (Regulation M), effective September 4, to establish a 10 per cent marginal reserve requirement on certain foreign borrowings, primarily Euro-dollars, by member banks and on the sales of assets by member banks to their foreign branches.

December

Announced revised guidelines covering foreign credit and investments by US banks and other financial institutions.

Authorised Federal Reserve Banks, effective immediately and until April 1, 1970, to provide, in accordance with certain specified principles, emergency credit facilities to non-member depositary institutions, if the need should arise.

1970

January

Increased maximum interest rates payable by member banks on time and savings deposits, effective January 21. This action, in combination with a minor further amendment on February 26 (retroactive to January 21) bringing rates on multiple-maturity deposits in line with those on single maturities, set the following maximum rates:

1. Passbook savings, raised from 4 to 4.5 per cent.
2. Other types of consumer-type deposits—those of less than $100,000—raised as follows:

Maturity	Rate (per cent)	
	New	Previous
Multiple-maturity:		
30-89 days	4.50	4.00
90 days to 1 year	5.00	5.00
Single-maturity:		
30 days-1 year	5.00	5.00
Single- and multiple-maturity:		
1 to 2 years	5.50	5.00
2 years or more	5.75	5.00

3. Time deposits of $100,000 or more, raised as follows:

Maturity	Rate (per cent)	
	New	Previous
30-59 days	6.25	5.50
60-89 days	6.50	5.75
90-179 days	6.75	6.00
180 days to 1 year	7.00	6.25
1 year or more	7.50	6.25

May

Reduced the margin requirements on loans by banks, brokers and dealers, and other lenders for the purpose of purchasing or carrying registered equity securities from 80 to 65 per cent.

Reduced the margin requirements on such loans by these lenders against securities convertible into registered equity securities from 60 to 50 per cent.

June

Suspended limitations on the maximum rate of interest member banks may pay on single-maturity deposits or $100,000 or more that mature 30 days or more but less than 90 days after date of deposit.

August

Reduced reserve requirements against time deposits in excess of $5 million at each member bank from 6 to 5 per cent and applied a 5 per cent reserve requirement on funds obtained by member banks through the issuance of commercial paper by their affiliates, both actions to become effective in the reserve computation period beginning October 1 and be applicable to such deposits and commercial paper outstanding in the week beginning September 17.

November

Reduced discount rates from 6 to 5¾ per cent at 6 Reserves Banks, effective November 11. (By November 16, the 5¾ per cent rate was in effect at all Reserve Banks.)

Amended rules governing member bank reserves (Regulation D) and foreign branches of member banks (Regulation M), effective January 7, 1971, to (1) raise from 10 to 20 per cent the reserve ratio applicable to a member bank's Euro-dollar borrowings to the extent that they exceed a specified reserve-free base and (2) apply an automatic downward adjustment feature to the minimum reserve-free bases applicable to Euro-dollar borrowings.

Reduced discount rates from 5¾ to 5½ per cent at 5 Reserve Banks, effective December 1. (By December 11, the 5½ per cent rate was in effect at all Reserve Banks.)

1971

January

Reduced the discount rate from 5½ per cent to 5¼ per cent at 10 Reserve Banks, effective January 8. (By January 15, the 5¼ per cent rate was in effect at all Reserve Banks.)

Amended Regulation M to permit US banks to count toward maintenance of their reserve free Euro-dollar bases any funds invested by their overseas branches in Export-Import Bank securities offered under the programme announced on January 15 by the Export-Import Bank. For those banks that have had a minimum (3 per cent of deposits) reserve-free base, postponed for 4 weeks, through the computation period of February 17, 1971, the application of the automatic downward adjustment of their bases.

Reduced the discount rate from 5¼ per cent to 5 per cent at 6 Reserve Banks, effective January 19. (By January 29, the 5 per cent rate was in effect at all Reserve Banks.)

February

Reduced the discount rate from 5 per cent to 4¾ per cent at 11 Reserve Banks, effective February 13. (By February 19, the 4¾ per cent rate was in effect at all Reserve Banks.)

April

Amended Regulation M to permit US banks to count toward maintenance of their reserve-free Euro-dollar bases any funds invested by their overseas branches in US Treasury securities offered under the programme announced on April 1 by the Treasury.

150

July

Raised the discount rate from 4¾ per cent to 5 per cent at 4 Reserve Banks, effective July 16. (By July 23, the 5 per cent rate was in effect at all Reserve Banks.)

August

Amended the continuing authority directive with respect to domestic open market operations to authorise outright operations in Federal agency securities.

November

Reduced the discount rate from 5 per cent to 4¾ per cent at 7 Reserve Banks, effective November 11. (By November 19, the 4¾ per cent rate was in effect at all Reserve Banks.)

December

Reduced the margin requirement for purchasing or carrying stocks from 65 per cent to 55 per cent, effective December 6.

Reduced the required deposit on short sales from 65 per cent to 55 per cent, effective December 6.

Reduced the discount rate from 4¾ per cent to 4½ per cent at 4 Reserve Banks, effective December 13. (By December 24, the 4½ per cent rate was in effect at all Reserve Banks.)

1972

June

Amended Regulation D to apply the same reserve requirements to member banks of like size, regardless of the bank's location, to become effective in two steps in late September and early October.

November

Increased the margin requirements for credit extended to finance the purchase or carrying of stock from 55 to 65 per cent.

1973

January

Raised the discount rate from 4½ to 5 per cent, effective January 15 at all Reserve Banks.

February

Raised the discount rate from 5 to 5½ per cent, effective February 26 at 4 Reserve Banks and by March 2 at the others.

April

Requested commercial banks to establish "appropriate loan commitment policies" to avoid over-commitment of resources.

Amended the rules governing the discount window (Regulation A), primarily to provide special "seasonal lending arrangements" to smaller banks.

Raised the discount rate from $5\frac{1}{2}$ to $5\frac{3}{4}$ per cent, effective April 23 at 7 Reserve Banks and by May 4 at the others.

May

Raised the discount rate from $5\frac{3}{4}$ to 6 per cent, effective May 11 at 11 Reserve Banks and on May 18 for the other.

Increased from 5 to 8 per cent the marginal reserve requirements on funds raised through large CDs or similar instruments, including commercial paper raised by bank affiliates and, for the first time, sales of finance bills.

Reduced from 20 to 8 per cent the reserve requirement on certain foreign borrowings of US banks, primarily Euro-dollars.

Suspended Regulation Q ceilings on large CDs maturing in 90 days or more.

Urged large non-member banks to co-operate with the Board in limiting expansion of bank credit.

June

Raised the discount rate from 6 to $6\frac{1}{2}$ per cent, effective June 11 at 10 Reserve Banks and by June 15 at the others.

July

Raised the discount rate from $6\frac{1}{2}$ to 7 per cent, effective July 2 at all Reserve Banks.

Increased reserve requirements by $\frac{1}{2}$ percentage point on all but the first $2 million of net demand deposits at member banks.

Increased Regulation Q ceilings, establishing the following schedule of maximum rates for "consumer" deposits:

Maturity	Rate (per cent)	
	New	Previous
Passbook accounts	5.0	4.5
90 days to 1 year	5.5	5.0
1 year to $2\frac{1}{2}$ years	6.0	5.5
		(1 to 2 years)
$2\frac{1}{2}$ years and over	6.5	5.75
		(2 years and over)
4 years and over, minimum denomination of $ 1,000	no ceiling	5.75

August

Raised the discount rate from 7 to 7½ per cent, effective August 14 at 10 Reserve Banks and by August 23 at the others.

September

Increased the marginal reserve requirements on large CDs and similar instruments from 8 to 11 per cent.

A REVIEW OF THE CHANGING STRATEGY
OF OPEN MARKET OPERATIONS[1]

INTRODUCTION

The purpose of the present appendix is to give a brief account of the conduct of open market operations (henceforth OMO) based on published material. Since 1969 the Federal Open Market Committee (FOMC) has modified its operating targets in the direction of greater emphasis on monetary aggregates. This review is therefore divided into two parts: 1960-69 and 1970-71. Since both the formulation and the implementation of an OMO policy involves several controversial issues relating to the conduct of discretionary monetary action, the review cannot be comprehensive; it is rather a set of notes on selected aspects of OMO policy and conduct, examined under the following sub-headings:

1. How does the FOMC formulate its policy?
2. How is policy transformed into operating targets?
3. What technical problems are involved in the definition of operating targets?
4. What is the relationship between considerations arising out of 1-3 and the economic impact of OMO?

THE FOMC DIRECTIVE: 1960-1969

The FOMC directive consists of two parts:

i) a review of recent economic and financial developments concluding with a brief statement concerning the FOMC's ultimate targets; followed by
ii) the FOMC's instructions, in the light of (*i*), which guide the Account Manager in his operations. In recent years these instructions have generally been given in terms of money market conditions and since 1966, one or more monetary aggregates, typically bank credit.

INFORMATION AND POLICY FORMULATION WITH RESPECT TO ULTIMATE TARGETS

Since lags are involved in influencing aggregate demand through monetary policy, and since the FOMC is concerned with ultimate targets

---

1. A helpful account of the development of FOMC policies is to be found in Brimmer [10].

which are, themselves, lagged on aggregate demand, the FOMC needs forecasts of the economy for at least a 3-4 quarter horizon. Detailed forecasts based on the judgement of specialist Federal Reserve staff are provided on the basis of one or more policy options. The outcome is thus a consensus staff forecast. But FOMC members have additional sources of information from which they may derive their own views of the future development of the economy. Given these detailed forecasts, the FOMC has, in principle,

a) to determine its priorities between competing ultimate objectives, and

b) to translate these into a meaningful set of instructions to the desk.

The directives contain no means of identifying the FOMC's view on the technical "trade-offs" among the competing ultimate targets defined by the structure of the economic system. Nor do the directives contain any sure means of identifying the FOMC's preferences on ultimate objectives or even changes in them. To be sure, it is possible to draw inferences from the fact that while the FOMC directive typically contains a reference to each ultimate target, targets do not always appear in the same order. A change in the order of reference *may* reflect a change in the order of preference made after consideration of the (consensus) trade-offs. There is, however, no means of knowing whether this is so. These points aside, the FOMC reaches a consensus view regarding ultimate objectives. Its next task is to give this view an operational content.

PART II OF THE FOMC DIRECTIVE: INSTRUCTIONS TO THE DESK

The FOMC view regarding ultimate targets is given in the last paragraph of Part I of the directives. The function of Part II is to transform this view into operational guidance for the desk. Since the last sentence simply defines the FOMC stance for "stabilisation policy" purposes, two elements are inescapably involved in this translation. The first element requires the "stabilisation stance" to be transformed into values, or more probably ranges of values, for price and quantity variables which the desk is to influence, the *operating targets*.[2] The second element requires "adjustment" of these ranges or values to take account of initial conditions in financial markets—insofar as they are known—and any special difficulties which it is believed are likely to arise in the period before the next FOMC meeting. Both elements involve complex issues. For example, under the second heading, Part II of the directive must take account of the impact of Treasury debt operations and any associated "even-keeling" requirement; the possibility of a temporary liquidity crisis or unusual strain

---

2. This is the usual terminology for financial variables which are (*i*) strongly influenced by changes in the main instruments of monetary policy and (*ii*) links in the transmission mechanism by which policy effects spread through financial and real markets. The values (ranges) of the operating targets conveyed in the instructions to the Desk have little economic significance *per se;* they are communicating devices required to make policy operational. No distinction is made in this Appendix (or in the text itself) between operating and intermediate targets, because the dividing line is essentially arbitrary. As analysed in the literature, intermediate targets meet (*i*) and (*ii*) above, but they are further removed from policy influences than the operating targets. Usual examples of intermediate targets are monetary aggregates and long-term interest rates.

156

in a particular market; and the risk of the emergence of "disorderly market conditions". It follows that Part II of the FOMC directive must be regarded as the "consensus transformation" of the "stabilisation" judgement of Part I into operational terms subject to the constraints imposed by Treasury policy on the one hand, existing and foreseeable market conditions on the other and finally to the overriding lender of last resort responsibility. Stated in this way, it is easy to see how complex are the issues involved and why, on occasions, the FOMC fails to attain unanimity.

Throughout most of the 1960s, Part II of the directive took the form of requiring the desk to "maintain", "ease" or "tighten" money market conditions. After the introduction of the so-called "proviso clause", the directive took the same form, but added "provided" some specified aggregate (typically bank credit) "does not deviate significantly from projections". From published information it is impossible to ascertain the values (ranges) assigned to those variables in terms of which "money market conditions" are defined or even to identify, unambiguously, the relevant variables. The following sections identify the principal issues involved on the basis of certain explicit assumptions.

Money Market Conditions

It is argued in the main text that "money market conditions" is a function, not necessarily invariant, of net free reserves, the Federal funds rate and the Treasury bill rate.[3] These variables are, however, representative of a much larger group including also member bank borrowings and rates charged on call loans to government bond dealers. In an exact world, net free (and unborrowed) reserves would be related, by invariant asset demand functions, to the two interest rate variables. Hence the three main operational targets would collapse to one and the Desk would have one instrument, the Federal Reserve security portfolio, and one operating target which, in principle, it could determine exactly. But in the real world in which the Desk must operate invariant asset demand functions do not exist. Hence, in practice, a given range[4] of net free reserves may co-exist with very different Federal funds rates. In such a case, a conflict arises which the manager must resolve by following either a rate or quantity strategy, and perhaps giving emphasis to one rate (or quantity) rather than another. Thus in the general case, the definition of policy in terms of money market conditions will *not* leave the desk with any simple mechanical rule of action. Skilled interpretation of the FOMC directive will usually be required. Moreover, the selected resolution of any rate/quantity conflict carries economic implications, as will be discussed later.

Even on the assumption that any rate/quantity conflict has been resolved, a technical problem exists because none of the three variables in terms of which money market conditions are here defined is under the immediate control of the Desk. Consider, for example, a quantity target such as net free reserves, defined as the difference between unborrowed and

---

3. Axilrod [4] puts special emphasis on the Federal funds rate and net free reserves. Young [101] stresses the multi-dimensional nature of money market conditions.
4. Typically variables are not defined as numbers but as ranges. This procedure makes some allowance for the stochastic nature of the underlying functions and reduces the frequency of conflicts. It does not, however, ensure the absence of conflicts.

required reserves. Under present arrangements required reserves are based on previous deposits totals and are thus predetermined. Changes in unborrowed reserves, however, depend not only upon Federal Reserve security transactions but on changes in all other items in the sources and uses of the base: for example, float, currency held by the public, and Treasury cash holdings. Insofar as these "market" elements are incorrectly forecast, over any operating period, control of unborrowed reserves will be less than perfect. The degree of control over the two short-term rates is more nearly complete; information about them is always available, and if the Federal Reserve were firmly determined to achieve any particular value of one of these rates, it would have the means to do so. But in general the implementation of instructions regarding money market conditions involves

   a)   their definition;
   b)   interpreting "easier" or "tighter" in terms of this definition;
   c)   decisions, with economic implications. concerning the resolution of possible conflicts; and possibly
   d)   technical difficulties of implementation.

It may be concluded that, as a proximate target of policy, money market conditions—though its meaning may be clear to the FOMC—is imprecise and cannot be given an unambiguous interpretation from any published directive.

MONETARY AGGREGATES AND THE PROVISO CLAUSE

Through 1969, the aggregate most commonly mentioned in the proviso clause was "bank credit". This variable is measured from the liabilities side of the banks' balance sheet.[5] Originally, the proxy was simply total member-bank deposits; it has now been refined to make allowance for non-deposit sources of bank funds and is referred to as "the adjusted credit proxy". In general, given the prevailing definition, the proviso clause was symmetric in the sense that the desk was expected to make money market conditions "easier" if the rate of growth of the proxy fell "significantly" short of its "projected" growth or "tighten" conditions if it "significantly" exceeded the rate projected.

The origin or time horizons of the projected rates are not inferable from the directive. According to Axilrod [4] the projection was generally for one month and based upon an interpretation of the money market conditions defined in the first section of Part II. The directive contains no information regarding the size of a deviation which must be considered significant nor of the time-scale involved in its definition; i.e., whether the Desk should revise money market conditions if significant errors appeared after 1, 2 or 3 weeks. As the Desk's control over even unborrowed reserves is not perfect, it seems plausible to suggest that its control over the bank credit proxy—which in terms of any very short period such as a week will presumably lag unborrowed reserves—is less secure, even if the change in the proxy is a relatively stable function of the current and

---

5. This practice is due to the more speedy availability of deposit data. The proxy will be inadequate insofar as member and non-member banks' behaviour differs.

past changes in unborrowed reserves.[6] If this suggestion is correct, fairly large percentage errors in the "bank credit proxy" must be accepted. Moreover, though the Desk's control of bank credit must depend on the method by which the bank credit proxy is calculated, the estimates available to the Desk may themselves have an error. If so, there may be, in addition to uncertainty regarding the response of the proxy to security purchases or sales, uncertainty about what is happening to bank credit.

It seems reasonable to infer from this analysis that the bank credit proxy and other monetary aggregates were primarily used, in the first three years after the addition of the proviso clause to the directive, "as a variable for testing the consistency between money market conditions and projected developments in the real economy",[7] i.e. as an indicator rather than as a target in itself. If the selected monetary aggregate(s) rose significantly faster (or more slowly) than projected, this was interpreted as evidence that GNP was also developing more strongly (or weakly) than anticipated. But the deviations had to be significant and sustained. There is no record that the FOMC precisely defined "significant" or "sustained". Within a single policy period the Desk's information about recent movements in monetary aggregates is subject to sizeable error; how large these errors may be in practice may be inferred from Davis [16] and Friedman [34]. It is doubtless these considerations, among others, which cause Holmes [49] to suggest that significant cumulative errors are required to influence operations. In short, it appears legitimate to conclude that the proviso clause only infrequently had an operational significance and accordingly to interpret open market operations throughout the period 1960-69 primarily in terms of money market conditions.

THE IMPLICATIONS FOR OPEN MARKET STRATEGY OF REGULATION Q MAXIMA

There is one consideration, the use of Regulation Q maxima, which suggests that this interpretation is not the only possible one. The aim in the two periods of Q effectiveness in 1966 and 1969 was to restrain the growth of bank lending, and it would appear that the bank credit proxy in these two phases of restraint took on the character of an additional target. It may be instructive to consider what difference the existence of Regulation Q maxima may have made to the conduct of open market operations and to the impact on bank lending in the two periods of restraint, on the assumption that the Federal Reserve was aiming to let money market conditions (in particular short-term market interest rates) develop in either case as actually observed. As Treasury bill and other short-term market interest rates rise above Q maxima, bank customers switch out of certificates of deposit into Treasury bills. To the extent that banks cannot attract non-deposit funds to offset this run-off, they will reduce their earning assets. If they sell exactly the type of short-term marketable assets which the non-bank public is now demanding, there will be no further effects; required reserves will decline with the run-off of CDs, but

---

6. Some evidence regarding the size of the errors involved is given by Davis [6] on the assumption that the current period change in unborrowed reserves is precisely controllable. Davis, of course, stresses that the assumption is not realistic.

7. Axilrod [4] p. 20. See also pages 160-161 for a discussion of the possible target role of the monetary aggregates.

if money market conditions are kept unchanged by the authorities, this modest effect will be offset.[8] A more likely hypothesis is that some of the assets unloaded by the banks have a longer maturity than those demanded by the public and that some of them will be non-marketable. If so, the existence of the Q maxima reinforces the upward pressure on longer-term interest rates; long rates will tend to rise relative to short. There will also be a somewhat slower increase in lending through some combination of tighter rationing and higher lending rates. The net effect on demand of these shifts is deflationary, since expenditure decisions are more closely related to longer-term interest rates.[9] As the FOMC is assumed to aim for the same course of short-term interest rates whether Regulation Q maxima are effective or not, larger open market sales will have to be undertaken in periods of Q effectiveness to offset the tendency for bill and other rates to fall as a result of the excess of purchases by the non-banking public over the sales by the banks. Thus Q effectiveness enables the FOMC to engage in larger open market sales and to reduce non-borrowed reserves without any impact on the short-term rates.[10] Thus, the periods of Q effectiveness modified the context of open market operations slightly; the argument outlined suggests that Regulation Q was seen as an instrument which increased the scope for influencing bank credit by manipulation of the traditional short-term instruments.

MONEY MARKET CONDITIONS AS AN OPERATING TARGET

The interval between FOMC meetings is three to four weeks. This interval will be hereafter called the *policy period* and each week within it the *short period*. On the assumption that the earlier analysis in this Appendix is broadly correct, the implications, for each of these periods, of the dominance of the money market conditions targets must now be reviewed. Outside an exact theoretical model, the Federal funds rate and net free reserves will not be uniquely related, despite a close correlation between them. Moreover, it seems safe to suggest that the shorter the time period over which a relationship is sought, the less predictable any such relation will be. Hence within any *short period,* the rate/quantity dilemma seems certain to arise. The Desk is given daily estimates of net free reserves, but these estimates are subject to considerable error.[11] Reliable data on rates are of course available on a continuous basis, but they will at times reflect erroneous estimates by the banks of their reserve position. For

---

8. The effect is bound to be modest, since the ratios required against time (and savings) deposits are small. Some of the freeing of reserves may be offset if some bank customers shift from CDs into demand deposits against which the required ratio is about three times as large.

9. As explained in Part III, page 67, no clear evidence is available that changes in the degree of rationing of bank loans have had any significant effect on private expenditures though the authorities were apparently working on the assumption that there were such effects in 1966 and possibly also in 1969.

10. It is a weakness of some of the available literature on the effects of Regulation Q that it assumes non-borrowed reserves to be constant. If the FOMC is following a given course with respect to short-term rates, these rates, *excess* reserves, and possibly also net free reserves, may be assumed constant; non-borrowed reserves will be smaller because of the decline in required reserves.

11. See Friedman [34], pp. 127-28, for information bearing on this point.

example, on any day the Federal funds rate may open at a low figure, but the Desk's own estimate of free reserves may be so low as to be inconsistent therewith, suggesting that the funds rate is likely to rise. In such a situation, the Desk's free reserves estimate is a better guide to short-run open market operations than the initial Federal funds rate. In general, the two dimensions of money market conditions supplement each other. From the viewpoint of the FOMC it would appear that reliance on a rate interpretation leaves a minimum of discretion to the Desk; but the tendency in recent years seems to be in the direction of allowing wider fluctuations in the Federal Funds rate, in recognition that strong attention to day-to-day or even week-to-week fluctuations may prevent the desk from responding to money market developments in a proper way. Whether a rate or a reserves interpretation is relied on, dominance of money market conditions as an operating target implies that policy will have an accommodative element. In both cases shifts in the public's demand for currency are accommodated automatically; to the extent that the relationship between free reserves and short-term interest rates is stable the FOMC may expect to achieve approximately similar results by instructing the Desk to maintain the weekly average of the Federal funds rate or of free reserves. The one situation in which a policy formulated strictly in terms of rates would have a larger element of accommodation is in the case of a shift in the banks' demand for free reserves; such a shift would not be accommodated if the FOMC had instructed the desk to keep free reserves constant. If the shift is random, i.e. not related to changes in deposits, there is little reason not to accommodate it; preventing the banks from adjusting reserves would magnify the destabilising initial effect on interest rates and ultimately income. To the extent that such shifts are important, the use of a reserves target supplies more misleading information than a rate target.

The conclusion that open market operations had a very important element of accommodation is supported by additional institutional considerations. In any financial system, seasonal and random shifts in demand for reserves will occur. In some systems they are accommodated by seasonal and occasional borrowing, direct or indirect, from the central bank. In the United States, however, the discount mechanism is not automatic and is subject to rules regarding legitimate access. Moreover, banks typically prefer not to borrow, perhaps partly because of the form of discount window surveillance. It follows that seasonal movements must either be offset by accommodating open market operations or else be adapted to by the market participants via seasonal fluctuations in rates and reserve positions. But, as already indicated, the Federal Reserve is concerned to maintain orderly markets. It thus finds it convenient to accommodate seasonal and other random demand shifts. A very similar argument applies to "even-keeling" though action of this kind is not generally undertaken where bill issues are involved.

Over the period of 3 to 4 weeks between FOMC meetings, discretionary changes in money market conditions have on a number of occasions been an objective of policy and thus of open market operations. But the extent of rate adjustment was often constrained by concern with orderly money markets and the interpretation of this concept in terms of "acceptable" rates of change in key rates. In particular, the desire of the FOMC to

161

avoid sharp changes in the week-to-week level of the Federal funds rate,[12] which would otherwise tend to move most widely in response to changes in money demand and supply, tended to give policy an accommodative element even in periods when short-term rates were allowed to "firm" or "ease", as well as in some periods of "stable" rates. The implication with respect to the monetary aggregates is that in phases of discretionary changes in money market conditions the element of discretion is a function of the time periods involved and is considerably greater over a month than over a week. Even within a month, the behaviour of the monetary aggregates is likely to be rather erratic; indeed, this is what the data show. The longer the time period involved, the larger becomes the discretionary element in both reserves and in monetary aggregate. This relationship suggests that week-to-week or even month-to-month changes in these magnitudes had a considerable accomodative element during the period of emphasis on money market conditions, and that, for the purpose of interpreting policy, it is quarterly or even longer movements in aggregates which are of greater relevance.

CONCLUSION: 1960-69

In these years FOMC policy was formulated in terms of a money market conditions target. The introduction of the proviso clause seems to have had relatively little influence on the conduct of open market operations between FOMC meetings. During such shorter intervals it therefore defined an *indicator* rather than a *target*. Over time spans longer than a month, the aggregates, notably the "bank credit proxy", may have served in part also as a target during the years 1966-69, particularly in the two phases of restraint. At times the interpretation of money market conditions by the desk was typically in terms of rates rather than quantities. Within any policy period, open market operations largely accommodated reserve movements. Though there is no reason that a concentration on money market conditions should lead necessarily to apparently inappropriate cyclical movements in aggregates, it is possible that in practice it did.

SOME THEORETICAL CONSIDERATIONS IN CHOOSING BETWEEN RATES AND AGGREGATES AS TARGETS

The selection of interest rates rather than aggregates as optimal operating targets over the policy period implies the view that instability in the money demand and supply functions is a more important source of economic instability than instability in expenditure functions. This empirical proposition has long been the subject of dispute. It is now frequently argued, for example by Poole [84] and [85], that the appropriate operating target is an aggregate, usually M_1, or alternatively, that the "single target" strategy should be abandoned in favour of a definition embracing *both* an aggregate *and* an interest rate target. Simulations of "rules" of this type have been undertaken by, *inter alia,* Poole [84] and [85] and Pierce [82]. They

---

12. The short-term volatility of the Federal funds rate has increased somewhat in recent years relative to the period up to 1969, though less than may have been anticipated by the FOMC at the time of the transition to a strategy based more on monetary aggregates.

suggest that some rather simple rules, in particular an interest rate rule —allowing for an upward drift of rates during the 1960s—constrained by a permissible range of variation for M_1, might have performed rather well.

However, simulations are of only limited help in this context for two reasons. First, the monetary authority needs to select an intermediate variable as a target only because it is uncertain of the structure of the economic and financial system. Clearly, if no uncertainty existed, the transmission between the monetary policy instrument and any ultimate target variable would be known and there would be no need to select some intermediate variable as an operating target. Generally, however, simulations are non-stochastic in that the parameters of the model are treated as exact. Secondly, the parameters are treated as independent of the policy actually pursued. This may, in practice, be an important limitation. Hence simulations can only provide estimates, with unknown variances, of the consequences of following defined policies on what may be a strong assumption, *viz* that the behaviour of the system and its parameter estimates are independent of the policies followed.

Alternatively, following Kareken *et al.* [61], one may think of two alternative models determining a single target variable (say, nominal GNP $= Y$).

These models are:

$$Y = a_o - a_1 r + a_2 Z + v_1 \tag{1}$$

where $Z =$ a vector of exogenous variables beyond the influence of the Federal Reserve;

$r =$ the interest rate;

$v_1 =$ error

and

$$Y = b_o - b_1 r + b_2 Z + u_1 \tag{2}$$
$$r = m_o + m_1 Y - m_2 M + u_2 \tag{3}$$

where $M =$ nominal money supply, and u_1 and u_2 are errors.

Relations (1) and (2) are identical in appearance; but (1) is a reduced form which suggests that the interest rate is directly an instrument variable, while (2) is part of a slightly more fully specified model which recognises in (3) that one way of operating on rates is by manipulating M. (2) and (3) yield a new reduced form (4):

$$Y = \frac{b_o - b_1 m_o}{1 + b_1 m_1} + \frac{b_1 m_2}{1 + b_1 m_1} M + \frac{b_2}{1 + b_1 m_1} Z +$$
$$\frac{1}{1 + b_1 m_1} (u_1 - b_1 u_2) \tag{4}$$

From each of (1) and (4) it is possible to develop a function relating the expected value of Y to its variance. These functions, or opportunity loci, can then, as Kareken *et al.* [61] demonstrate, be estimated upon the basis of the FMP model by making estimates of the variances of the structural relations. If one locus (say, the M locus) dominates the other in the sense that for any expected value of Y its variance is less, then that potential target variable is superior to the other, provided *both* can be controlled by the Federal Reserve *with the same degree of accuracy*.

The last point seems either to be overlooked—or at least not explicitly included—in Kareken's formal presentation of the problem. It may, however, be of importance, since in setting r equal to (say) r*, the Federal Reserve will find:

$$r = r^* + e_1 \tag{5}$$

Similarly, in setting M, it will find:

$$M = M^* + e_2 \tag{6}$$

If the error in controlling the interest rate (e_1) is small relative to the error in controlling the money stock (e_2), as indeed is bound to be the case if one compares,[13] say, the Treasury bill rate and M_1, this advantage may outweigh any calculated superiority of the monetary aggregate as an operating target. As argued below (page 168) it is not possible to assert with any confidence that one of the two is always superior. The best one can hope for is some view as to the average properties of one as against the other. But there may be reasons to expect these averages of observed past behaviour in financial and real markets not to apply in a particular policy phase. A further complication in interpreting past evidence on the errors in (1) and (4)-(6) is that these errors may not be unaffected by a change in operating strategy. Nevertheless, the theoretical framework outlined in the present section is a useful background to the modifications of policy observable in recent years.

THE MODIFICATION OF FOMC POLICY FROM 1970

Since 1970 the FOMC has placed more emphasis on the rate of growth of monetary aggregates (including money supply—M_1 and M_2—and the bank credit proxy) as operating targets, while retaining a money market conditions constraint; see page 166. This modification of procedures is consistent with the view that, on average, the instabilities of equation (1) are large in relation to those of (4) over the policy period between FOMC meetings but also that the relationship between (5) and (6) is not such as to reverse the implications of the judgement. The development of policy in 1970-71 will be reviewed below, in the light of this outline of the Federal Reserve position and the theoretical judgements which presumably underpin it.

The gradual shift in emphasis with respect to operating targets seems to have begun at the January 1970 FOMC meeting and become fully explicit in March 1970. Thus the January directive stated:

"System open market operations [...] shall be conducted with a view to maintaining firm conditions in the money market: provided, however, that operations shall be modified if money and bank credit appear to be deviating significantly from current projections."

Then in March 1970 it stated:

"To implement this policy, the Committee desires to see moderate growth in money and bank credit over the months ahead. System

---

13. It may be pointed out that this comparison is biased in favour of the interest rate target. The interest rates that matter in private expenditure functions are long-term ones, e.g. corporate bond and mortgage rates, which, as explained in Part III, are only very imperfectly controllable by means of the policy instruments or short-run operating targets. Though the long-term rates still have a high degree of predictability because they are to such a large extent determined by past history, they are probably even less subject to policy influences in the short run than are the monetary aggregates.

open market operations [...] shall be conducted with a view to maintaining money market conditions consistent with that objective."

Since the February directive stated its objectives in terms of "money market conditions" but added "Operations shall be modified promptly to resist any tendency for money and bank credit to deviate significantly from a moderate growth path"—an unusually firm statement of the "proviso" clause—it seems reasonable to argue that from January through March 1970, the FOMC was gradually modifying its position. Throughout the remainder of 1970 the directives were typically constructed in terms of moderate growth in money and bank credit, though, for reasons mentioned in Part IV(c), the May-July directives made special mention of the need to moderate excessive pressures in financial markets. During 1971, the formal wording of Part II of the directive varied somewhat. Aggregates were mentioned first on nine occasions, and "money market conditions" and reserves on four; both short-term rates and reserves were clearly under careful observation in these. Fuller examination of the context, however, suggests that the main targets were seen by the Committee to be aggregates; money market conditions were to be adjusted to be consistent with the policy for aggregates. Given this conclusion, a number of issues now arise:

a) Which aggregate (or aggregates) dominated FOMC policy formation?

b) Over what period of calendar time were target growth rates in the defined aggregates specified?

c) What procedure was adopted by the FOMC to deal with failures, on the part of the Desk, to move along the specified path?

The first of these questions is, obviously enough, the counterpart to the problem of defining money market conditions. The issue arises because the candidate aggregates M_1, M_2 and the adjusted credit proxy, do not grow at the same or, particularly in the short-run, even closely correlated rates. Thus the counterpart to the price/quantity dilemma under the money market conditions regime is an M_1, M_2 bank credit dilemma under an aggregate regime. For technical reasons—see Davis [16], Friedman [34], Maisel [70] and Holmes [49]—the Desk is unlikely to attain, in each of the monthly FOMC policy periods, any given target growth rate. On the other hand, over a somewhat longer period such as a quarter, it is reasonable to expect a closer approximation to any planned outcome. It thus seems likely that FOMC policy will be *conceived* in terms of (say) target growth rates defined over quarters but *specified*, in Part II of the directives, in terms of monthly (policy period) growth rates. Since to meet a quarterly growth target, given positive errors in (say) the growth of M_1 in the first two months (policy periods), might require a sharp *fall* in M_1 in month three, it is important to know how errors are in fact dealt with. Attachment to arithmetic accuracy might have severe destabilising effects on the monthly growth rate and thus, presumably, on money market rates. These considerations clearly give an incentive to smooth the correction of past errors over longer time spans than the policy period.

Aggregates as Targets

The phrase generally used in Part II of the FOMC directive is "monetary and credit aggregates". No more precise definition is provided and the only source of inference is the background discussion and Part I of the directive. The discussion commonly, but not invariably, reports growth rates over the past month (and sometimes over the past quarter) for each of M_1, M_2 and the proxy. In the same way, all three frequently receive mention in Part I of the directives. It thus seems that the FOMC, in its approach to aggregates takes an eclectic stand precisely as it did in its earlier definition of "money market conditions". This may involve the Desk in a contradiction if, for example, the rate of growth of M_1 were substantially exceeding its projection, M_2 falling substantially short, and the proxy roughly on track. In such cases the sense of the discussion at the previous FOMC meeting might give the account manager some guidance; if not, the conflict would have to be resolved through the daily conference call among Committee members.

Discussion at FOMC meetings during 1970-71 appears to have proceeded on the basis of estimated past monthly and quarterly growth rates in aggregates and staff projections, on specified assumptions regarding money market conditions, of growth rates in the following quarter, and against longer-run projections for the economy. In describing its own decision, the FOMC frequently referred to growth rates "over the months ahead". This horizon is assumed here to mean 3-6 months. Given this interpretation, the FOMC directive instructs the Desk to conduct its operations in a manner which will attain "moderate", "more moderate" or "greater" growth in monetary and credit aggregates over the months ahead. Thus, at each FOMC meeting, policy is specified for *one* month in terms of a (set of) projected growth rate(s) for a horizon of some *3-6 months,* and the quantitative description of these target paths is roughly translatable into "stable", "firming" and "easy" posture. It is not generally possible, from published information, to infer how far the target growth rates were adjusted on the basis of growth recorded in the recent past. The error adjustment procedure, if any, thus remains a matter for conjecture.

EXPERIENCE WITH AGGREGATES: 1970-71

With the 1970 increase in emphasis on aggregates, the modus operandi of the FOMC still seems to have entailed an implicit consideration of money market conditions because the degree of fluctuation in these conditions was constrained in the short run. In sanctioning changes in money market conditions, the FOMC was typically very cautious both in order to avoid "whip-sawing" in short-term rates and because, on many occasions, it felt constrained by pressures, actual or expected, in particular markets.[14] Given the apparent caution in adjusting money market conditions, observed growth rates are bound in the short term to reflect mainly demand elements and, insofar as these were unstable, to exhibit fairly severe fluctuations.

In adopting its new procedure, the FOMC faced additional problems arising from difficulties with data and from repeated revision of staff projections. Since the format of and information contained in FOMC reports both vary, it is not possible to summarise the evidence on these

---

14. Cf. the FOMC reports for 10th March and 23rd June, 1970.

points in a single table. Nevertheless, some suggestive illustrations can be provided with the help of a paper by Holmes [50].

a) The first estimate of the rate of growth in M_1 for 1970.I was 2 per cent (March, FOMC); this estimate was later revised to 4. In September it was reported that M_1 data were biased, and the growth rates for 1970.I and II were both revised upwards by about 1 per cent, while that for 1970.III was revised down by 1 per cent. In December the average rate of growth in each of the first three quarters of 1970 was put at 6.0 per cent—a figure not easy to reconcile with the earlier estimates.

b) In 1971 the first staff projection for the rate of growth in M_1 in 1971.II was slightly above 7 per cent (March). This figure became 8 per cent in April, 9 per cent in May and 12 per cent in June despite the fact that the FOMC was attempting from April onwards to reduce the growth rate through a policy of "firming". Apparently the main explanation of these discrepancies is to be found in somewhat faster growth of money incomes and lower interest rates in early 1971 than expected at the time projections were made, rather than in any major unexplained shift in the demand for money.

It thus seems that, for much of 1970-71, the FOMC was trying to control growth rates in aggregates despite the fact that:

i) it was often uncertain how fast the aggregates had been and were growing;

ii) there were unforeseen demand shifts;[15] and

iii) the response of aggregates to action by the desk was typically lagged.[16]

In these circumstances, it would clearly be a mistake to assume that the recorded growth rates in the main aggregates, which are set out, for example, in Chart 18 of the text of the present study, reflect FOMC intentions closely in the short run. The monthly growth rates show that there was wide variation in all three aggregates with the smallest spread of rates displayed by the M_1 series. This in itself is not surprising since both the M_2 series and that for the bank credit proxy are more strongly influenced by changes in the extent of intermediation.

Particular interest attaches to the period following April 1971, in which policy was "firming" as the FOMC, seriously disturbed by the high rates of growth recorded in February and March, sought to reduce the rate of expansion in M_1 below the staff's conditional projection (initially 8 per cent). Though interest rates in general, and money market rates in particular, rose sharply in the summer of 1971, the rate of growth in M_1 rose also. Staff projections were repeatedly revised upwards and the growth rate of M_1 in 1971.II actually exceeded the rates which, in

---

15. "M_1 did respond to variations in the public's demand for it for precautionary and other reasons that are imperfectly understood." Holmes [50] p. 361.

16. "M_1 did not respond quickly to the changing impact of open market operations in reserves and interest rates." "Recent experience suggests that M_1 responds slowly to changes in non-borrowed reserves and the Federal Funds rate initiated by System Open Market Operations." Holmes [50] p. 361. The same author puts the lag in M_1 response at 4-6 months.

1970.I, had given the FOMC cause for concern.[17] Thus FOMC "firming" coincides with the highest rates of growth in M_1, though with very sharply reduced rates of growth in M_2. It appears from FOMC reports that the planning of aggregate policy was primarily conducted with quarterly growth rates in mind. For obvious reasons these rates tend to be smoother than those revealed by monthly data, though they too display a fair measure of fluctuation. Moreover, it is clear from evidence already quoted that they did not, at least in 1971, correspond at all closely with FOMC intentions. In September 1971, the staff projection for 1971.IV was that M_1 would grow a good deal more slowly than in 1971.III while 1971.III would, in its turn, reveal a rate of growth very substantially lower than the 11.5 per cent of 1971.II. The FOMC then decided on a policy of cautious "easing" aiming at a rate of growth in excess of the 3 per cent conditionally projected by the staff. In fact, the rate of growth in M_1 in 1971.IV was only slightly above 1 per cent—*below* the initial staff projection. In conclusion, it appears that in 1971 the rate of growth in M_1 was:

    a)   initially (1971.I) faster than the FOMC desired or expected;

    b)   in 1971.II even faster despite the FOMC policy of firming;

    c)   in 1971.IV slower than expected and substantially slower than desired despite a policy of "easing".[18]

The rationale of selecting aggregates as operating targets is, as already mentioned, that instability in the demand for money, over a period of one or two quarters, is *typically* less than instability in expenditure functions, so that concentrating on aggregates reduces the risk of a major error in policy direction. This proposition, if correct, does not necessarily hold for any short run of policy periods, say the months of the second half of 1971. It is to be interpreted as applying on average over a large number of policy periods. It is interesting that some FOMC members on various occasions in 1970 and 1971 urged greater reliance upon money market conditions as an operating target. It is obvious that the predictability of the demand for money was lower in 1971 than usually, probably in large measure because of the general uncertainties during most of that year. In these circumstances, the FOMC may, on hindsight, have little reason to regret that it failed to keep the aggregates on a smooth course, whether the main reason at the time was to be found in technical inability to do so, some adjustment in the target growth rates, or, most likely, a combination of these two factors. The FOMC may also have come to hold the view that relatively wide movements in the growth rate of the aggregates for one or two quarters would not be important if they were offset later; see below.

An Optimal Strategy for the Monetary Aggregates?

It cannot, then, be determined to what extent observed developments in M_1 in 1971 deviated from what the FOMC wished at the time. Nor is it possible to resolve, even with the full benefit of hindsight, what would

---

17. Cf. FOMC reports for 4th May and 8th June 1971.

18. Towards the end of 1971 there appears to have been a downward shift in the demand for money not readily accounted for by existing models of the money market, though some of it may be seen as a lagged response to the high interest rates prevailing earlier in the year.

have been an optimal strategy for M_1; for the year as a whole the increase in M_1 of approximately 6 per cent could be interpreted to have turned out about right. Simulation experiments provide some insight; those reported in Part III suggest that a shift in Federal Reserve credit leads over time to changes in M_1. The response is modest in early quarters but builds up strongly; so also does the response of aggregate demand to changes in M_1. In such a situation any attempt to use monetary action to promote a smooth recovery from recession appears to require an oscillating growth rate for M_1. To have an appreciable early effect on aggregate demand, the rate initially would have to be considerable. But, if it were sustained, excess demand would be created; the rate must therefore be reduced. The lagged effects of reduction must then be offset by a further acceleration. If other exogenous variables do not change significantly, an oscillatory path for M_1 appears necessary for a while, until longer-run equilibrium values of the growth rates of money incomes and M_1 are approached. Since such oscillations will tend to be associated with fluctuations in money market rates, a minimal requirement is that the oscillations should be dampened. These results, which have been demonstrated by Poole [85], make it clear that fluctuations in observed growth rates for the monetary aggregates are not in themselves a basis for criticism of policy. But beyond these generalities it is difficult to define an optimal strategy; it will depend on several factors among which the most important are the speed with which it is hoped to restore "full employment", the attitude to deviations from this and other important policy targets, the behaviour of other exogenous variables—or forecasts of them if one is searching for an *ex ante* strategy—and the extent to which fluctuations in money market conditions are acceptable. No quantification of these factors is possible despite the explicitness and detail of available material on policy formation; and no comparison of observed M_1 growth rates and an optimal rate can be made in these circumstances.

This somewhat agnostic attitude to the problem of selecting an appropriate growth rate for M_1 or other aggregates has been criticised severely by economists of a "monetarist" persuasion. Indeed, the Federal Reserve has been constantly challenged to justify why it allowed M_1 to fluctuate so sharply in 1971. It may therefore be of some interest that it is not only simulations with the FMP model which suggest that the costs to the US economy of erratic developments in monthly or quarterly growth rates of M_1 are likely to be small for the reasons outlined in the previous paragraph; similar conclusions may be derived from monetarist models. Pierce and Thomson [82] report the results of simulating, on the model developed at the Federal Reserve Bank of St. Louis, for 1972-73 the effects of a smooth 6 per cent growth rate and various fluctuating growth rates around the same average. It turns out that it is only when a growth rate of 10 per cent is maintained for three or four quarters, followed by a below-trend growth of 2 per cent over a similar number of quarters, that significant differences in real GNP, prices and employment emerge. This finding suggests that "a latitude for errors exists for short-term money growth provided that the average growth rate over as long a period as one year equals the desired growth."[19]

19.   Pierce and Thomson [83] p. 23.

Partly because of the special circumstances of 1970-71, partly because of the inconclusive nature of the search for an optimal aggregate strategy, it is not safe to draw any general conclusions about FOMC experiences since the movement to an aggregate-based policy in early 1970. Indeed, since the end of the period here under study, FOMC procedures have evolved further in a way that underlines a continuing readiness to experiment with the formulations of the directive. The new element is a greater emphasis on reserves in the interpretation of money market conditions. The February 1972 policy record is particularly instructive in this respect:

"In continuation of a discussion begun at a meeting on the previous day, the Committee considered the relative merits of money market conditions and various measures of member bank reserves as 'operating targets'—that is, as variables for guiding day-to-day open market operations in the effort to achieve its intermediate monetary objectives and, in the process, contribute to the Nation's basic economic goals. Some arguments were advanced in favor of placing about the same degree of emphasis on money market conditions as had been customary prior to the meeting on January 11. However, the Committee concluded that in the present environment it was desirable to increase somewhat the relative emphasis placed on reserves while continuing to take appropriate account of money market conditions. Committee members believed that doing so would enhance their ability to achieve desired intermediate monetary objectives. These include the performance of various measures of money stock and bank credit that are supported by reserves as well as interest rates and over-all liquidity and credit conditions. At the same time, the members believed that reserve-supplying operations should be conducted so as to avoid disturbing effects in money and credit markets.

At this meeting the Committee decided to express its reserve objectives in terms of reserves available to support private non-bank deposits—defined specifically as total member bank reserves less those required to support Government and interbank deposits. This measure was considered preferable to total reserves because short-run fluctuations in Government and interbank deposits are sometimes large and difficult to predict and usually are not of major significance for policy. It was deemed appropriate for System open market operations normally to accommodate such changes in Government and interbank deposits."

The increasing emphasis on a reserves (quantity) interpretation of money market conditions within an aggregate-based strategy[20] has a theoretical justification somewhat analogous to the one reviewed in the interest rate versus aggregates discussion above. If there were an exact relationship between the selected short-term rates and M_1 and between the selected

---

20. In practice the FOMC proceeds by determining ranges of permissible variation in (i) reserves against private non-bank deposits, (ii) the Federal funds rate, and (iii) a monetary aggregate, typically M_1. The range of variation for the (weekly average of) the Federal funds rate is typically wider than under the previous money market conditions regime and more likely to be exceeded in cases of conflict with the reserves and M_1 targets.

reserve concept—RPD for short—and M_1 it would make no technical difference whether the authorities were aiming to control the money stock through RPD or the Federal funds rate. In the stochastic relationships prevailing in the real world, the degree of predictability of M_1 in the two relations is unlikely to be the same, and a substantive choice is therefore involved. The issue may be illustrated by a simple model of the supply and demand for money taken from Pierce and Thomson [83]:

$$M_d = a_1 Y - a_2 r + u \qquad (7)$$
$$M_s = b_1 R + b_2 r + v \qquad (8)$$
$$M_d = M_s \qquad (9)$$

Money demand (M_d) is assumed to be a function of nominal income and short-term interest rates, while money supply depends on reserves (RPD) and the short rate; both relations include an error term. The market is assumed to be in equilibrium. One may solve this little model for reserves and interest rates as alternative "policy instruments". It will then emerge that, if the error in the money demand function (u) is large relative to that of money supply (v), control through r will cause relatively large errors in attaining target levels for the money stock. That error is dampened if R is the operating target. If on the contrary, the money demand relation is less unstable than the supply relation, the degree of control over the money stock is increased by using an operating target in terms of the interest rate. Experience has demonstrated that large errors are to be expected in predicting short-run changes in both money supply and demand, even when models considerably more refined than (7)-(9) are used. The empirical evidence as to which of them is less unstable remains inconclusive. Indeed, it may be difficult to see how it could be otherwise, since control of the money stock has at no time been the sole aim to which the operating targets among money market conditions have been geared. For this reason the FOMC has understandably selected a blend of reserves and interest rates as operating targets. Nevertheless, the movement towards greater emphasis on a reserve interpretation in 1972 implied that the FOMC was sufficiently impressed by observed instability in the money demand function during the previous one or two years to think that it was the more unstable. But, as in the case of interest rates versus aggregates, this is not a question which can be settled once and for all; it is bound to be under continuous examination.

A recent statement from the FOMC suggests that although the emphasis on RPD did not assure any high degree of control over quarterly growth rates in M_1, the approach "proved a workable means of providing operational instructions to the Manager" ([26], June 1973, p. 415). But the experiences also "again cast doubt on whether M_1 alone was performing adequately as an indicator of the thrust of monetary policy" (ibid.), and the statement suggests that it may be worthwhile to watch the behaviour of other monetary aggregates, i.e. M_2 and the bank credit proxy, more carefully in the future.

Appendix III

RESIDENTIAL INVESTMENT
AND THE UNITED STATES HOUSING MARKET

INTRODUCTION

This brief Appendix has two aims:

a) To give a short review of the principal characteristics of the United States housing market and the consequential cyclical performance of residential investment.

b) To indicate the role of financial factors in explaining fluctuations in residential investment.

Beyond that, the Appendix also gives a short account of some institutional problems relating to the mortgage market which, in recent cycles, have raised difficulties for the conduct of monetary policy. In general, throughout this Appendix, housing is defined to exclude mobile homes though these have rapidly increased in importance in recent years and now account for nearly one third of new single family units.

Chart A shows the share of residential construction expenditure in:

i) GNP; and

ii) gross private investment in fixed capital.

Typically both series show a declining trend since the beginning of the 1950s so that, by 1970-71, the share of residential investment in GNP was not much more than half that of 1950. Indeed the downward trend in the proportion of residential investment to GNP explains most of the decline in the proportion of gross private investment to GNP. From Chart A it is clear that, on average, the importance of residential construction in total demand has been declining.

CYCLES IN RESIDENTIAL CONSTRUCTION

Chart 2[1] shows investment in residential construction (annual rates at current prices) plotted against the NBER cyclical peaks and troughs and a somewhat arbitrary dating accepted in the present study for the mini-recession of 1966-67. Two conclusions emerge immediately:

a) the housing cycle does not, typically, coincide with the general cycle;

b) investment in housing frequently moves contracyclically.

In addition, the chart suggests that, in the two most recent recessions,

---

1. Of the main text.

173

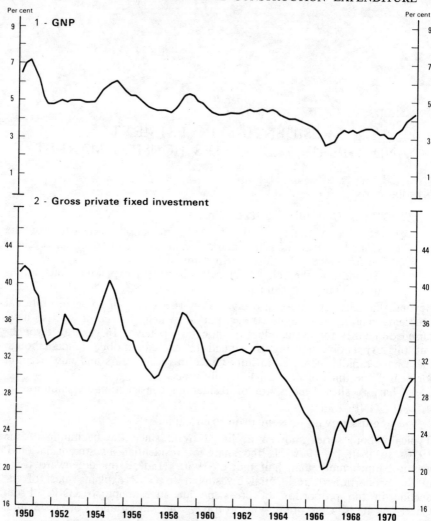

Source: Survey of Current Business.

1966-67 and 1969-70, the contracyclical element was rather less marked than in previous fluctuations.

A more detailed examination of the relative contribution of changes in residential construction to changes in GNP suggests the following conclusions:

> *i)* There is no single timing pattern relating fluctuations in residential construction to fluctuations in aggregate demand. Thus in the 1948-49 recession, housing expenditures led the general cycle by about one quarter; by contrast, in the 1953-54 recession

174

housing expenditures actually expanded. Again, in 1969-70, housing expenditures turned down about two quarters before the cyclical peak and turned up about one quarter before the cyclical trough.

ii) Timing correspondence is closest in the mini-recession of 1966.

iii) Typically, though 1966 and 1969 are exceptions, changes in housing expenditure have contributed rather little to cyclical movements in either aggregate demand or gross private fixed investment during business cycle phases.

iv) Despite *(iii)* it is nevertheless the case that the fluctuations in the rate of housing expenditures have been severe if measurement is taken from the phases of its own cycle. Thus peak to trough fluctuations (in current dollars) have typically been of the order of 18-20 per cent and, even in 1969 when the Federal government took active steps to insulate the mortgage market, expenditures declined by about 15 per cent from 1969.II to 1970.III. This is a significant point since housing investment is socially and politically important while the construction industry typically suffers from a relatively high average rate of unemployment as well as a relatively severe range of fluctuations.[2]

THE CYCLICAL PROCESS IN HOUSING

The most sensitive indicator of the demand/supply situation in the housing market is the number of starts ($\equiv S$). Residential construction expenditures could be regarded as a distributed lag on starts. Hence if I_h is defined as gross expenditure on residential construction,

$$I_h (t) \equiv \varnothing (t) \sum_{i=0}^{i=n} a_i S (t-i) \tag{1}$$

where the function $\varnothing$ is inserted to take account of changes in the value of a typical start. As the average size or cost per area unit increases, the relation between starts and expenditures is gradually inflated through the presence of this term.

Since I_h is a rather stable function of current and past values of S, the simplest way to formalize the housing market is to provide an explanation for starts. A method of doing this is to recognise that the demand for starts—by households—essentially reflects a discrepancy between the desired stock of housing (H*) and the actual stock (H). A rather general set of hypotheses would suggest a demand function of the form:

$$H^*_t = h[Y_p, P_h, \pi, P_c, r_m, \text{Pop}, m] \tag{2}$$

where $Y_p \equiv$ permanent income
$P_h \equiv$ supply price of new houses
$\pi \equiv$ rental rate of return on existing houses
$P_c \equiv$ prices of other goods and services entering household consumption

---

2. These aspects of the housing cycle have been studied intensively in recent years. A report on ways to moderate fluctuations in construction of housing was submitted by the Board of Governors of the Federal Reserve System to Congress in early 1972 [28].

$r_m \equiv$ mortgage rate
Pop $\equiv$ population
m $\equiv$ rate of family formation.

This type of formulation would give:

$$S^d_t = f[H^*_t — H_t]$$

$$= f (h[Y_p, P_h, \pi, P_c, r_m, Pop, m] — H_t) \qquad (3)$$

The implications of this function are interesting. The demographic variables (Pop and m) appear to change only rather slowly. Moreover, whatever the income elasticity of the demand for housing—which is in dispute—permanent income probably responds fairly slowly to changes in observed income. Hence though Y_p, Pop and m may dominate the market in the long run, their short-run importance will be small. By definition

$$\pi \equiv \frac{\text{Rent}}{P_h}$$

Typically rents are rather sticky prices since contracts are sometimes long, and there are often social inhibitions concerning rapid rent increases even where legal restraints are absent. The rental rate (π) is thus likely to be a somewhat slow-moving variable. The function thus implies that short-run fluctuations in S^d_t are likely to result in the main from fluctuations in r_m.[3]

Though this approach seems reasonable, at least as a first approximation, it should be obvious that (3) implicitly assumes a perfect capital market and, in particular, a perfect mortgage market since only r_m—the nominal interest cost of mortgages—appears in it. This position is untenable. Mortgage rates are notoriously sticky, and mortgage lenders commonly engage in rationing devices. Thus (3) will be applicable, if at all, only in circumstances in which the mortgage market imposes no constraints.

To see what this implies, one can transform (3) into a demand for mortgages ($\equiv M^d_t$). A simple way of doing this would be to write:

$$M^d_t = \alpha . \oslash (t) S^d_t \qquad (4)$$

It is immediately clear that (4) is applicable to short-run behaviour if, and only if,

$$M^d_t = M^s_t$$

where M^s_t is the supply of mortgage finance. In general, and particularly in periods of monetary restraint, one cannot expect this condition to be met. Hence, M^d_t will be restrained to M^s_t and the resultant (restricted) equation for housing starts will be:

$$S^{dr}_t = \frac{M^s_t}{\alpha . \oslash (t)} \qquad (5)$$

---

3. The formulation (3) assumes that the interest rate relevant for housing starts is the mortgage rate. To the extent that the construction of houses is financed temporarily through other channels, e.g. bank loans, which are subsequently repaid when the mortgage is raised, the role of the cost factor may be somewhat mis-specified.

Analytically this formulation is somewhat crude since α, somewhat cavalierly assumed to be a parameter, strictly needs to be explained. It serves, nevertheless, as a useful first approximation in that it asserts the dominant role of M_t^s, a financial variable, in explaining S_t^d in the short-run and thus, by implication, of the institutional arrangements in the mortgage market. It must be noted, however, that (5) holds only in a situation of excess demand for mortgage finance. If there is no excess demand, the equation becomes irrelevant: there are no availability effects. But there will still be interest-rate effects; see equation (3) above. And housing investment might still fluctuate cyclically due to cost-of-borrowing effects.

Strictly speaking the analysis is incomplete in that it fails to specify a supply function for S_t. Since most houses are constructed by speculative builders who have no identified client at the time of the start, any S_t^s function would involve a theory of builders' behaviour. Such a theory, at least at the present level of generality, could be constructed without much difficulty. It is unnecessary, however, provided one is prepared to assume that:

$$S_t^s \geqslant S_t^d \geqslant S_t^{dr} \tag{6}$$

for, if this holds, observed starts (S_t) will equal the lesser of the two specified demand quantities. If this inequality is acceptable in most short-run situations, it is possible to concentrate attention on the mortgage market, the typical short-run determinant of observed starts.

THE MORTGAGE MARKET AND THE CYCLICAL PROCESS

The previous section set out a schematic account of the US housing market and concluded that short-run fluctuations in housing starts were:

i) generally to be explained by financial variables; and
ii) in particular to be explained by conditions in the mortgage market.

These conditions, insofar as they form part of the conventional wisdom, are uncontroversial. It is therefore comforting to be able to report that, though econometric work on the United States housing sector has been, speaking generally, rather unsuccessful in identifying the *precise* role of financial variables and in providing useful forecasting relationships, most studies put general emphasis on the role of financial variables.

On *a priori* grounds the financial variables which seem likely to influence starts are:

i) the mortgage rate;
ii) the discount on government guaranteed mortgages;
iii) the required deposit (equity) on a typical house purchase and other non-rate elements;
iv) the flow supply of finance to mortgage lenders.

The mortgage rate has already been discussed. It remains only to examine the hypothesis that the interest elasticity of starts should be relatively high for the following reasons:

a) Houses are long-lived assets, and thus the desired *stock* of houses is likely to be interest sensitive, and
b) The annual flow increase in the stock (a function of current

177

TABLE A. THE STOCK OF HOUSING

	Estimated Stock of Houses[1] First Quarter (Thousands of units)	Per cent Increase from Previous Year
1960	58,326	—
1961	59,151	1.41
1962	60,023	1.47
1963	61,041	1.70
1964	62,232	1.95
1965	63,371	1.83
1966	64,472	1.74
1967	65,249	1.21
1968	66,170	1.41
1969	67,384	1.83
1970	68,631	1.85

1. Figures for 1960 and 1970 are Census estimates and include mobile homes. Estimates for intervening years assume a constant rate of net removals over the 10 year interval, and gross additions equal to the number of new starts, including mobile home shipments, during the previous calendar year.

Source: L. Gramley [34].

and lagged starts) is typically between 1-2 per cent of the stock (see Table A).

It is also the case that, because of the existence of a rental market which is fairly well organised, house purchases may rather readily be postponed while interest costs form a larger part of rental expenditure. There is some econometric evidence to support the hypothesis of high interest elasticity. References are to be found in Gramley [36]. Since discounts are a way of raising the effective mortgage rate while leaving the market rate unaltered, the remarks concerning interest elasticity refer—a fortiori—to any variation in discounts.

The schematic account on pages 175-177 implies that the mortgage rate adjusts slowly to excess demand/supply situations. Precisely why this should be the case is not known. Nevertheless there are many possible explanatory factors. Among them are:

    i) the existence of usury laws in most states—more than half with ceilings less than 9 per cent;

    ii) social pressures against high mortgage rates;

    iii) the ability of lenders to tighten non-price terms in the typical mortgage contracts, e.g. by:

        a) requiring higher standards of credit worthiness;

        b) shortening repayment periods; or

        c) demanding higher initial deposits.

Thus far published econometric studies have not succeeded in separating the influence of non-rate variables from rates, though there is some evidence that starts are significantly influenced by changes in *(iii) (b)* and *(iii) (c)* as well as by the mortgage rates; cf. for example Brady [8], Huang [52] and Silber [92]. On balance it seems reasonable to argue that both price

178

and non-price elements play a part in the response of starts. This, of course, implies that the market is not cleared in the usual sense, and this in turn implies that the margin between mortgage rates and rates on competing assets should tend to narrow as rates rise. Since all US rates exhibit a strong upward trend over the last ten years, this is not an easy matter to establish. Chart B, however, does not contradict the hypothesis and, for some periods, provides support.

If the time series are difficult to interpret on the issue of cyclical movements in rate margins, they seem extremely clear on the relationship between mortgage borrowing and residential construction expenditure. This was displayed in Chart 6 to the main text. This chart, though its moving average basis must obscure the niceties of timing, nevertheless powerfully suggests:

i) a very close correlation between mortgage borrowing and resi-
    dential construction; and

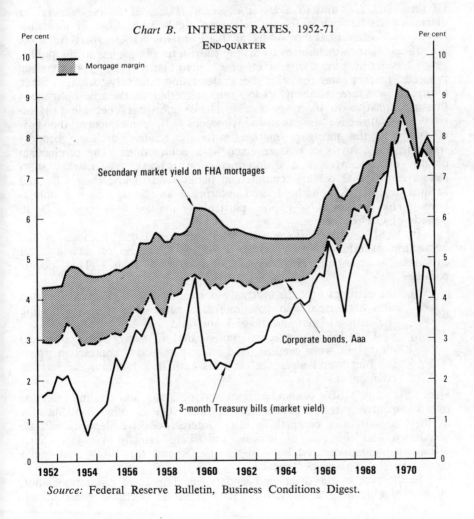

Chart B. INTEREST RATES, 1952-71
END-QUARTER

Source: Federal Reserve Bulletin, Business Conditions Digest.

ii) that the financial series leads the expenditures series typically by one or two quarters.

Since mortgage lending depends upon the flow supply of funds to lending institutions and their portfolio choices, the supply side of the mortgage market is examined in the following section. The form, extent and consequences of Federal government intervention in the market are considered in a later section.

THE SUPPLY OF FUNDS TO THE MORTGAGE MARKET

The principal (non-governmental) lenders in the mortgage market are, in order of importance (Table B):

- *i)* the savings and loan associations (SL's);
- *ii)* the commercial banks;
- *iii)* the mutual savings banks (MSB's); and
- *iv)* the life offices.

Of these *(ii), (iv)* and to a lesser degree *(iii)* are, of course, general or diversified lenders while *(i)* are relatively highly specialised in mortgage lending. Moreover, as borrowers all these intermediaries, apart from the life offices, finance themselves by selling short-term obligations to the public.

Consider now the stylised facts of a United States cycle. As expansion proceeds, market rates rise with short rates rising relatively to long. Since mortgage rates are relatively sticky, rates on other marketable obligations thus rise relative to mortgage rates. Hence mortgages become progressively less attractive as expansion proceeds. In consequence, the flow of funds to the mortgage market suffers a relative decline. Broadly speaking the analysis can be reversed in a contraction. The mechanism of this decline involves a disintermediation process. As market short rates rise above Q ceilings, commercial banks tend to lose their CDs and savings deposits as households and enterprises switch into market obligations. This process is, of course, particularly marked with larger CDs in periods of Q effectiveness.

Both SL's and MSB's are typically unable, either because of the imposition of rate ceilings or because of the stickiness of their interest earnings, to compete effectively against market rates. This occurs because:

- *a)* the earnings on their mortgage portfolios are, in effect, a weighted sum of current and past mortgage rates, the weights reflecting the dating of past mortgage loans; and
- *b)* in United States practice (unlike that in some other countries) mortgages are a genuine fixed-interest long-term contract in which the borrower hedges not only his cash flow but also the interest component.

Hence SL's and MSB's cannot, without making losses and eroding reserves, offer competitive rates on shares and deposits. On the other hand, insofar as they do *not* offer competitive rates, interest-sensitive deposits will be withdrawn and the rate of deposit and share growth curtailed. Such disintermediation occurred both in the 1950s and the 1960s, but much more severely in the latter decade.

In the case of the diversified lenders, the impact of disintermediation on mortgage lending tends to be exacerbated by portfolio substitutions.

180

TABLE B. MORTGAGE TRANSACTIONS
Seasonally adjusted annual rates[1]

	1959 II	1959 III	1959 IV	1960 I	1960 II	1960 III	1960 IV	1961 I	1961 II	1961 III	1961 IV	1962 I	1962 II
Mortgage lending by: 1. Commercial banks	n.a.	2.4	2.0	0.4	0.8	1.2	0.4	—	2.8	1.8	2.2	2.4	4.7
2. Non-bank financial sector	n.a.	11.2	8.8	8.4	10.0	10.8	9.6	8.4	12.0	10.8	12.2	10.6	13.7
3. FHLB lending to savings & loan associations	n.a.	1.2	1.2	-2.4	0.8	—	0.8	-2.0	1.6	0.9	1.2	0.3	1.2

	1965 I	1965 II	1965 III	1965 IV	1966 I	1966 II	1966 III	1966 IV	1967 I	1967 II	1967 III	1967 IV	1968 I
Mortgage lending by: 1. Commercial banks	2.5	2.8	3.7	3.4	2.6	3.0	1.9	1.9	1.0	1.4	3.4	4.0	2.9
2. Savings & loan associations	7.9	7.6	7.4	7.3	7.5	3.4	0.1	0.6	3.1	5.2	7.6	7.8	7.2
3. Mutual savings banks	2.6	2.5	2.8	2.8	1.8	1.1	1.8	1.7	1.9	1.9	1.7	1.6	1.0
4. Life offices	1.7	1.0	1.0	1.0	1.5	0.7	0.4	-0.1	0.5	-0.3	-0.9	-0.9	-0.2
5. Federal agencies	0.9	0.5	1.0	-0.1	0.4	-0.6	-0.9	-1.1	0.3	1.3	-0.2	0.1	3.9
6. FHLB lending to savings & loan associations	1.5	1.5	0.5	-0.8	2.8	1.8	1.1	-2.0	-2.8	-6.3	-1.1	0.1	3.7
7. Sum of 5 + 6	2.4	2.0	1.5	-0.9	3.2	1.2	0.2	-3.1	-2.5	-5.0	-1.3	0.2	

	1968 IV	1969 I	1969 II	1969 III	1969 IV	1970 I	1970 II	1970 III	1970 IV	1971 I	1971 II	1971 III	1971 IV
Mortgage lending by: 1. Commercial banks	4.0	4.3	3.3	2.1	2.1	1.0	0.6	1.1	0.9	3.7	7.0	6.0	n.a.
2. Savings & loan associations	8.5	9.1	9.5	7.0	5.5	3.0	4.9	9.3	11.7	12.6	18.3	18.8	n.a.
3. Mutual savings banks	2.1	1.6	1.5	1.1	1.4	0.2	1.1	1.1	1.3	0.9	1.0	1.3	n.a.
4. Life offices	-0.9	-0.7	-0.6	-0.8	-2.1	-1.3	-1.2	-1.2	-1.8	-1.5	-2.1	-2.2	n.a.
5. Federal agencies	1.9	0.9	1.1	0.7	0.4	0.6	0.9	1.7	1.0	1.4	0.9	-1.1	n.a.
6. FHLB lending to savings & loan associations	0.3	2.9	3.1	5.3	4.8	4.4	0.8	0.3	-0.2	-1.2	-10.8	0.7	n.a.
7. Sum of 5 + 6	2.2	3.8	4.2	6.0	5.2	5.0	1.7	2.0	0.8	0.2	-9.9	-0.4	n.a.

1. Seasonally adjusted data not available before 1961 III.
Source: Federal Reserve Bulletin.

Typically, in periods of restraint, commercial banks seek to maintain their lending to non-financial business by:

a) selling or reducing their rate of acquisition of Federal and state and local government obligations;

b) reducing their rate of new lending to finance companies; and

c) reducing their rate of mortgage acquisition.

MSB's were, until about 1967, relatively highly specialised in the mortgage market. Since 1967 they have, by contrast, moved into corporate securities. Though there is not great evidence of adverse switching by MSB's in 1969, this development clearly increases the probability of such adverse portfolio adjustments in the future. Finally, life offices, who acquired residential mortgages at an average annual rate of $2.6 billion from 1964-66 have virtually abandoned this form of lending: purchases in recent years have averaged only about $0.4 billion.

Thus the cyclical process itself, in view of the relative changes in market rates which accompany it:

i) tends to encourage disintermediation and reduce the flow of finance to institutions which engage in mortgage lending in the upswing; while

ii) this process has been exacerbated on occasions and particularly in 1966-69 by the impact of Regulation Q ceilings.

The result has been cyclical fluctuations in both the flow of funds to the leading intermediaries and in the flow of mortgage lending.

FEDERAL INTERVENTION IN THE MORTGAGE MARKET

There is a considerable extent of Federal regulation and intervention (direct and indirect) in the mortgage market. This can be classified in two main forms.[4]

i) action designed to improve the structure of the market: for example by developing a secondary market in mortgages; and

ii) action designed to offset the impact of fluctuations in the flow of private finance to the financial institution operating in the market.

In addition, Regulation Q ceiling rates on small CDs and time and savings deposits have been used to "protect" SL's and MSB's from the consequence of excessive competition by commercial banks. Federal intervention

---

4. The operations of the various Federal government agencies straddle these activities.

Generally speaking the Veterans' Administration (VA) Guarantees and the Federal Housing Administration (FHA) insurance schemes reduce risk and improve marketability. Their impact in this respect is buttressed by the work of the Federal National Mortgage Association (FNMA or "Fannie Mae") and the Government National Mortgage Association (GNMA or "Ginnie Mae") which provide a secondary market for mortgages guaranteed by the VA, FHA, and Farmers' Home Administration Board.

The Federal Home Loan Banks (FHLB) were created in 1932 to provide credit for private non-bank mortgage lending institutions, e.g. savings and loan associations and mutual savings banks. Initially, the FHLB's seem to have been conceived as specialised lenders of last resort. In recent years their activities have expanded considerably and expansion in their lending to SL's has become of increasing importance in offsetting fluctuations in fund flows to these institutions.

typically takes the form of the direct purchase of mortgages by Federal agencies and the indirect purchases represented by loans made by the FHLB in the SL's. The relevant information (from quarterly estimates of flows of funds) is set out in Table B, which covers three periods of steep decline in mortgage borrowing: 1959-60; 1965-66; and 1969-70. The inferences are too clear to need extensive comment. The main points are:

  i)   the growing sensitivity of SL share inflows—as measured by the percentage decline in their rate of growth over the relevant periods;

  ii) the lesser—but nevertheless considerable—declines in the rate of growth in MSB deposits;

  iii) the considerable increase in the scale of Federal intervention and, in particular, of FHLB lending to SL's.

SOME CONCLUSIONS

As indicated, fluctuations in residential construction in recent years have been procyclical rather than anticyclical. For example, it can be argued that the policy-generated mini-recession of 1966-67 was conducted only at the cost of a sharp fall in construction expenditure and a near financial crisis in the SL industry. It can also be argued that similar consequences might well have arisen in 1969 had not the scale of Federal support for the mortgage market very markedly increased. The present position of the United States authorities appears to be that:

  i)   recent fluctuations in the rates of residential construction are on a scale unacceptable on social grounds; but

  ii) some degree of cyclical fluctuation must be accepted; and

  iii) fluctuations may be beneficial if the housing investment cycles revert to their earlier, relatively anticyclical timing.

Essentially, events in the 1960s demonstrate that, as the economy approaches a situation of overall excess demand (1965-68), the business sector is typically able to compete financial (and hence real) resources away from the housing sector through the interest rate mechanism. This in turn suggests that, where market rates are permitted to vary widely during the cycle, sensitive responses by the housing sector can, in the near future, only be mitigated by Federal support since they result basically from the institutional structure of the mortgage market. That structure could scarcely be modified rapidly even if general agreement existed (which is probably not the case) concerning the appropriate modifications.

On the assumption that Federal support for the mortgage market in an attempt to reduce fluctuations will increase, it follows that, for any given degree of demand restraint, either:

  a)   interest rates will have to rise further in order to reduce other demand components, including expenditure on consumer durables and business investment in fixed capital; or

  b)   more extensive use will have to be made of anticyclical fiscal policy.

Moreover, it seems likely, if (b) is excluded, that since investment in housing responds rather rapidly to monetary policy, there will be some lengthening of the lags in the response of aggregate demand to monetary action and a decline in the impact on demand of any given change in interest rates. This weakening of the impact of monetary policy would require a greater rise in rates for any given degree of restraint. Accordingly the important conclusions are:

  i) increasing Federal intervention in the mortgage market will result in the need to tolerate wider fluctuations in market interest rates;

  ii) the shift in FOMC policy towards greater emphasis on monetary aggregates and its likely consequence that interest rates will tend to fluctuate more makes acceptance of these wider fluctuations more probable; and

  iii) the growth in Federal intervention is likely to lengthen the lags in monetary policy.

Appendix IV

OPERATION TWIST
AND US CAPITAL MOVEMENTS

INTRODUCTION

Following the recession of 1960-61, the US authorities attempted to maintain a general position of monetary ease while at the same time keeping short-term rates at a level in relation to rates ruling overseas which would reduce the rate of capital outflow from the United States. Since monetary ease entails cyclically low long rates, the first requirement of any such policy was to modify (twist) the rate structure so that any given level of long-term rates would be associated with a higher level of short rates than might typically—in the light of past experiences—be expected to prevail. Accordingly, the proximate objective of "Operation Twist" may be defined as being to modify the rate structure so as to reduce the yield gap (=long rate *minus* short rate) prevailing at any given level of the long rate. In the same way the ultimate objective of Operation Twist may be defined as being to reduce the rate of capital outflow from the United States from the level which would have obtained in the absence of any change in the rate structure.

THE TECHNIQUE OF OPERATION TWIST

An increase in the extent of intermediation will generally be associated with a relative strengthening of the long market against the short. Furthermore, economic theories of the rate structure, particularly those which derive from the Hicks [47] version of the expectations theory, suggest that the yield gap, frequently called the "long-short differential", should be a function of the distribution of outstanding debt between "long" and "short" maturities.[1] It is therefore not surprising that Operation Twist, which appears to have occurred through 1961-64, relied in the main upon:

i)   the encouragement of intermediation; and
ii) the modification of the maturity pattern of outstanding Federal debt in a way tending to raise short rates relative to long.

The main elements in *(i)* were:

a)   the increase in Regulation Q maxima which increased the ability of the banks to compete for time deposits;

---

1. In theory, "debt" in this context should include at least all public sector debt. In practice, data problems commonly restrict analyses to consideration of central government debt.

185

b) the exemption of time deposits of foreign governments and certain foreign institutions from Q maxima for a period of three years; and

c) a reduction in the reserve ratio required against time deposits.

The chronology of these events is set out in Appendix I.

As indicated, an increase in Q maxima typically enables the banks to compete more effectively with thrift institutions in general and savings and loan associations in particular, as well as with market obligations. Since shifts of funds *from* thrift institutions *to* banks must be expected to entail asset effects which operate against the authorities' objectives over this period, the techniques employed to increase bank competitiveness were probably to some extent constrained. Nevertheless, it is clear that:

a) 1961-64 did display a considerable growth in bank intermediation; while

b) the flow of funds to thrift institutions was well maintained.[2]

The observed growth in intermediation is, however, in part simply a reflection of the cyclical process which, for example, generated a sharp fall in short rates in 1960 before the Federal Reserve had embarked upon the "Twist" policies. To allocate the growth of intermediation in 1961-64 between these policies and the usual cyclical responses would require a well specified model with good coefficient estimates. No such model is available. It seems, however, safe to say that not all of the observed expansion in intermediation is attributable to Federal Reserve attempts to twist the rate structure.

At the same time as the Federal Reserve acted so as to promote intermediation, it modified its open market techniques by abandoning "bills only" and purchasing coupon issues. Moreover, over the same period, the US Treasury concentrated its borrowing requirements, as far as possible, at the short end of the maturity spectrum. The net result of these complementary actions on the maturity composition of Federal debt is set out in Table C.[3]

The Effects on the Rate Curve

There are three types of information relevant to the assessment of the impact of these techniques on the rate curve or, more precisely, the long-short differential. They consist of:

a) evidence from econometrically estimated equations specified by reference to a theory of the term structure;

b) evidence derived from equations which, while relatively empty of economic hypotheses, can be used to forecast the rate curve or changes in it;

c) inspection of time series.

Under (*a*) the literature is extremely extensive and the survey reported

---

2. It can be, and has been, argued that this result constituted something of a triumph for Regulation Q in that mortgage rates declined and the flow of funds to the mortgage market was well maintained.

3. It is important to note that these figures are somewhat artificial in that they take no account of the maturity distribution within defined maturity classes. More refined data is given in Modigliani and Sutch [78]. In fact the changes in maturity pattern were small.

TABLE C.   MARKETABLE SECURITIES HELD BY PRIVATE INVESTORS

END-MONTH, PER VALUE

| | 1960 | | | | | | | |
| | March | | June | | September | | December | |
	$ bill.	%	$ bill.	%	$ bill.	%	$ bill.	%
Maturity: within 1 year....	54.7	35.9	48.5	32.4	53.3	35.2	57.1	37.2
1-5 years	61.8	40.5	64.5	43.1	60.6	40.0	59.2	38.6
5-10 years	18.2	11.9	18.5	12.4	19.5	12.9	15.9	10.3
Over 10 years ...	17.7	11.6	18.1	12.1	18.0	11.9	21.3	13.9
[of which over 20 years] ...							[9.8]	[6.4]
Total..............	152.5	100.0	149.5	100.0	151.4	100.0	153.5	100.0

| | 1961 | | | | | | | |
| | March | | June | | September | | December | |
	$ bill.	%	$ bill.	%	$ bill.	%	$ bill.	%
Maturity: within 1 year....	57.7	38.1	63.3	41.8	65.1	41.8	65.5	41.3
1-5 years	51.4	33.9	47.9	31.6	51.4	33.0	55.8	35.2
5-10 years	23.4	15.4	21.7	14.3	18.1	11.6	16.0	10.1
Over 10 years ...	19.0	12.5	18.5	12.2	21.1	13.5	21.3	13.4
[of which over 20 years] ...							[11.3]	[7.1]
Total..............	151.5	100.0	151.4	100.0	155.7	100.0	158.6	100.0

| | 1962 | | | | | | | |
| | March | | June | | September | | December | |
	$ bill.	%	$ bill.	%	$ bill.	%	$ bill.	%
Maturity: within 1 year....	67.8	42.8	68.1	43.1	66.0	41.6	67.9	41.8
1-5 years	49.5	31.3	47.4	30.1	46.7	29.4	49.4	30.4
5-10 years	19.4	12.2	21.6	13.7	27.3	17.2	29.2	18,0
Over 10 years ...	21.7	13.7	20.4	4.9	5.8	11.7	16.1	9.9
[of which over 20 years] ...	[12.7]	[8.0]	[12.7]	[8.1]	[12.9]	[8.1]	[12.9]	[7.9]
Total..............	158.3	100.0	157.4	100.0	158.8	100.0	162.5	100.0

| | 1963 | | | | | | | |
| | March | | June | | September | | December | |
	$ bill.	%	$ bill.	%	$ bill.	%	$ bill.	%
Maturity: within 1 year....	62.1	38.3	61.9	38.6	62.3	38.8	65.0	40.1
1-5 years	49.2	30.4	48.1	30.0	45.4	28.3	47.9	29.5
5-10 years	32.8	20.2	32.3	20.1	33.8	21.1	30.5	18.8
Over 10 years ...	17.9	11.0	18.0	11.3	18.9	11.8	18.7	11.6
[of which over 20 years] ...	[13.0]	[8.0]	[11.8]	[7.4]	[12.8]	[8.0]	[12.6]	[7.8]
Total..............	162.1	100.0	160.4	100.0	160.5	100.0	162.1	100.0

| | 1964 | | | | | | | |
| | March | | June | | September | | December | |
	$ bill.	%	$ bill.	%	$ bill.	%	$ bill.	%
Maturity: within 1 year....	63.2	38.9	61.6	38.6	61.1	37.8	65.3	40.0
1-5 years	49.3	30.3	48.8	30.6	42.7	26.4	48.0	29.4
5-10 years	30.8	19.0	30.1	18.9	37.7	23.3	31.5	19.3
Over 10 years ...	19.2	11.9	19.1	11.9	20.1	12.5	18.4	11.3
[of which over 20 years] ...	[13.1]	[8.1]	[13.0]	[8.1]	[14.0]	[8.7]	[13.9]	[8.5]
Total..............	162.4	100.0	159.6	100.0	161.5	100.0	163.3	100.0

Source: Federal Reserve Bulletin.

187

here must be incomplete. Under *(b)* two references are made in this report. Consideration of *(a)* necessarily calls for a brief review of the theory of the rate curve which will be set out below.[4]

THE THEORY OF THE RATE CURVE

On the hypothesis of rational behaviour, any portfolio manager will adjust his holdings of financial assets until the expected rate of return (including expected capital gains or losses) from each type of asset, adjusted for the "uncertainty" involved, are equal. To simplify matters, assume the portfolio consists entirely of government debt. Further assume that the total of debt which is to be held by the representative portfolio owner is D_j. Then:

$$D_j \equiv C_j + S_j + L_j \tag{1}$$

where:

$C_j \equiv$ demand government debt (currency);
$S_j \equiv$ short-term debt;
$L_j \equiv$ long-term debt.

The total amount of debt, D_j, is clearly determined by the budget restraint of the individual. Hence only *two* of the three elements on the right-hand side of (1) are independent. It thus follows that:

$$X_1 = \frac{S_j}{D_j} \text{ and } X_2 \equiv \frac{L_j}{D_j}$$

are choice variables and $X_o \equiv \dfrac{C_j}{D_j}$ is then determined from the condition:

$$X_o + X_1 + X_2 \equiv 1 \tag{2}$$

The problem for the portfolio manager (in this example) is to choose X_1, X_2 so as to maximise utility, where utility is a function of the expected rate of return and "riskiness" of the selected portfolio. It is also clear that if D_j is replaced by W_j (the total wealth of the portfolio owner) and if other financial assets (e.g. equities) are admitted into the analysis, the problem is capable of generalisation to portfolio choices as a whole. Clearly, given this description of the problem, we must expect the chosen X_1 and X_2 to be functions of:

i) the expected rates of return on S and L; and
ii) the index of "riskiness" attached to S and L.

If now *all* managers are rational (in the sense defined) and have identical expectations regarding the capital gains on long-term debt, equilibrium entails:

$$r_1 = r_2 + g_2 + l \tag{3}$$

where:

$r_1 \equiv$ expected rate of return on short debt over the holding period;
$r_2 \equiv$ market yield on long debt;
$g_2 \equiv$ expected percentage capital gain (or loss) on long debt over the holding period; and
$l \equiv$ a liquidity premium on long debt due to the greater riskiness of its expected holding-period return $(r_2 + g_2)$.

---

4. For a fuller survey of this theory consult Malkiel [71] and Telser [94].

So far no index of "riskiness" has been defined. It is now common, however, following Markowitz [72] and Tobin [97] and [98] to make use of a one-period portfolio selection model in which portfolio managers identify the "expected" return on the portfolio with the mathematical expectation (mean), and "riskiness" with the variance. If this is done, we have:

$$\widehat{r_1} = r_2 + \widehat{g_2} + [X_1, \ X_2, \ \sigma_{11}^2, \ \sigma_{12}^2, \ \sigma_{22}^2] \tag{4}$$

where:

$\sigma_{11}^2 \equiv$ variance of $\widehat{r_1}$
$\sigma_{22}^2 \equiv$ variance of $(r_2 + \widehat{g_2})$
$\sigma_{12}^2 \equiv$ co-variance.

The meaning of (3) and (4) may need a little explanation. In the *individual* experiment the manager chooses X_1, X_2 given $\widehat{r_1}$ and $r_2 + \widehat{g_2}$. In the market experiment all managers together ($\equiv$ the private sector) *have* to hold debt in the proportions X_1, X_2 determined by the authorities' debt policy. In this case it is the rates (r_1, r_2) which are determined by the requirement of equilibrium. Thus rewriting (3) to yield a single dependent variable (the long-short differential) gives:

$$r_2 - \widehat{r_1} \equiv \begin{array}{c} \text{expected} \\ \text{long-short} \\ \text{differential} \end{array} = -\widehat{g_2} - l \tag{5}$$

which states that the yield differential depends upon the expected capital loss $(-\widehat{g_2})$ and the liquidity premium which, since l depends on X_1 and X_2, gives the yield differential as a function of debt policy. These points are explained more fully below and in Rowan and O'Brien [87].

As is shown in Rowan and O'Brien [87] and [88], this approach easily yields a rate structure equation of the form:

$$r_2 = \widehat{r_1} - a_1\widehat{g_2} + a_2X_1 \ [\sigma_{11}^2 - \sigma_{12}^2] + a_3X_2 \ [\sigma_{22}^2 - \sigma_{12}^2] \tag{6}$$

where: a_1 is a function of taxation policy and reflects the relative rate of taxation on coupon income and capital gains; a_2, a_3 are functions of both taxation policy (as defined) and the parameters of the (assumed) utility function. Generally we expect $a_1 > 1$ since capital gains are typically taxed at a lower rate than income. We also expect a rise in the proportion of long debt (X_2) to *raise* the yield differential and a rise in the proportion of short debt (X_1) to reduce it.

Since $\dfrac{\delta \ (r_2 - \widehat{r_1})}{\delta X_2} = a_3 \ [\sigma_{22}^2 - \sigma_{12}^2]$ this suggests that we should

expect $a_3 > 0$ on the plausible assumption that $\sigma_{22}^2 > \sigma_{12}^2$. Similarly we expect $a_2 > 0$ since if $\sigma_{22}^2 > \sigma_{12}^2$ then $\sigma_{11}^2 < \sigma_{12}^2$.

If we now assume:

$$\widehat{r_1} = r_1$$

that is, the expected short-term yield equals the current short-term yield, then (6) can obviously be used to yield an equation for the long-short differential. That is

$$r_2 - r_1 \equiv \text{long-short differential}$$

$$= - a_1\widehat{g_2} + a_2X_1 \ [\sigma_{11}^2 - \sigma_{12}^2] \\ + a_3X_3 \ [\sigma_{22}^2 - \sigma_{12}^2] \tag{7}$$

189

which shows that the differential is a function of:

1. expectations;
2. the risk indices $(\sigma_{ij}{}^2)$;
3. the maturity pattern of the debt (X_1, X_2).

To be made operational, this model must be treated as follows:

i) X_1, X_2 must be made observable. This is usually done by the simplification of identifying

$$D \equiv \sum_{j=1}^{j=n} D_j \quad \text{with central government debt;}$$

ii) X_1, X_2 must either be explained (as must D) by debt supply functions or treated as exogenous (the typical procedure of most investigators);

iii) $\widehat{g}_2$ must be defined in terms of observable variables. This is usually done by hypothesizing:

1. $-\widehat{g}_2 = f[r_2 - r_2{}^*]$ where $r_2{}^*$ is the historical expectation of r_2;
2. making $r_2{}^*$ some distributed lag function of:
   a) past values of r_1 (as is done by Modigliani and Sutch and Gibbs); or
   b) past values of r_2 (as is done by Rowan and O'Brien);

iv) the $\sigma_{ij}{}^2$ must also either:

1. be defined in terms of observable variables and consistently with the prior specification of r^* (Gibbs and Rowan and O'Brien); or
2. be implicitly treated as constraints (Modigliani and Sutch and de Leeuw).

Once these steps have been taken, algebraic manipulations of the equation yield a reduced-form regression equation with specified error properties. From this it is, in principle, possible to obtain estimates of:

$$\frac{\delta(r_2 - r_1)}{\delta X_i} \equiv \text{response of yield differential to (exogenous) changes in maturity patterns.}$$

The necessary procedures and their interpretations are fully set out in Rowan and O'Brien and Modigliani and Sutch.

Slightly more complex hypotheses, involving lagged adjustment of private sector portfolios, extend the reduced forms by including terms in:

$$\frac{\delta(r_2 - r_1)}{\delta \Delta X_i} \equiv \text{response of yield differential to a change in the rate}$$

of change of the maturity pattern.

The volume of work undertaken with rate curve models along lines similar to this is very considerable. No very complete review can be attempted here. Thus far, however, no investigator has succeeded in demonstrating any significant value for $\dfrac{\delta(r_2 - r_1)}{\delta X_i}$ from models of this type. Moreover, there are some theoretical difficulties with the best known US studies which cover the relevant period—those of Modigliani and Sutch [78] and [76].[5]

---

5. See, for example, Telser [94] and Wallace [99].

A suitably cautious conclusion is that, apart from de Leeuw [17], who finds a small transitory effect (i.e. an almost significant coefficient for $\dfrac{\delta\,(r_2 - r_1)}{\delta\,\Delta\,X_i}$) there is no evidence from rate structure equations of a measurable impact on the long-short differential of changes in the proportion of debt outstanding.[6]

An alternative approach is to develop a theory which requires no hypothesis about expectations, but merely a hypothesis—typically of the error learning type—about the way in which they are revised. The seminal work here is due to Meiselman [75] whose basic regression equation is:[7]

$$r_1\,(t+n)_t - r_1\,(t+n)_{t-1} = a_n + b_n E\,(t)$$

where: $E\,(t) = r_1\,(t)_t - r_1\,(t)_{t-1}$ and
where: $r_1\,(t+n)_t \equiv$ the rate on a one (short) period loan expected at time t to rule in period $t+n$
and $\quad r_1\,(t)_t \quad =$ the rate on a one period loan expected at time t to rule in period t, i.e. the current short rate.

This hypothesis can be extended to include the debt structure (as for example by Wallance [99]) by writing:

$$r_1\,(t+n)_t - r_1\,(t+n)_{t-1} = a_n^1 + b_n^1\,E\,(t) \qquad (8)$$
$$+\,c_n\;\frac{M\,(t+n)_t}{M\,(t)_t} - \frac{M\,(t+n)_1}{M\,(t-1)_{t-1}}$$

where: $M\,(t+n)_t \equiv$ outstanding US government marketable securities at time t which mature on or after time $t+n$.

Wallace found small but significant value for c_n for selected values of n. It is his results—and perhaps those of de Leeuw [17] and Scott [91]—which provide the only theoretically based econometric evidence for statistically significant values of $\dfrac{\delta\,(r_2 - r_1)}{\delta\,\Delta\,X_i}$.

Forecasting Equations

A simple forecasting[8] equation can be used to explain the rate structure. Thus we might write:

$$r_2\,(t) - r_2\,(t-1) = a_1 + \sum_{i=o}^{i=n} b_i\,r_1\,(t-i) - r_1\,(t-i-1) \qquad (9)$$

where the b_i defines some unspecified distributed lag function. If b_i for all $i = 1, 2... n$ are set to zero, (9) reduces to the equation employed by Hamburger and Latta [42] which is:

$$r_2\,(t) - r_2\,(t-1) = a_1 + b_o\,[r_1\,(t) - r_1\,(t-1)] \qquad (10)$$

---

6. Nor do the residuals suggest any significant influence for elements of "Twist" other than maturity change.

7. At the cost of introducing some spurious correlation, this equation can be transformed into:
$$r_2\,(t) - r_2\,(t-1) = a^{11}_n + b^{11}_n\,E\,(t)$$
and thus into a rate structure form.

8. The term "forecasting" is not used in any critical sense. It simply implies that the underlying economic theory does not impose restraints on the b_i of their distribution.

This equation can, of course, readily be converted into an equation explaining $r_2(t)$. If this is done it reduces to a special case of the reduced form of the rate structure equations but with the terms involving the X_i and σ_{ii}^2 omitted.[9] Forecasting equations of this type perform relatively satisfactorily. Indeed it is generally the case that, when the terms in X_i and σ_{ii}^2 are omitted, the explanatory power of the Hamburger forecasting equation is statistically not inferior to apparently more sophisticated equations containing distributed lag expectation hypotheses of the form used by Modigliani and Sutch [78] and [76], Rowan and O'Brien [87] and [88] or Gibbs [35].

Apart from suggesting that economists have, as yet, no very reliable theory of interest rate expectations, Hamburger's equation can be used as an admittedly rather weak test of the impact of Operation Twist. To do this the equation to predict the yield gap can be written:

$$r_2(t) - r_1(t) = a_1 + (b_o - 1)\ r_1(t) - b_o r_1\ (t-1) + r_2\ (t-1) \qquad (11)$$

The parameter b_o has no precise theoretical interpretation. It summarises, however, the structure and typical response of the market. Where the incidence of changes in Regulation Q maxima, reserve requirements and modification of maturity patterns are occurring as part of Operation Twist, some change in b_o should therefore be expected. Some rather weak evidence concerning Operation Twist is obtained by using the equation to forecast the yield gap and then examining the residuals to see whether they are generally negative in the relevant period. The Hamburger and Latta equation is used below to predict the US yield gap from the second quarter of 1959 to the fourth quarter of 1966. The residuals are also plotted on Chart C.

The fit of the Hamburger-Latta equation is impressive. However, examination of the residuals from 1960.IV to 1963.IV does not suggest any great dominance of negative errors such as we would expect if debt and other policies had significantly and persistently modified the yield gap. It would indeed be generous to suggest that there is any strong evidence of an influence of debt policy. Furthermore, what evidence there is suggests that if there was any such influence, it probably occurred in the first half of 1961 and almost certainly did not exceed one-tenth of one percentage point. It should, of course, be emphasised that this test is relatively weak largely because, in economic terms, b_o is undefined and therefore one cannot be sure how b_o should respond to the set of measures constituting Operation Twist.

INSPECTION OF TIME SERIES

While theoretically specified econometric rate structure equations yield small and unreliable estimates of the impact of Operation Twist, the Hamburger and Latta equation suggests a short-lived change not exceeding 0.1 per cent. A similar (very rough) estimate can be derived from the residual of the Modigliani and Sutch equation with the X_i terms omitted. A final method of looking for the impact of the policy is to attempt to draw inferences from the time series themselves. This is the most subjective and potentially most dangerous method, since what is sought is an estimate of a partial derivative and what is observed is a total derivative. Never-

---

9. For a simple explanation see Hamburger [39].

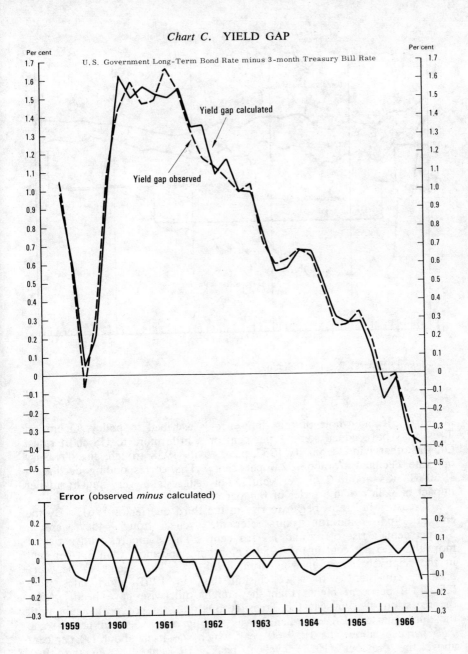

Chart C. YIELD GAP

U.S. Government Long-Term Bond Rate minus 3-month Treasury Bill Rate

Yield gap calculated

Yield gap observed

Error (observed *minus* calculated)

theless, it may help us to set at least an upper bound to the impact of policy.

Chart D shows the behaviour of selected interest rates during the period 1960-64; and Chart E shows the behaviour of selected rates over the longer period covering the cycles of 1953-54, 1957-58 and 1960-62. From these Charts it is clear that the Treasury bill rate, which fell below 1 per cent in both the 1954 and 1958 troughs, remained at 2 per cent

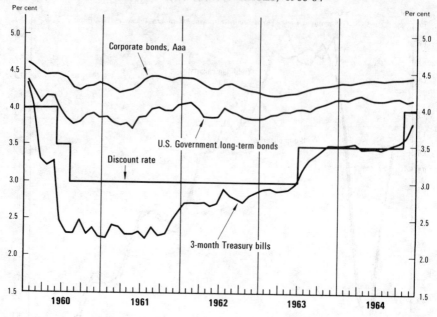

Source: Federal Reserve Bulletin.

in 1961. If the whole of this difference is ascribed to policy, Operation Twist may have added some 1 per cent or a little more to US short rates. On the other hand, from its 1957 peak to its 1958 trough, the Treasury bill rate declined by about 2.6 per cent. The corresponding decline in 1960-61 was about 2.25 per cent. This suggests a very much smaller impact of policy of the order of 0.4 per cent.

Treasury bill rates began to rise in the third quarter of 1961. By the end of 1964—some four years after the cyclical trough—they were at 3.8 per cent, a rise of around 1.7 per cent. This compares with a rise of more than 2.5 per cent in the 1954-57 upswing and more than 3.4 per cent in the relatively short upswing from 1958-60. This seems to be, very broadly, consistent with a conclusion that, in 1961, short rates were 0.5 — 1.0 per cent higher than they might otherwise have been. After the recession of 1960-61, the Treasury bill rate did not peak again until the third quarter of 1966 when it was slightly below 5.5 per cent—some 0.75 per cent above the 1959-60 peak which was itself about 1.0 per cent above the previous (1957) cyclical peak. In general, from the 1961 trough through 1964, corporate bond yields were stable or slightly falling, municipal bond yields were typically falling, and Treasury bond yields were only slightly rising. Thus, the rise in the short rate after the third quarter of 1961 was not, as a whole, reflected in the behaviour of long rates.

In short, whether one looks at initial levels, recession declines or increases in upswings, the Treasury bill rate seems to have been between 0.4 and 1.0 per cent *above* what past experience in similar cyclical phases

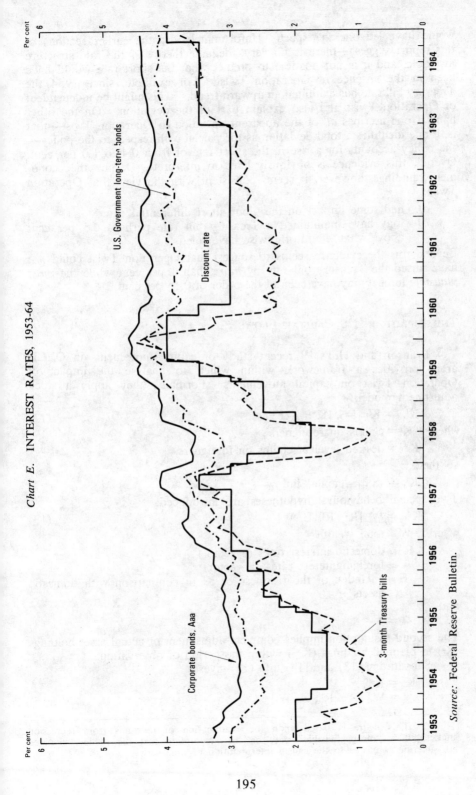

Chart E. INTEREST RATES, 1953-64

Source: Federal Reserve Bulletin.

195

would have led one to expect. Unfortunately—as the earlier sections of this report suggest—there is no very adequate theory of the rate structure available, and it is not possible to predict what the short rate would have been in the absence of Operation Twist. For example, since 1954 the Treasury bill rate has exhibited an upward trend. This might be independent of Operation Twist and also explain part of the deviation. On the other hand if one ascribes *all* of the apparent deviation to Operation Twist—that is, if one identifies a total deviation as the partial with respect to the policy— the policy accounts for a rise in the short rate of from 0.4 to 1.0 per cent. Overall, this evidence is obviously hard to interpret. Despite the econometric findings, however, it seems consistent with the view that Operation Twist:

a) had some impact on the "long-short differential"; and

b) may have maintained a Treasury bill rate perhaps 0.5 per cent above what would otherwise have ruled.

Beyond this the evidence seems to suggest that Operation Twist could *not* have raised the Treasury bill rate by *more* than 1 per cent while the *most plausible* impact may have been of the order of 0.15 per cent.[10]

The Impact on US Capital Flows

Branson and Hill's [9] recent study of capital movements in OECD areas provides a framework within which to analyse the impact of Operation Twist on capital movements. Formally, they apply a stock adjustment model:

$$K^f_t - K^f_{t-1} = \lambda \, [K^{*f}_t - K^f_{t-1}] \qquad (12)$$

where: K^f = claims on foreigners

K^{*f} = desired level of claims on foreigners

so that:

$$K^f_t - K^f_{t-1} \equiv \text{capital inflow}$$

Two special behavioural hypotheses are introduced:

$$K^{*f}_t = W^f \, [R^d, R^f, E, W] \qquad (13)$$

where: $W \equiv$ total wealth

$R^d \equiv$ domestic interest rates (a vector)

$R^f \equiv$ foreign interest rates (a vector)

$E \equiv$ an index of the riskiness of K^f in comparison with domestic assets

and

$$\lambda = 1 \qquad (14)$$

The second assumption implies complete adjustment of actual asset holdings (K^f) to planned holdings (K^{*f}) within the period of observation.

Substituting (13) and (14) into (12) gives:

$$K^f_t = K^{*f}_t$$
$$= W^f_t \, [R^d_t, R^f_t, E_t, W_t] \qquad (15)$$

---

10. This figure is based upon the examination of residuals from regression studies. It is "most plausible" only on the assumption that the models involved are superior as guides to the causal interpretation of time series.

whence:
$$K^f_t - K^f_{t-1} = W^f_t [R^d_t, R^f_t, E_t, W_t]$$
$$- W_{t-1}^f [R^d_{t-1}, R^f_{t-1}, E_{t-1}, W_{t-1}] \qquad (16)$$

For estimation purposes this is linearised to given an equation of the form:
$$\Delta K^f_t = a_o + a_1 \Delta (WR^d)_t + a_2 \Delta (WR^f)_t + a_3 \Delta (W,MI)_t + a_4 \Delta (WV^d)$$
$$+ a_5 \Delta (WV^f)_t + a_6 \Delta W_t + a_7 \Delta (W^2)_t + D \qquad (17)$$

where the new variables are defined as:

MI $\equiv$ the Jaffee-Modigliani credit rationing index
$V^d \equiv$ US income velocity of money
$V^f \equiv$ UK income velocity of money
D $\equiv$ a dummy representing US capital account measures taken after 1963.

After considerable experimentation, Branson and Hill arrive at a set of equations with partial derivatives evaluated at the December 1969 value of W (Table D). From this table, we have:

$$\frac{\delta \text{ KA}}{\delta \text{ RT}^{\text{US}}} = \$2.57 \text{ billion}$$

Thus *if* Operation Twist raised the US Treasury bill rate by 1 per cent, the *ceteris paribus* increase in the capital inflow is \$2.57 billion. This inflow would be concluded by the end of three quarters and by far the greater part of it by the end of two quarters.

To this calculation we need to make two corrections:

i) a "scale" correction to allow for the fact that:
$$\frac{\text{W (1961-63)}}{\text{W (1969)}} < 1; \text{ and}$$

ii) an "interdependence correction" to allow for the fact that most of the "independent" variables are, in practice, functionally related to RT^{US}.

A plausible value for $\dfrac{\text{W (1961-63)}}{\text{W}}$ is approximately 0.6. The main "independent" variables likely to be related to RT^{US} are:

i) RT^{CN} (Canadian Treasury bill rate);
ii) RED (Euro-dollar rate);
iii) V^{US}; and
iv) V^{CN}

According to Branson and Hill two plausible relationships are:
$$\frac{\delta \text{ RED}}{\delta \text{ RT}^{\text{US}}} \simeq 1.0$$
$$\frac{\delta \text{ V}^{\text{US}}}{\delta \text{ RT}^{\text{US}}} \simeq 0.1$$

since the responsiveness of RED to US short rates has grown through 1961-70—the former estimate is likely to be too large. There is no information given on the response of RT^{CN} or V^{CN}. But since there is usually a close relationship between RT^{US} and RT^{CN}, we may not be much in error if we take
$$\frac{\delta \text{ RT}^{\text{CN}}}{\delta \text{ RT}^{\text{US}}} \simeq 1.0$$

TABLE D. STOCK-SHIFT MULTIPLIERS OF CHANGES IN MONETARY VARIABLES
$ MILLIONS, QUARTERLY RATES NOT SEASONALLY ADJUSTED

Capital Flow Item in US Balance of Payments	Mean Quarterly Flow 1960. I to 1969. IV	Multipliers* for								
		Treasury Bill Rates			Euro-$ Deposit Rates	UK Long-term Govt. Bond Yield	Index of US Credit Rationing	Income Velocity of Money		
		US	UK	Canada				US	UK	Canada
Private Short-term Claims	210.8	257.6 (3)	-156.1 (2)							
Private Long-term Portfolio Claims	278.7				-247.0 (2)		13.6 (1)	222.2 (1)		
Short-term Liabilities to Private	552.4	1,176.7 (1)					79.4 (2)			
Long-term Portfolio Liabilities	320.9				-216.6 (2)	-808.5 (2)		379.7 (1)	-148.7 (2)	
Errors and Omissions	255.5	1,131.3 (2)		-345.8 (1)	-628.8 (2)				-133.8 (5)	-353.7 (2)
Net Financial Capital Account		2,565.6 (2)	-156.1	-345.8	-1,092.4	-808.5	93.0	601.9	-282.6	-353.7

* Multipliers are the product of estimated regression coefficients and a scale variable; a positive sign indicates an increased capital inflow from an increase in the relevant variable. The numbers in parentheses indicate the maximum time (in quarters) for the stock shifts to be completed. The source document provides a detailed description.

Source: Branson and Hill [9], pp. 25-26.

On these assumptions we have:

$$\frac{dKA}{dRT^{US}} = 0.6$$

$$\frac{\delta KA}{\delta RT^{US}} + \frac{\delta KA}{\delta RT^{CN}}\frac{dRT^{CN}}{dRT^{US}} + \frac{\delta KA}{\delta RED}\frac{dRED}{dRT^{US}} + \frac{\delta KA}{\delta V^{US}}\frac{dV^{US}}{dRT^{US}}$$

$$= 0.6\,[2565.6 - 345.8 - 1092.4 + 601.9]$$

$$= 0.6\,[1729.3]$$

$$= \$1{,}037.5 \text{ million}$$

It thus appears that a one per cent rise in RT^{US} generates an inflow of some \$1 billion which occurs mainly in the first two quarters after the change in RT^{US} and is completed by the end of the third. Since our calculation makes no allowance for any change in V^{CN} or any change in UK variables, both of which would have a negative influence on KA, this is probably the upper limit of the influence of Operation Twist.

As we have seen, our best guess at the impact of Operation Twist on RT^{US} is 0.15 per cent. On this basis Operation Twist generated a once-and-for-all capital inflow of \$0.16 billion, most of which probably occurred in 1961—a period for which Modigliani and Sutch's rate equation tends to overpredict the long-short rate differential by some 0.12 per cent.[11] Alternatively, if we prefer a time series guess at the impact of Operation Twist we have an upper limit of \$1 billion and a most plausible estimate of \$0.5 billion on the basis of the discussion on pages 194-196.

CONCLUSIONS

Despite the relatively small change in the debt maturity pattern engineered by the Federal Reserve, there is some rather weak evidence to suggest that Operation Twist raised the Treasury bill rate relative to long-term rates. The upper limit of this effect could not have exceeded one per cent: a more plausible estimate would lie close to 0.15 per cent. Tentatively accepting this estimate suggests, on the basis of Branson and Hill's results, once-and-for-all inflows of capital into the United States of no more than \$1 billion, with the most plausible range lying between \$125 and \$500 million and perhaps with \$160 million as the most likely guess. It must, however, be admitted that these conclusions are extremely tentative.

11. This estimate—like Hamburger's—would suggest a once-and-for-all inflow of some \$125 million.

BIBLIOGRAPHY

[1] ANDERSEN, L.C., "Additional Evidence on the Reverse Causation Argument," *Federal Reserve Bank of St. Louis Review*, August 1969.

[2] ANDERSEN, L.C. and JORDAN, J.L., "Monetary and Fiscal Actions: A Test of Their Relative Importance," *Federal Reserve Bank of St. Louis Review*, November 1968.

[3] ARGY, V. and HODJERA, Z., "Financial Integration and Interest Rate Linkages in the Industrial Countries 1958-71," *Mimeo*, International Monetary Fund (DM/72/66), July 1972.

[4] AXILROD, S.H., "The FOMC Directive as Structured in the late 1960's: Theory and Appraisal," in *Open Market Policies and Operating Procedures—Staff Studies*. Federal Reserve Board, July 1971.

[5] BISCHOFF, C.W., "A Model of Non-Residential Construction in the US," *American Economic Review*, May 1970.

[6] BLACK, S.W., "An Econometric Study of Eurodollar Borrowing by New York Banks and the Rate of Interest on Eurodollars," *Journal of Finance*, March 1971.

[7] BOUGHTON, J.M., *Monetary Policy and the Federal Funds Market*. Duke, 1972.

[8] BRADY, E.A., "An Econometric Analysis of the US Residential Housing Market," Working Paper No. 11. Federal Home Loan Bank Board, 1971.

[9] BRANSON, W.H. and HILL, R.D., "Capital Movements in the OECD Area," *OECD Economic Outlook, Occasional Studies*, December 1971.

[10] BRIMMER, A., "The Political Economy of Money, Evolution and Impact of Monetarism in the Federal Reserve System," *American Economic Review*, May 1972.

[11] BRUNNER, K., "Monetary Analysis and Federal Reserve Policy", in *Targets and Indicators of Monetary Policy*. Chandler, 1969.

[12] BRUNNER, K. and MELTZER, A.H., "The Nature of the Policy Problem," in *Targets and Indicators of Monetary Policy*. Chandler, 1969.

[13] BRYANT, R.L. and HENDERSHOTT, P.H., "Financial Capital Flows in the Balance of Payments of the United States: An Explanatory Empirical Study," *Princeton Studies in International Finance*, No. 25, 1970.

[14] COOPER, J.P. and FISHER, S., "Simulations of Monetary Rules in the FRB-MIT-Penn Model," *Journal of Money, Credit and Banking,* May 1972.

[15] CROCKETT, J., FRIEND, I. and SHAVELL, H., "The Impact of Monetary Stringency on Business Investment," *Survey of Current Business,* August 1967.

[16] DAVIS, R., "Short-run Targets for Open Market Operations," in *Open Market Policies and Operating Procedures—Staff Studies.* Federal Reserve Board, July 1971.

[17] De LEEUW, F., "A model of Financial Behaviour," in J.S. Deusenberry, *et al.* (eds.), *The Brookings Quarterly Econometric Model of the United States,* Chicago 1965. (Hereinafter, "Brookings Model.")

[18] De LEEUW, F. and GRAMLICH, E., "The Federal Reserve—MIT Econometric Model," *Federal Reserve Bulletin,* January 1968.

[19] De LEEUW, F. and GRAMLICH, E., "The Channels of Monetary Policy," *Federal Reserve Bulletin,* June 1969.

[20] ECKSTEIN, O. and FELDSTEIN, M., "The Fundamental Determinants of the Interest Rate," *Review of Economics and Statistics,* November 1970.

[21] *Economic Reports of the President,* Annual Reports, 1960-71.

[22] EDWARDS, F., "More on Substitutability Between Money and Near-Monies," *Journal of Money, Credit and Banking,* August 1972.

[23] FAIR, R.C., "Disequilibrium in Housing Models," *Journal of Finance,* May 1972.

[24] FEDERAL RESERVE BANK OF NEW YORK, *Annual Reports,* 1960-71.

[25] FEDERAL RESERVE BOARD, *Annual Reports,* 1960-71.

[26] FEDERAL RESERVE BOARD, *Federal Reserve Bulletin,* monthly.

[27] FEDERAL RESERVE BOARD, *Federal Reserve System: Purposes and Functions.* Washington, 1963.

[28] "Ways to Moderate Fluctuations in Housing," *Federal Reserve Bulletin,* March 1972.

[29] FEIGE, E., "Alternative Temporal Cross-Section Specifications of the Demand for Demand Deposits," paper presented at the Money Study Group Conference, Bournemouth, February 1972.

[30] FEIGE, E., *The Demand for Liquid Assets: A Temporal Cross-Section Analysis.* Prentice Hall, 1964.

[31] *Financial Structure and Regulation,* Report from the President's Commission, Washington, D.C., December 1971.

[32] FISHER, G. and SHEPPARD, D., "Effects of Monetary Policy on the United States Economy: A Survey of Econometric Evidence," *OECD Economic Outlook, Occasional Studies,* December 1972.

[33] FISHER, R.M. and SIEGMAN, C.J., "Patterns of Housing Experience During Periods of Credit Restraint in Industrialised Countries," *Journal of Finance,* May 1972.

[34] FRIEDMAN, B.M., "Tactics and Strategy in Monetary Policy," in *Open Market Policies and Operating Procedures—Staff Studies*. Federal Reserve Board, July 1971.

[35] GIBBS, H.J., "The Term Structure of Interest Rates: A Portfolio Selection Approach." *Unpublished M. Sc. Dissertation*. University of Southampton, 1968.

[36] GRAMLEY, L.H., "Fluctuations in Housing Construction," *Mimeo*, 1971.

[37] GRAMLICH, E.M., "The Usefulness of Monetary and Fiscal Policy as Discretionary Stabilisation Tools," *Journal of Money, Credit and Banking*, August 1971.

[38] GRAMLICH, E.M. and JAFFEE, D.M. (eds.), *Savings Deposits, Mortgages and Housing; Studies for the Federal Reserve-MIT-Penn Economic Model*. Lexington, 1972.

[39] HAMBURGER, M.J., "Expectations, Long-term Interest Rates and Monetary Policy in the United Kingdom," *Bank of England Quarterly Bulletin*, September 1971.

[40] HAMBURGER, M.J., "The Lag in the Effect of Monetary Policy," *Federal Reserve Bank of New York Review*, December, 1971.

[41] HAMBURGER, M., "The Demand for Money by Households, Money Substitutes and Monetary Policy," *Journal of Political Economy*, December 1966.

[42] HAMBURGER, M. and LATTA, C., "The Term Structure of Interest Rates: Some Additional Evidence." *Journal of Money, Credit and Banking*, February 1969.

[43] HANSEN, B., *Fiscal Policy in Seven Countries*, OECD, March 1969.

[44] HENDERSHOTT, P.H., "Neutralisation of the Money Stock," *Federal Reserve Bank of St. Louis Review*, May 1971.

[45] HENDERSHOTT, P.H., *The Neutralised Money Stock: An Unbiased Measure of Federal Reserve Policy Actions*. Irwin, 1968.

[46] HENDERSHOTT, P.H., "The Structure of International Interest Rates, The US Treasury Bill Rate and the Eurodollar Deposit Rate," *Journal of Finance*, September 1967.

[47] HICKS, J.R., *Value and Capital*, Oxford, 1946.

[48] HOLLAND, R.L., "The Federal Reserve Discount Mechanism as an Instrument for Dealing with Banking Market Imperfections," *Journal of Money, Credit and Banking*, May 1970.

[49] HOLMES, A.R., "Operational Constraints on the Stabilisation of Money Supply Growth," in *Controlling Monetary Aggregates*. Federal Reserve Bank of Boston, 1969.

[50] HOLMES, A.R., "Open Market Operations and the Monetary and Credit Aggregates—1971," *Federal Reserve Bulletin*, April 1972.

[51] HOMA, K.E. and JAFFEE, D.W., "The Supply of Money and Common Stock Prices," *Journal of Finance*, December 1971.

[52] HUANG, D.S., "The Short-run Flows of Non-farm Residential Mortgage Credit," *Econometrica*, April 1966.

[53] JAFFEE, D.M., *Credit Rationing and the Commercial Loan Market.* Wiley, 1971.

[54] JAFFEE, D.M. and MODIGLIANI, F., "A Theory and Test of Credit Rationing," *American Economic Review,* December 1969.

[55] Joint Economic Committee of Congress, *Staff Report on Employment, Growth and the Price Level,* Washington, D.C., 1959.

[56] JORGENSON, D.W., "Anticipations and Investment Behaviour," in *Brookings Model* [17].

[57] JORGENSON, D.W., "Capital Theory and Investment Behaviour," *American Economic Review,* May 1963.

[58] JORGENSON, D.W. and SIEBERT, C.D., "A Comparison of Alternative Theories of Corporate Investment Behaviour," *American Economic Review,* September 1968.

[59] JORGENSON, D.W. and STEPHENSON, J., "The Time Structure of Investment Behaviour in US Manufacturing," *Review of Economics and Statistics,* February 1967.

[60] KALCHBRENNER, J.H., "A Model of the Housing Sector," in Gramlich, E. and Jaffee, D.M. (eds.), *Savings Deposits, Mortgages, and Housing.* Lexington, 1972.

[61] KAREKEN, J., MUENCH, T., SUPEL, T. and WALLACE, N., "Determining the Optimum Monetary Instrument Variable," in *Open Market Policies and Operating Procedures—Staff Studies.* Federal Reserve Board, July 1971.

[62] KAREKEN, J. and SOLOW, R.M., "Lags in Monetary Policy," in E.C. Brown (ed.), *Stabilisation Policies.* Prentice-Hall, 1963.

[63] KERAN, M.W., "Neutralisation of the Money Stock-Comment," *Federal Reserve Bank of St. Louis Review,* May 1970.

[64] KERAN, M.W. and BABB, C., "Explanation of Federal Reserve Actions," *Federal Reserve Bank of St. Louis Review,* October 1969.

[65] LAFFER, A.B. and RANSON, R.D., "A Formal Model of the Economy," *Journal of Business,* July 1971.

[66] LEE, T.H., "Alternative Interest Rates and the Demand for Money: The Empirical Evidence," *American Economic Review,* December 1967.

[67] LOTZ, F., "Techniques of Measuring the Effects of Fiscal Policy," *OECD Economic Outlook, Occasional Studies,* July 1971.

[68] LOVELL, M.C., "Factors Influencing Investment in Inventories," in *Brookings Model* [17].

[69] MAISEL, S., "Non-Business Construction," in *Brookings Model* [17].

[70] MAISEL, S., "Controlling Monetary Aggregates," in *Controlling Monetary Aggregates.* Federal Reserve Bank of Boston, 1969.

[71] MALKIEL, B., *The Term Structure of Interest Rates.* Princeton, 1960.

[72] MARKOWITZ, H., *Portfolio Selection.* Wiley, 1959.

[73] MAYER, T., "The Federal Reserve's Policy Procedures," *Journal of Money, Credit and Banking,* August 1972.

[74] McGouldrick, P.F. and Peterson, J.E., "Monetary Restraint, Borrowing and Capital Spending by Large States and Local Governments," *Federal Reserve Bulletin*, July 1968.

[75] Meiselman, D., *The Term Structure of Interest Rates.* Prentice-Hall, 1962.

[76] Modigliani, F., "Monetary Policy and Consumption—The Linkages via Interest Rate and Wealth Effects in the FRB-MIT-Penn Model," in *Consumer Spending and Monetary Policy. Federal Reserve Bank of Boston*, 1972.

[77] Modigliani, F., Cooper, J.R. and Raasche, R., "Central Bank Policy, the Money Supply and the Short-Term Rate of Interest," *Journal of Money, Credit and Banking*, June 1970.

[78] Modigliani, F. and Sutch, R., "Debt Management and the Term Structure of Interest Rates: An Empirical Analysis of Recent Experience," *The Journal of Political Economy*, supplement, August 1967.

[79] Modigliani, F. and Sutch, R., "Innovations in Interest Rate Policy," *The American Economic Review*, May 1966.

[80] Okun, A., "Rules and Roles for Fiscal and Monetary Policy," in P.F. Diamond (ed.), *Issues in Fiscal and Monetary Policy: the Eclectic Economist Views the Controversy.* De Paul University, 1971.

[81] Peterson, J.E., "Response of State and Local Government to Varying Credit Conditions," *Federal Reserve Bulletin*, March 1971.

[82] Pierce, J., "Some Rules for the Conduct of Monetary Policy," in *Controlling Monetary Aggregates.* Federal Reserve Bank of Boston, 1969.

[83] Pierce, J. and Thomson, T., "Controlling the Money Stock," Paper presented at the Konstanz Seminar, June 1972.

[84] Poole, W., "Alternative Paths to a Stable Full Employment Economy," *Brookings Papers on Economic Activity*, No. 3, 1971.

[85] Poole, W., "Rules-of-Thumb for Guiding Monetary Policy," in *Open Market Policies and Operating Procedures—Staff Studies.* Federal Reserve Board, July 1971.

[86] Raasche, R.H. and Shapiro, H., "The FRB-MIT Econometric Model: Its Special Features," *American Economic Review*, May 1968.

[87] Rowan, D.C. and O'Brien, R.J., "Expectations, the Interest Rate Structure and Debt Policy," in K. Hilton and D.F. Heathfield, (eds.), *The Econometric Study of the United Kingdom.* London, 1970.

[88] Rowan, D.C. and O'Brien, R.J., "Expectations and the Rate Structure," *Essays in Honour of Viti de Marco.* Italy, 1970.

[89] Ruebling, C.E., "RPDs and Other Reserve Operating Targets," *Federal Reserve Bank of St. Louis Review*, August, 1972.

[90] Saving, T., "Monetary Policy Targets and Indicators," *Journal of Political Economy*, August 1967.

[91] Scott, R., "Liquidity and the Term Structure of Interest Rates," *Quarterly Journal of Economics*, February 1965.

[92] SILBER, William L., "An Econometric Model of the Mortgage Market," in A. Samatz (ed.), *Cyclical and Growth Problems Facing the Savings and Loan Industry.* Bulletin No. 46-47, Institute of Finance, New York University.

[93] SPRINKEL, B.W., *Money and Stock Prices.* Irwin, 1964.

[94] TELSER, L.G., "The Term Structure of Interest Rates," *Journal of Political Economy*, August 1967.

[95] TEIGEN, R.L., "An Aggregate Quarterly Model of the US Monetary Sector," in *Targets and Indicators of Monetary Policy.* Chandler, 1969.

[96] THOMSON, T.D., PIERCE, J.L. and PARRY, R.T., "A Monthly Money Market Model," *Mimeo,* paper given at the Konstanz Seminar, June 1972.

[97] TOBIN, J., Article in F.R.P. Brechling and P.H. Hahn (eds.), *The Theory of the Rate of Interest.* Macmillan, 1966.

[98] TOBIN, J., "Deposit Interest Ceilings as a Monetary Control," *Journal of Money, Credit and Banking,* February 1970.

[99] WALLACE, N., "Comment," *Journal of Political Economy,* August 1967.

[100] WOOD, J., Article in *Monetary Process and Policies: A Symposium.* Irwin, 1967.

[101] YOUNG, R., "Monetary Policy and Its Instruments in the United States." International Monetary Fund, 1974.

[102] YOUNG, R. and YAGER, C., "The Economics of 'Bills Preferably'," *Quarterly Journal of Economics,* August 1960.